A TELEPSYCHOLOGY CASEBOOK

A TELEPSYCHOLOGY CASEBOOK

USING TECHNOLOGY ETHICALLY AND EFFECTIVELY IN YOUR PROFESSIONAL PRACTICE

EDITED BY
LINDA F. CAMPBELL, FRED MILLÁN, AND JANA N. MARTIN

American Psychological Association • Washington, DC

Published by
American Psychological Association
750 First Street, NE
Washington, DC 20002
www.apa.org

To order
APA Order Department
P.O. Box 92984
Washington, DC 20090-2984
Tel: (800) 374-2721; Direct: (202) 336-5510
Fax: (202) 336-5502; TDD/TTY: (202) 336-6123
Online: www.apa.org/pubs/books
E-mail: order@apa.org

In the U.K., Europe, Africa, and the Middle East, copies may be ordered from
American Psychological Association
3 Henrietta Street
Covent Garden, London
WC2E 8LU England

Typeset in Meridien by Circle Graphics, Inc., Columbia, MD

Printer: Sheridan Books, Chelsea, MI
Cover Designer: Mercury Publishing Services, Inc., Rockville, MD

Library of Congress Cataloging-in-Publication Data
Names: Campbell, Linda Frye, 1947- editor. | Millán, Fred, editor. | Martin, Jana N., editor.
Title: A telepsychology casebook : using technology ethically and effectively in your professional practice / edited by Linda F. Campbell, Fred Millán, and Jana N. Martin.
Description: First Edition. | Washington, DC : American Psychological Association, [2017] | Includes bibliographical references and index.
Identifiers: LCCN 2016059929 | ISBN 9781433827068 | ISBN 1433827069
Subjects: LCSH: Psychologists—Professional ethics. | Psychology—Standards. | Information technology—Moral and ethical aspects.
Classification: LCC BF76.4 .T45 2017 | DDC 150.28/4—dc23 LC record available at https://lccn.loc.gov/2016059929

British Library Cataloguing-in-Publication Data
A CIP record is available from the British Library.

Printed in the United States of America
First Edition

http://dx.doi.org/10.1037/0000046-000

We dedicate this book to our families, who support all our efforts with their love, patience, and encouragement—Karen and Jeff Vasquez, Greg, Lee, and Alan Campbell; Emily, Marcus, Freddy, Matthew, and Maria Millán; Mackenzie, Madison, and Jerry Martin—and to our colleagues, whose concern for the well-being of others and quest for advancing our profession are an inspiration.

Contents

Contributors

Margo Adams Larsen, PhD, Virtually Better, Inc., Decatur, GA

Deborah C. Baker, JD, Practice Directorate, American Psychological Association, Washington, DC

Linda F. Campbell, PhD, Department of Counseling and Human Development Services, University of Georgia, Athens

Bruce E. Crow, PsyD, Warrior Resiliency Program, Regional Health Command—Central, U.S. Army Medical Command, Fort Sam Houston, TX

Stephen T. DeMers, EdD, Chief Executive Officer, Association of State and Provincial Psychology Boards, Peachtree City, GA

Eric A. Harris, EdD, JD, The Trust, Rockville, MD

Cindy Juntunen, PhD, Counseling Psychology and Community Services, University of North Dakota, Grand Forks

Julie M. Landry Poole, PsyD, ABPP, Warrior Resiliency Program, Regional Health Command—Central, U.S. Army Medical Command, Fort Sam Houston, TX

Jana N. Martin, PhD, Chief Executive Officer, The Trust, Rockville, MD

Russell McCann, PhD, VA Puget Sound Health Care System—Seattle Division; Department of Psychiatry and Behavioral Sciences, University of Washington, Seattle

Stephen McCutcheon, PhD, VA Puget Sound Health Care System—Seattle Division; Department of Psychiatry and Behavioral Sciences, University of Washington, Seattle

Fred Millán, PhD, ABPP, NCC, Department of Psychology, State University of New York at Old Westbury

Thomas W. Miller, PhD, ABPP, Institute for Health, Intervention and Policy, University of Connecticut; Department of Gerontology, College of Public Health, and Department of Psychiatry, College of Medicine, University of Kentucky

Ronald S. Palomares, PhD, Department of Psychology and Philosophy, Texas Woman's University, Denton

Sara Smucker Barnwell, PhD, Department of Psychiatry and Behavioral Sciences, University of Washington, Seattle; Independent Practice, Seattle, WA

Preface

In 2010 and earlier, psychologists became more and more aware of the increasing provision of services via various telecommunications technologies. Web searches produced huge results for all types of services and fees; however, there was little structure or regulation to oversee or ensure quality of care. These activities were known by a host of names, all meaning health service practice by telecommunications. Some of these terms are *telemental health, telemedicine, telehealth,* and *telepractice*. During this time, other health professions were developing policies or guidelines for telecommunication practices to address the issues as well.

Dr. Melba J. T. Vasquez, who had been recently elected president-elect of the American Psychological Association (APA), was well aware of these developments. Because of the far-reaching nature of telecommunications, she realized that this new extension of practice would significantly involve licensure laws and malpractice insurance. Thus, she created a task force to develop guidelines for psychologists as the profession entered the age of telecommunications. This task force included representatives with a broad array of perspectives, including individuals from APA to provide the membership perspective, individuals from the Association of State and Provincial Psychology Boards (ASPPB) to provide the regulatory perspective, and individuals from the American Insurance Trust (The Trust) to provide the risk management perspective. The cochairs of the task force were Linda F. Campbell, PhD (appointed by Dr. Vasquez to represent APA); Fred Millán, PhD (representing ASPPB); and Jana N. Martin, PhD (representing The Trust). The cochairs, in turn, selected members of the task force, which included Terry S. Gock, PhD; Colonel Bruce E. Crow, PsyD (ret.); Margo Adams Larsen, PhD; Sara Smucker Barnwell, PhD; Joe S. Rallo, PhD; Eric A. Harris, EdD, JD; and Thomas W. Miller, PhD. The task force received excellent support from staff of APA (Ronald S. Palomares, PhD, Joan Freund, and Jessica Davis) and ASPPB (Stephen T. DeMers, EdD; Alex M. Siegel, PhD, JD; and Janet Pippin Orwig, MBA).

One of the first decisions of the task force was to select a name for practice via telecommunications technologies by psychologists. They wanted a clear connection with the discipline and coined the term *telepsychology*, which has, in fact, become the standard name for any services provided via telecommunications technologies by psychologists.

Frankly, there was concern at the time about whether three discrete professional organizations could collaborate, come to consensus, and avoid the traps of competition, pursuits of influence, or incompatible goals and values. Interestingly, the task force not only avoided all of those obstacles but completed its work with a unanimous recommendation for the telepsychology guidelines—and it did so in the shortest period of time of any APA-related task force that has produced guidelines!

On July 31, 2013, at the APA Annual Convention in Honolulu, Hawaii, the Guidelines for the Practice of Telepsychology were approved by a wide margin by the APA Council of Representatives. Subsequently, the ASPPB Board of Directors and The Trust Board of Directors also approved the guidelines that summer. Since then, the guidelines have been widely disseminated, have been the subject of many presentations to educate the psychological community, and have stimulated work toward possible regulatory changes which could allow the legal interjurisdictional practice of telepsychology.

This casebook is the next step in encouraging and highlighting the proper practice of telepsychology. It focuses on the applicability of the guidelines in various settings in which psychologists practice.

A TELEPSYCHOLOGY CASEBOOK

Linda F. Campbell, Fred Millán, and Jana N. Martin

Introduction

Dr. Bailey was intrigued with the concept of "telepsychology," which increasingly popped up on electronic mailing lists and in e-mails with colleagues. However, she had no interest in developing a telepsychology practice. Her office was in Northern California, and many of her clients in sales and consultation traveled for several weeks at a time within the state. Dr. Bailey often had telephone sessions with her clients and occasional e-mail exchanges. Still, she did not consider this practice to be telepsychology because there was no web camera or other Internet conferencing technology and because she was not practicing interjurisdictionally (i.e., across a state line). Furthermore, she did not worry about any ethical or legal issues specific to her telephone sessions and e-mails because she believed that her skills and knowledge with in-person practice applied the same way to these other activities. Then one day, she was shocked to learn that any electronic communication, including telephone and e-mail, was considered *telepractice*. Dr. Bailey consulted the American Psychological Association (APA; Joint Task Force for the Development of Telepsychology Guidelines for Psychologists, 2013) *Guidelines for the Practice of Telepsychology*, only to find many factors at play that she had not considered (e.g., confidentiality, security of transmission, standards of care, disposal of e-mails).

http://dx.doi.org/10.1037/0000046-001
A Telepsychology Casebook: Using Technology Ethically and Effectively in Your Professional Practice, L. F. Campbell, F. Millán, and J. N. Martin (Editors)

Dr. Bailey's reactions are not uncommon. Psychologists have received the development of telepsychology as they have other new and emerging aspects of practice—with interest, skepticism, curiosity, dread, appreciation, reluctance, enthusiasm, anxiety, and other reactions that span the emotional range. To be sure, the practice of videoconferencing as a means of delivering psychological services has previously not been widely known to psychologists except in special settings, such as the military. In contrast, the practice of using the telephone to communicate with clients is years old. Although both of these activities are considered telepsychology, many psychologists have not thought of their use of the telephone in that way. Recently, we, the volume editors, were presenting a symposium on telepsychology when a woman in the back of the room raised her hand and said, "I've been talking on the phone with my clients since 1954. Am I practicing telepsychology?" We not only answered her question in the affirmative but also declared her a "pioneer in telepsychology"!

Telepsychology is "the provision of psychological services using telecommunication technologies" (Joint Task Force for the Development of Telepsychology Guidelines for Psychologists, 2013, p. 791). It is not a specialty. It is not a separate domain of practice. Telepsychology is an extension of the broad and general practice of psychology. This conceptualization of telepsychology as an extension of psychologists' current practice is a valuable perspective to take in that the application of telepsychology to practice is not to change fundamental competence, modality of practice, therapeutic approach, or other building blocks of psychologists' practice. Rather, telepsychology offers an opportunity for psychologists to apply their skills, their ethical decision-making, and the profession's standards of care to technology-assisted practice.

As new practice opportunities emerge for psychologists with the growth of telecommunications technology, so too emerge new responsibilities. Psychologists must now become knowledgeable of new developments, regulations, and guidelines; develop new skill sets; become equipped with risk management strategies; and understand how all of this is integrated with their ethics code.

Increasing interest in telepsychology within the psychological community is evidenced by the special sections and special issues in APA journals and other citation sources, including the following:

- Special Issue: Advances in Telehealth and Telepsychology. *Psychological Services, 10*(3), August 2013
- Special Section: Telepractice. *Professional Psychology: Research and Practice, 45*(5), October 2014
- Special Issue: Telehealth and Technology Innovations in Professional Psychology. *Professional Psychology: Research and Practice, 42*(6), December 2011
- Special Section: Visions for the Future of Professional Psychology. *Professional Psychology: Research and Practice, 43*(6), December 2012
- Special Section: Telepractice. *Professional Psychology: Research and Practice, 45*(5), October 2014
- Special Issue: Training and Professional Development. *Psychotherapy, 50*(2), June 2013

The purpose of this casebook is to help psychologists understand how standards of practice apply to telepsychology and to offer ways in which psychologists may think about ethical decision-making regarding their movement into telepsychology.

The foundation of this book is the *Guidelines for the Practice of Telepsychology* (hereafter referred to as "the guidelines"; see the Appendix, this volume), which were created jointly by APA, the Association of State and Provincial Psychology Boards (ASPPB), and The Trust. The guidelines are designed to facilitate practice, much as record-keeping guidelines, multicultural guidelines, and others are meant to improve the efficiency, effectiveness, and competence in our practice. They are aspirational in intent and not intended to be mandatory or exhaustive and may not apply to every professional and clinical situation. They are not definitive and are not intended to take precedence over the judgment of psychologists (APA, 2017). Guidelines are critically important because telepractice incorporates many aspects of in-person practice but in an unfamiliar and nonintuitive manner for some people. It is no coincidence, then, that seven of the eight guidelines are also current sections or standards of the *Ethical Principles of Psychologists and Code of Conduct* (APA, 2017). These are Competence, Standards of Care, Informed Consent, Confidentiality, Testing and Assessment, Security and Transmission of Data, and Disposal of Data. There is also a new guideline on the concept of Interjurisdictional Practice. Each guideline is represented in a chapter and highlighted in the case studies. It is important for psychologists to familiarize themselves with all of the guidelines and to think about how each affects their particular practice decisions. Problems of confidentiality breaches, clients with limited technical proficiency, concerns about safe transmission of electronic messages, and appropriate disposal of information are but a few considerations for telepractitioners. The guidelines build on our existing ethics code both to provide a safety net and to lead us toward greater competency in practice.

The format of this casebook is similar to that of the guidelines. All APA Guidelines are developed from a template, and this template stipulates that a guideline be presented in two sections. The first section is the Rationale, which explains why the guideline is necessary, what purpose it serves, and how it facilitates practice. The Rationale also identifies the expectations the profession has of the psychologist practicing that guideline and describes specific actions as examples of enacting the Rationale. The second section of the guideline is the Application, which does just that—it answers the question of how psychologists are to implement or "apply" the guidelines. Examples are offered, and decision-making factors are presented.

Each chapter covers a guideline. The chapter begins with the specific guideline, the rationale for the guideline, and introductory remarks that set the context for understanding what the psychologist is to do regarding the guideline. Next are case studies that identify the setting; the scenario; key elements, challenges, and decision factors; options available to the psychologist; and the best decision possible. The chapter ends with the key points from all case studies. The key points provide guidance on how to generalize and apply the various thought processes and decisions to other situations the psychologist may encounter.

Although the casebook has a similar format to the guidelines, the casebook goes beyond the guidelines by providing a structure and method for working from the global situation or dilemma down to the actual decisions that must be made. It provides a more detailed discussion of how to think through the scenarios presented.

This casebook is written for psychologists in all settings and in all areas of practice. The case studies therefore include independent practice, organizational/consulting, counseling centers, academic settings, public sector agencies, hospitals, Veterans Administration facilities, military sites, and other settings in which psychologists practice. Cases vary also in types of dilemmas to demonstrate the variety of scenarios that can occur involving each of the guidelines.

Telepsychology is often discussed as though the services were uniformly practiced and in similar settings when, in fact, the challenge of this emerging medium is just the opposite. The practice of telepsychology ranges from the solo independent practitioner whose access to technology is a phone, e-mail, and possibly texting, to the Department of Defense in which synchronous videoconferencing is conducted between military personnel in Austin, Texas, and a soldier in Afghanistan. Further challenges lie in the ever-changing status of technology so that what is "state of the art" today is not tomorrow.

We tried to represent this broad range of activities and settings in the casebook. Every chapter could not incorporate every practice setting; however we, the editors, hope that the cases will be relevant and familiar and that the readers can relate to the cases in a way that lends guidance and helps each individual develop a decision-making model to integrate telepsychology into his or her professional practice.

References

American Psychological Association. (2017). *Ethical principles of psychologists and code of conduct* (2002, Amended June 1, 2010 and January 1, 2017). Retrieved from http://www.apa.org/ethics/code/index.aspx

Joint Task Force for the Development of Telepsychology Guidelines for Psychologists. (2013). Guidelines for the practice of telepsychology. *American Psychologist, 68,* 791–800. Retrieved from https://www.apa.org/pubs/journals/features/amp-a0035001.pdf

Sara Smucker Barnwell, Russell McCann, and Stephen McCutcheon

Competence of the Psychologist

1

> Psychologists who provide telepsychology services strive to take reasonable steps to ensure their competence with both the technologies used and the potential impact of the technologies on clients/patients, supervisees, or other professionals.
>
> —Guideline 1, *Guidelines for the Practice of Telepsychology*

Rationale

> Psychologists have a primary ethical obligation to provide professional services only within the boundaries of their competence based on their education, training, supervised experience, consultation, study, or professional experience. As with all new and emerging areas in which generally recognized standards for preparatory training do not yet exist, psychologists utilizing telepsychology aspire to apply the same standards in developing their competence in this area. Psychologists who use telepsychology in their practices assume the responsibility for assessing and continuously evaluating their competencies, training, consultation, experience, and risk management practices required for competent practice. (Joint Task Force for the Development of Telepsychology Guidelines for Psychologists, 2013, p. 798)

Ethical Principles of Psychologists and Code of Conduct, Standard 2, addresses the expectations of all psychologists in attaining and maintaining competence

http://dx.doi.org/10.1037/0000046-002
A Telepsychology Casebook: Using Technology Ethically and Effectively in Your Professional Practice, L. F. Campbell, F. Millán, and J. N. Martin (Editors)

in their professional activities (American Psychological Association [APA], 2017). Psychologists provide services "only within the boundaries of their competence, based on their education, training, supervised experience, consultation, study, or professional experience" (p. 4). Even in emerging areas where recognized standards might not yet exist, "psychologists nevertheless take reasonable steps to ensure the competence of their work and to protect clients/patients, students, supervisees, research participants, organizational clients, and others from harm" (p. 5).

The following applications are examples of the means by which competency is evidenced in the practice of telepsychology. The applications illustrate competence through supervision, practice, determining technology appropriateness, and emergency service. Psychological practice is a complex endeavor that requires extensive training to achieve competence. This is particularly true when using new and innovative technologies in delivering health care.

Case Study 1: Supervision

The advent of telepsychology offers the opportunity to harness telecommunication technologies to serve patients, psychologists, and psychology trainees. *Supervision* refers to

> a distinct professional practice employing a collaborative relationship that has both facilitative and evaluative components, that extends over time, which has the goals of enhancing the professional competence and science-informed practice of the supervisee, monitoring the quality of services provided, protecting the public, and providing a gatekeeping function for entry into the profession. (APA, 2014)

The APA Commission on Accreditation (CoA; APACoA, 2014) identified "telesupervision . . . [as] clinical supervision of psychological services through asynchronous audio and video format where the supervisor is not in the same physical facility as the trainee." The CoA (APACoA, 2014) further defined that "in-person supervision is clinical supervision of psychological services where the supervisor is physically in the same room as the trainee." Providing supervision services over the telephone, Clinical Video Telehealth technology (CVT), e-mail, text, and other online modalities creates the opportunity to disseminate quality training opportunities despite barriers of geographic distance, physical mobility challenges, or other barriers.

SETTING: POSTDOCTORAL SUPERVISION IN A VA HOSPITAL PROGRAM

The Telehealth and Rural Outreach postdoctoral training program (TROP) through the Department of Veterans Affairs (VA) offers postdoctoral training intended to instill advanced competencies in health service psychology (HSP) with a focus on the provision of psychological services using telehealth technologies. The 1-year fellowship emphasizes the provision of evidence-based treatments to medically underserved veteran populations (e.g., rural, recently returning, female, Native American). Using secure CVT, the postdoctoral fellows deliver individual, couples, and group therapy to veterans in VA medical centers and community-based outpatient clinics. Training emphasizes clinical skills and practical considerations specific to telehealth (e.g., clinical skills that differ from face-to-face care, security measures, risk management) and clinical skills training for the provision of evidence-based treatments.

Although the VA telehealth program is specific, the scenario is illustrative of the essential elements of using telecommunication technologies during training supervision.

SCENARIO

Dr. Shante Adrian was a fellow in the telehealth program. She possessed interests in telepsychology, rural health, program administration, and evidence-based PTSD care and sought to advance her broad array of competencies, with a particular focus on provision of services in these areas to rural veterans. After meeting with the training director (TD), Dr. Adrian selected the TROP's team lead as one of her primary supervisors for the fellowship. The supervisor's background (telepsychology and evidence-based PTSD care) aligned well with Dr. Adrian's interests. The supervisor's duties as program administrator required regularly scheduled days working off-site with rural partner clinics that posed logistical challenges.

KEY ELEMENTS, CHALLENGES, AND DECISION FACTORS

The prospect of working with a supervisor who regularly traveled off-site posed important questions regarding the nature of supervision and the costs and benefits of remote supervision. Could the supervisor competently meet Dr. Adrian's training needs while off-site? Should they conduct regularly scheduled supervision over telecommunication technologies, or would this modality be limited to additional, "as needed" meetings? What technology should the supervisor use to deliver supervision at a distance? What were the rules governing distance supervision? The supervisor worked closely with the Seattle VA TD and the VA Office of Academic Affiliations (OAA) to address these concerns. The CoA Implementation Regulation (IR) C-28 (APACoA, 2014) addresses telesupervision and the unique advantages of in-person supervision (e.g., the ability to perceive subtle interactions with a trainee, socialization opportunities, superior ability to observe trainees). IR C-28 of the Accreditation Standards instructs those considering offering telesupervision to develop a telesupervision policy that addresses a variety of considerations.

OPTIONS AVAILABLE TO THE PSYCHOLOGIST

Guided by the CoA Implementation Regulations (APACoA, 2014), the TD worked closely with the supervisor and facility leadership to develop a policy that addressed these concerns. The TD, supervisor, and supervisee created a training plan to deliver weekly in-person supervision with supplemental telesupervision.

COMPONENTS OF A TELESUPERVISION POLICY

The following policy was written in compliance with and application of the CoA Implementation Regulations:

- Telesupervision offers trainees the opportunity to experience CVT firsthand. The modality offers trainees consultation with Seattle VA supervisors whose role may require them to travel off-site.
- Telesupervision will continue to employ a competency-based approach to supervision (see Falender & Shafranske, 2008).
- Telesupervision may not account for more than 50% of the minimum required supervision hours (e.g., 1 of the 2 weekly supervision hours). Telesupervisors use telesupervision to augment in-person supervision and conduct the majority of their supervision in person.
- Postdoctoral fellows with an interest in telehealth may participate in telesupervision.
- The relationship between supervisor and supervisee will be initiated at Seattle VA, and the majority of supervision will occur at Seattle VA.
- When a supervisor travels off-site, she will designate an on-site supervisor to assist the trainee in case of emergency.
- The supervisee may seek nonscheduled supervision at any time from the on-site supervisor when the primary supervisor is off-site and/or for supplemental telesupervision. The authority of the primary supervisor will be authoritative in cases of conflict.
- All telesupervision will occur over secure, encrypted, synchronous CVT provided through the VA Information Technology infrastructure or via the telephone (i.e., not text or e-mail).
- A telesupervisor must receive the recommended trainings in CVT (e.g., online courses with the VA Learning Management System, meeting with the Telemental Health team).

Soon after the telesupervision policy was established, a situation arose that would demonstrate its value. Dr. Adrian received her first telehealth referral. The client, a middle-aged man initially evaluated at his local VA community-based outpatient clinic, agreed to receive CVT services at his local clinic. This clinic had limited mental health staff resources, and a telehealth consult could facilitate the provision of prolonged exposure for PTSD. His provider, Dr. Adrian, delivered care from her office at the Seattle VA while the client attended care at his local, rural clinic. Dr. Adrian received basic training in telehealth provision, including technology use, safety planning, and other fundamentals required in advance of seeing a first client.

The first session with this client occurred on a day when the supervisor would be working off-site. Dr. Adrian was familiar with the telesupervision policy, as well as the protocol for obtaining on-site supervision, if needed. Upon arriving for his first session, the client appeared uncomfortable. A nurse from his local clinic greeted him and seated him in a private room with CVT equipment. The nurse connected Dr. Adrian and the client via the CVT equipment and exited the room for privacy.

Although the client had agreed to CVT therapy previously and discussed reservations before seeing Dr. Adrian, he disclosed some reservations about therapy over CVT and sharing intimate information during the first few minutes of the session. Dr. Adrian managed the situation appropriately, balancing an exploration of his concerns with his right to elect in-person care. She suggested that they use the current session as a litmus test for his comfort and decide at the session's conclusion whether to proceed with a telepsychology intervention or refer the client back to in-person care at his local clinic. Consistent with empirical literature regarding clients' reports of high rapport with CVT providers (see Glueck, 2013), the client ultimately reported feeling very comfortable with Dr. Adrian as his provider and elected to remain on her service. After this experience, Dr. Adrian decided to seek supplemental supervision to discuss the experience. She contacted her supervisor to discuss the case over CVT that day.

Dr. Adrian communicated her reservations that although research indicates most clients feel comfortable with CVT care, she worried that her clients would not. She and her supervisor examined the benefits of CVT for the specific client (e.g., access to specialty care, convenience). They discussed the manner in which aggregate data could predict likely outcomes but that Dr. Adrian would need to monitor her client's comfort carefully and respect his preferences. They also reflected on the manner in which their supervision, often held over CVT, enjoyed levity, warmth, and other indicators of rapport. This fact, perhaps more than research, reassured Dr. Adrian of the potential for rapport over the modality.

Supervisee: I know research indicates that most clients feel comfortable with CVT by the end of the first session. But I am concerned that I will not *deliver* rapport.

Supervisor: You raise an important point. We know the aggregate data, but we can't be sure how he, as an individual, will react to the modality. Am I understanding that correctly?

Supervisee: Exactly. I haven't seen clients over CVT. The jump from theory to practice is hard—especially when it undermines my faith in my ability to establish an alliance with my client.

Supervisor: Just when you think you've covered the basics, we pull the rug out from under you!

Supervisee: (laughing) Exactly!

Supervisor: Only time will tell regarding this new client. But I wonder if this moment between us can inform our thinking regarding rapport.

Supervisee: I see your point. We're having a good discussion—just like our regular meetings. And we're laughing—something that requires us to feel a comfortable rapport. I disclosed something difficult to you, my supervisor: not feeling as competent as usual. That made me feel vulnerable. It felt like a bit of a risk, but an important one.

Supervisor: I really appreciate you highlighting that. It takes courage. Now we know each other in person as well. This certainly creates a foundation for rapport that is carried over to our video meetings. What could you do with this new client to help establish more foundational rapport over CVT?

THE BEST DECISION POSSIBLE

Psychologists of all experience levels ask whether CVT allows for the emotional connection achieved in person. Information is lost over CVT. Providers miss subtle shifts in body posture, changes in the client's facial expression, sensory cues (e.g., olfactory), and other valuable cues to the distance gap. But can we still convey warmth, acceptance, and caring? In conducting telesupervision, we have the opportunity to model rapport over CVT. The supervisor–supervisee relationship differs vastly from a psychologist–client relationship. Nonetheless, both relationships require acceptance, openness, and boundary-governed rapport. Telesupervision allows a trainee to experience the CVT milieu firsthand and engage in a process-oriented discourse over the modality. As technology is increasingly democratized and more and more human interaction occurs at a distance, the challenge to maintain connection, rapport, and understanding remotely is perhaps never more important.

Case Study 2: Independent Practice

The first guideline of Competence in the *Guidelines for the Practice of Telepsychology* (Joint Task Force, 2013) directs clinicians adopting telepsychology to "assume the responsibility for assessing and continuously evaluating their competencies, training, consultation, experience and risk management practices required for competent practice" (p. 793). This guidance is consistent with ethical standards related to emerging areas of practice, for which psychologists seek training, consultation, and supervision to enhance their competencies. Limited telehealth educational and training resources (Glueck, 2011) prevent some practitioners from adopting telehealth technology. Larger institutional practice environments may develop their own telepsychology training program. Practitioners in independent practice typically possess fewer resources. Psychologists may be uncertain how best to approach assessing their own competence or obtain training to augment their skills.

SETTING: INDEPENDENT PRACTICE

Dr. Joyce Hill was a psychologist with an independent practice that included herself and other, more junior therapists. Although her practice delivered services to urban clients, she had an interest in providing care to traditionally underserved communities in the state, including rural women. Dr. Hill pursued postdoctoral training in women's health in a rural community and was familiar with the challenges unique to delivering care to rural populations (e.g., distance from care, few providers, dual-role relationships in small communities).

Dr. Hill aimed to offer telepsychology interventions to facilitate quality care for women in a rural community with few resources. She hoped that others in her practice would share her enthusiasm and reasoned that telehealth could be a welcome opportunity to expand the client base for newer clinicians beginning their practice. She felt competent in technology basics (e.g., e-mail, maintaining her electronic medical records and website), but she possessed limited knowledge of telepsychology or how to approach its ethical implementation.

SCENARIO

Dr. Hill recalled that her state psychological association and malpractice insurance provider sponsored telepsychology presentations in recent years. Dr. Hill resided in a state where the state's psychological association demonstrated a committed interest in telehealth and developed resources to promote clinician competence in telehealth. Her state association referred Dr. Hill to a psychologist colleague with a telehealth consulting practice. She and the consultant met in person and over CVT for several additional meetings to identify a path to obtaining the training necessary.

KEY ELEMENTS, CHALLENGES, AND DECISION FACTORS

Dr. Hill and the consultant conducted a thorough needs assessment. Telepsychology is a broad and diverse category of technologies and clinical applications (Joint Task Force, 2013). Although there are fundamentals recommended for anyone interested in telepsychology (e.g., *Guidelines for the Practice of Telepsychology*, Joint Task Force, 2013; empirical literature review; American Telemedicine Association best practice guides, Grady et al., 2011), no single approach to training serves as a panacea to establish competency for all telepsychology applications. A thoughtful needs assessment thoroughly explores the psychologist's reasons for pursuing training; targets technologies that the psychologist intends to use; considers the psychologist's prior experience with the technology; and lays out the psychologist's plans to implement technology, including available training resources. Regardless of how much or how little competency psychologists have in technology, a needs assessment is the first step in determining the additional training, preparation, and experience needed for the chosen telepractice. Some of the determining factors are identification of client variables (e.g., culture, ethnicity, disability), client competencies (capabilities in using various levels of technology from the telephone, texting, e-mail, and social media to videoconferencing), and remote emergency services. Other factors include informed consent tailored for telepsychology practice and mutually agreed on understanding of the limits of confidentiality.

Independent practitioners further seek competency in securing, transmitting, and disposing of online information.

Rationale for Pursuit of Telepsychology

Dr. Hill hoped to deliver telepsychology services to once more offer care to rural communities. Discussion with the consultant revealed that Dr. Hill believed this modality would offer financial benefits to her practice because its client base would expand. They discussed the challenges she would face, including time and cost of attaining competence, identifying referrals in the rural community, coordinating care remotely, managing emergencies remotely, negotiating more complicated reimbursement processes, and negotiating the costs introduced by telepsychology (e.g., CVT software).

Technology Selection and Relevant Experience

Competence in telepsychology requires psychologists to determine which technologies need to be used to deliver care in order to focus training. Dr. Hill had read articles on CVT care and was enthused about this modality. Competence in telepsychology would therefore include a review of concerns specific to CVT. The community Dr. Hill hoped to serve had Internet access, but she was uncertain regarding the quality of connectivity there. For this reason, the consultant recommended expanding Dr. Hill's training to include an understanding of concerns specific to telephone use (e.g., types of telephony, concerns idiosyncratic to use of mobile devices, empirical literature on telephones) as an alternative if she experienced problems with CVT. Dr. Hill and other psychologists of varying levels of competency would be alert for loss of electronic connection with the client and would have a predetermined means of resolving the problem or an understanding with the client of next steps.

Dr. Hill had delivered telephone-based care throughout her clinical career. She routinely considered issues such as patient location while speaking on the telephone due to safety and privacy concerns. She had not previously considered interjurisdictional practice implications of speaking to clients over the telephone, although she typically spoke with clients located within her home state. Additionally, she was not in the practice of formally establishing and documenting safety plans for telephone-based clients, largely because these situations were rare and always in addition to in-person care. She was aware of how best to bill a telephone appointment. And she felt reasonably well apprised of the manner in which the empirical literature found equivalence for telephone-based interventions compared with traditional in-person care (see Dwight-Johnson et al., 2011).

In contrast, Dr. Hill had relatively little experience with CVT. She had used videoconferencing with friends and understood the fundamentals regarding operating the technology. However, she had not considered the specific concerns relevant to clinical applications (e.g., threats to privacy/confidentiality, information security, selecting a product appropriate for health care, safety planning for remote clients). For Dr. Hill, increasing her telepsychology competence would require training in CVT.

Implementation Plans

Some clinicians may elect to offer telepsychology to existing in-person clients. Dr. Hill, on the other hand, intended to identify new, remote clients who would otherwise not receive care. In her model, clients would be encouraged to visit her office in the urban community located 1 hour away for initial visits or supplemental in-person care as needed (e.g., emergencies, sessions to refresh assessment of telehealth appropriateness). Dr. Hill was open to seeing some clients who would only ever be served via CVT. For Dr. Hill, understanding the assessment of telehealth appropriateness at a distance (see *The Assessment of Suitability for Home Based Telemental Health*, Shore, 2011), the challenges of care termination in environments with few referral options, authenticating identity remotely, and other considerations unique to clients seen primarily at a distance were critical. Regular visits to the rural community she would serve would be scheduled to help her reaffirm relationships with referral resources and conduct initial telehealth appropriateness assessments with clients to prevent clients traveling to her urban office.

Dr. Hill realized that seeing patients remotely only would bring a level of monitoring and awareness (e.g., authenticating identity) that seeing patients intermittently in person and remotely would not duplicate. The mixed model of in person and remote would allow easier assessment of client status and use of in-person relational factors that may be important with specific types of cases or client preferences. Dr. Hill would assess the need for CVT for her intermittent in-person and remote clients and would determine if the ratio of in-person meetings would satisfy her need to assess and reassess the desirability and appropriateness of telepsychology from both the client and Dr. Hill's frame of reference.

Resources Available for Training

The training resources (e.g., time, finances, colleagues with experience) available to psychologists will significantly affect how they pursue competence. Psychologists in the Department of Veterans Affairs or Department of Defense health care systems will likely have access to large-scale institutional training resources (see the online courses in the VA Talent Management System), and may even be required to pursue these trainings. As a psychologist in independent practice, Dr. Hill was initially uncertain where to obtain quality information to pursue competence. She soon learned that she resided in a community with rich telehealth resources. She had already contacted her state psychological association and malpractice provider regarding her interest in telehealth and connected with a local colleague involved in telehealth. Dr. Hill possessed an academic affiliation with a local university but had been unaware of the university's telehealth research projects. She and the consultant discussed the value of reaching out to her departmental chair to inquire about opportunities in telehealth. She learned of a research consultation group that met with regularity at the university, as well as a clinical consultation group that met at a hospital affiliate of the university.

Not every psychologist resides in an area where telehealth resources are readily available. Increasingly, national training events, online telehealth communities, and online training certification programs offer a valid method for pursuing competence. Dr. Hill found herself hoping to pursue information specific to billing Medicare for telehealth appointments and was uncertain where best to pursue this information. Dr. Hill and the consultant reviewed several options for pursuing training remotely, including traveling to conferences for lectures and workshops, watching online webinars related to telehealth, attending her local state association convention meetings and lectures, participating in online telemental health consultation groups, or taking online courses.

OPTIONS AVAILABLE TO THE PSYCHOLOGIST

Dr. Hill and the consultant developed a personalized training plan that addressed her specific interests, technologies targeted, implementation plans, and available resources. The plan addressed fundamental information regarding the how-to mechanics of telepsychology and focused on information related to telehealth ethics (e.g., how to ethically implement care at a distance), information on rural health care, and financial information regarding telehealth, its costs, and typical approaches for billing telepsychology care (see Human Resources and Services Administration, 2015).

Dr. Hill's plan to pursue telepsychology competencies acknowledged myriad practical concerns, such as time and expense. She could gain much of her training through free and low-cost mechanisms (e.g., self-study, reviewing the extant literature, reviewing the *Guidelines for the Practice of Telepsychology*, joining the relevant professional organization special interest group). As a small business owner, Dr. Hill had limited time to pursue training and hoped to pursue these competencies efficiently. Workshops and online trainings incurred fees but saved valuable time.

Dr. Hill completed the recommended readings and trainings. She traveled to the rural clinic where she had pursued her postdoctoral training to establish her availability as a referral option and discuss how she might best serve the community via telepsychology. She successfully recruited several primary care providers to act as referral resources and established her practice as a partner in women's mental health. Her next steps were useful and appropriate whether Dr. Hill established a remote-only practice or a mixed model of intermittent in-person and remote practice. She reviewed several CVT products and ultimately selected a product designed for health care. She maintained contact with the consultant to discuss issues relevant to her first CVT and telephone cases and became a regular contributing member at her local telehealth clinical consultation group. She joined online consultation groups and became active on their electronic mailing lists and website forums. She became familiar with telehealth billing practices and billed insurance for clients when possible. With her competencies firmly established and maintained, Dr. Hill also became a resource to newer clinicians in her practice and other colleagues interested in telehealth.

Case Study 3: Technology Appropriateness

The *Guidelines for the Practice of Telepsychology* (Joint Task Force, 2013) emphasize the consideration of "current literature available, current outcomes research, best practice guidance and client/patient preference" (p. 794) when determining whether a telecommunication technology is suitable for use in clinical practice. A comprehensive approach to deciding when to use such a technology is critical to the competent practice of psychology because the answer to whether a modality is appropriate for a given patient is often, "It depends." Take, for example, a relatively established technology such as CVT. Research on CVT has generally established the effectiveness of this modality (Hilty et al., 2013), and no clinical groups have been identified for which CVT is wholly contraindicated (Turvey et al., 2013). Despite this, CVT may not be clinically indicated in all instances, such as when a client prefers in-person care, there is a lack of privacy at the location where the care would be received, the technology needed is not available, or there is a clinical issue that the provider judges would be best addressed in person.

SETTING: OUTPATIENT VA CLINIC

Dr. Sally Davis works as a clinical psychologist at a posttraumatic stress disorder (PTSD) clinic with a Department of Veterans Affairs VA Medical Center. Dr. Davis has received training through the VA on CVT, uses this modality with veterans on her panel, and brings up the possibility of home-based CVT to all veterans during intake and later during the course of treatment as indicated.

SCENARIO

Dr. Davis met with Mr. Salcedo, a 45-year-old Chicano combat veteran of the U.S. Army. Mr. Salcedo was discharged from the army subsequent to a diagnosis of PTSD after 13 years in service. He had four combat deployments and has multiple service-connected disabilities, including a 70% service-connected disability for PTSD. Mr. Salcedo has been employed as a truck driver since discharge. He lives with his spouse of 20 years and their three children, aged 10 to 18 years. Mr. Salcedo presented with symptoms of PTSD and depression and expressed interest in prolonged exposure (PE). Mr. Salcedo commented that it took about an hour and a half to drive to the intake appointment. The provider who referred him to the PTSD clinic indicated that video-based mental health services might be available.

KEY ELEMENTS, CHALLENGES, AND DECISION FACTORS

Considering Literature and Outcomes Research

Dr. Davis informed Mr. Salcedo that CVT might be an option and explored the appropriateness of this telecommunication technology with him. Dr. Davis began the process of determining the suitability of CVT for Mr. Salcedo by considering the literature and research base specific to the primary presenting problem, posttraumatic stress. She explained to Mr. Salcedo that research has largely found PTSD treatments delivered via CVT to be effective (Sloan, Gallagher, Feinstein, Lee, & Pruneau, 2011). She added that PE has been found to be equally effective when administered via CVT or in person (Yuen et al., 2015). It was emphasized that although research does not necessarily contraindicate the use of CVT for PE, some findings have been inconclusive and suggest the need for additional research.

Client–Patient Preference

Mr. Salcedo indicated that he was excited to hear CVT might be an effective way for him to get the care he was looking for without traveling hours back and forth for appointments. He expressed interest in receiving PE via CVT to his home from Dr. Davis, if possible.

Best Practice Guidance

Dr. Davis applied the American Telemedicine Association "Practice Guidelines for Video-Based Online Mental Health Services" (Turvey et al., 2013) by considering the veteran's technological competence, as well as the privacy and appropriateness of his home for care. Dr. Davis asked about Mr. Salcedo's experience with technology relevant to CVT. Mr. Salcedo noted a history of computer use, but he did not currently have a working computer at home. He described using a smartphone and high-speed Internet at home to browse the web and videoconference without difficulty. Dr. Davis was aware that the veteran's smartphone could be a possible option for CVT. She considered the small screen size on the smartphone and the limited research on the use of these devices for CVT (Luxton, Mishkind, Crumpton, Ayers, & Mysliwiec, 2012). As a result, she brought up the possibility of having the VA loan Mr. Salcedo an Internet-enabled tablet device to use for treatment. Had he declined videoconferencing care, Dr. Davis could have considered telephone-based care. Because Mr. Salcedo was amenable to videoconferencing care, Dr. Davis worked to consider the appropriateness of his environment for CVT. Mr. Salcedo described being at home alone during the day and did not anticipate interruptions during appointments.

Individual Characteristics

Dr. Davis continued by gathering unique individual characteristics to help further determine the appropriateness of this telecommunication technology. She considered cultural, linguistic, and socioeconomic factors that might influence the use of CVT. Using the work of Yellowlees, Marks, Hilty, and Shore (2008) to guide this process, she recalled research suggesting that Hispanic/Latino individuals were more likely relative to non-Hispanic/Latino Whites to have a high affinity for technology but were also likely to have decreased access to and skills with technology (Tolbert & Mossberger, 2006). She reflected on how this veteran used technology to communicate with relatives via CVT without incident. Furthermore, Mr. Salcedo has already expressed interest in meeting via CVT, which suggests the use of technology to communicate with a provider is consistent with his views on technology.

Dr. Davis then considered socioeconomic factors. Poverty has been discussed as a barrier to mental health care, both in person and otherwise (Yellowlees et al., 2008). Furthermore, those in poverty have been found not only to have lower utilization rates for mental health services but to have less access to technology as well. Limited financial resources might function as a barrier to CVT in terms of having a suitable location to receive the care, as well as access to the technology needed. When asked, Mr. Salcedo did not endorse concerns about money. Additionally, even if finances were an issue, CVT in this instance still could have been possible because the VA was able to send a device that includes its own Internet source. Resources such as tablets and the ability to provide Internet service are more readily available to practitioners in large-scale practice environments (e.g., hospitals, health care companies) and less financially viable for independent practitioners.

Other Individual Characteristics

Dr. Davis then considered other individual characteristics, such as medical and disability status and psychiatric stability, to assess the suitability of this modality for working with this veteran. She reviewed his medical record to screen for any factors that might affect the use of CVT. She noted that Mr. Salcedo has a service-connected disability for hearing loss. She asked him how this might affect his receiving care via CVT, and he commented that he finds it easier to communicate over technology relative to in person because he can turn the volume up on his speakers to hear someone better. She noted that the veteran is also service connected for a knee injury, and he described an added benefit of CVT being that he would not have to walk to and from his car as he would for a typical in-person appointment. No other medical issues germane to CVT were found in the veteran's medical record or were reported.

To evaluate for psychiatric stability, Dr. Davis first considered Mr. Salcedo's risk to self or others, being aware that responding to risks remotely can be more complex than doing so in person (e.g., Gros, Veronee, Strachan, Ruggiero, & Acierno, 2011). Mr. Salcedo endorsed thinking sometimes that he'd be OK if he "didn't wake up" from sleep but denied any current or prior thoughts, intent, or plans to harm himself or others. He also denied current or prior self-harm or nonmilitary violence toward others. Mr. Salcedo did not endorse a history of inpatient psychiatric care or emergency department visits related to behavioral health needs.

Dr. Davis informed Mr. Salcedo that emergencies that happen during the course of CVT can differ from those that might occur during an in-person visit. She gave an example of how hospital staff could be available to address a medical emergency if the veteran were sitting in her office, but if she were meeting the veteran via CVT, emergency services would need to be sent to his location.

OPTIONS AVAILABLE TO THE PSYCHOLOGIST

If the veteran and provider did not elect to proceed with this modality, they could have worked to consider alternatives. Potential alternative in-person treatment options for this veteran to receive PE could have included both VA and community-based locations. Given that Mr. Salcedo identified the distance to the clinic as a barrier to care, that option was clearly not ideal for him. Care in the community may have been a more compelling option for this individual and would realistically be reimbursed in such an instance by the VA; however, finding a provider trained in PE near the veteran's residence might have proven difficult.

When Dr. Davis and Mr. Salcedo were considering what technology to use, they could have settled on a non-CVT technology, such as the telephone or a virtual environment. There is research in support of the use of the telephone for a variety of presenting problems (Leach & Christensen, 2006), but at the time of this writing, there is no known research evaluating telephone-based delivery of PE. Although PE may well be successfully provided via telephone, the availability of research to support PE via CVT would likely make CVT a better choice.

THE BEST DECISION POSSIBLE

Dr. Davis reflected on all of the information discussed and determined that Mr. Salcedo was likely an appropriate candidate for home-based CVT. She explained that the CVT software used for care is compatible with the Health Insurance Portability and Accountability Act; however, there is always a risk when information travels over the Internet. Dr. Davis went on to talk about the benefits associated with CVT to the home, to include increased convenience and access care (Pruitt, Luxton, & Shore, 2014). Finally, she also informed Mr. Salcedo that the assessment of CVT appropriateness in clinical care is ongoing. Mr. Salcedo expressed his understanding of these concerns and was amenable to proceeding accordingly. Dr. Davis documented her rationale for using this modality for care with this veteran.

Case Study 4: Emergency Management

Remote emergency management poses unique challenges to clients and clinicians because it removes the safety conventions of in-person care. As an example, when care is provided to a client sitting in his or her home via a telecommunication technology, a clinician no longer has hospital or clinic staff onsite to assist in the event of a medical emergency. A clinician trained in basic life-saving skills cannot administer care or be an active aid in a psychiatric emergency (e.g., walking a client to the emergency department in a large hospital setting).

Challenges associated with remote emergency management are not limited to the instant the emergency occurs. An ethical psychologist may contend with challenges finding an acceptable alternative to telehealth if the modality is deemed inappropriate following an emergency. For example, a rural telehealth client requiring a higher level of care after an inpatient hospitalization may experience a dearth of in-person treatment options in his community. A return to in-person care could represent spending hours in a car to attend a single mental health visit or electing to terminate care entirely.

Given that an emergency response is more complex for a client seen via telecommunication technologies, it is perhaps no surprise that the telehealth literature has consistently pointed to the use of an emergency plan in practice (e.g., Gros et al., 2011; Luxton, O'Brien, McCann, & Mishkind, 2012). Consistent with this practice and the problems that can sometimes arise with discharge from telehealth care, the "Guidelines for the Practice of Telepsychology" (Joint Task Force, 2013) provide direction for psychologists using telecommunication technologies to competently establish an emergency plan and manage the discharge process.

SETTING: RURAL COMMUNITY–BASED CLINIC

Dr. Tom Marion was a counseling psychologist working at a highly rural VA community-based outpatient clinic (CBOC). Dr. Marion provided mental health services for a wide variety of presenting problems and frequently used telecommunication technologies (e.g., CVT, telephone, secure messaging) to improve clients' access to care.

SCENARIO

Dr. Marion met Ms. Alana Nieves, a 70-year-old Puerto Rican woman presenting with panic disorder, during his walk-in hours. Ms. Nieves lived alone in her home, which was situated in a rural location about 30 minutes from the CBOC. She expressed interest in therapy to help address panic attacks and scheduled a follow-up appointment to discuss treatment options.

The day before the follow-up, Ms. Nieves called Dr. Marion to reschedule the appointment, citing scheduling challenges. The rescheduled visit came and went, and Ms. Nieves again failed to appear at the clinic. Dr. Marion called to inquire about the two absences and hoped to reengage her in care. Ms. Nieves explained that she felt unable to attend appointments because of a secondary concern regarding driving safety and panic attacks. Dr. Marion provided psychoeducation on avoidance and how it functions to maintain anxiety. Ms. Nieves reported that the barrier felt insurmountable and indicated that she was no longer interested in pursuing care.

Dr. Marion asked if Ms. Nieves might be willing to receive care in her home using CVT, with the express intention of working toward in-person visits over time. Ms. Nieves was excited about this possibility and noted that this felt like an accessible compromise. Dr. Marion evaluated the suitability of the CVT modality for her and concluded it was appropriate. He indicated that before commencing CVT care, it would be important to collaboratively establish an emergency plan.

KEY ELEMENTS, CHALLENGES, AND DECISION FACTORS

Dr. Marion and Ms. Nieves developed an emergency plan specific to the provision of CVT care to her home. Dr. Marion confirmed the client's phone number and address as found in her medical chart and explained that accuracy of information is key to emergency planning. He asked if Ms. Nieves would like to identify someone as an emergency contact nearby during home-based appointments. She declined, noting that she did not wish to disclose being in therapy to others. Dr. Marion noted that although a local contact may be helpful in some situations, an emergency contact was not required to participate in home-based CVT. He reviewed what would happen in case of emergency and set expectations regarding how confidentiality would be managed (e.g., mandated reporting in emergencies, contacting emergency services to assist others). Dr. Marion documented the emergency plan and sent it to Ms. Nieves before their first CVT appointment. The following outlines Dr. Marion's process in developing the plan.

Step 1: Identify Resources and Prepare a Plan

The first step in Dr. Marion's emergency plan was to record the veteran's name, phone number, and address, which were confirmed over the telephone. Dr. Marion considered how emergency services might be provided to Ms. Nieves's home, where she would receive care via CVT. Dr. Marion was aware that some for-profit companies provide long-distance numbers to directly dial emergency response services, and at times these numbers can be found by searching online; however, he documented in the emergency plan to call 911 in the event of an emergency and ask to be connected to emergency services for the veteran's location. He chose this route because 911 would always reach emergency services, whereas direct-dial numbers could become outdated.

He then considered how he might pursue hospital admissions in Ms. Nieves's location. The CBOC itself did not have an emergency department. By searching online, Dr. Marion was able to identify the nearest medical facility to the veteran's location, an entry point for emergent medical and psychiatric presentations in that area. He added this hospital's name and address to the emergency plan.

Dr. Marion further considered any local referrals that would be relevant for Ms. Nieves. On each emergency plan he drafted, he included the toll free number to the Veterans Crisis Hotline, an emergency hotline established to manage psychiatric emergencies for veterans. He included this number on Ms. Nieves's plan, as well as the website for 211.org to provide the veteran with a means to research resources in her community as needed. Ms. Nieves elected not to identify a support person as an emergency contact, and thus Dr. Marion did not include such an individual on the emergency plan. He noted in the emergency plan that the client chose not to identify an emergency support person, and he documented their discussions regarding the potential benefits and risks of this choice.

Step 2: Communicate Plan

When Dr. Marion met with Ms. Nieves for her first appointment via CVT, he oriented her to the technology and verbally reviewed informed consent. They discussed the emergency plan and addressed Ms. Nieves's questions. They discussed the manner in which CVT care would act as an interim step to in-person care.

Step 3: Discharge the Plan

Dr. Marion worked with Ms. Nieves to develop a treatment plan that included the use of an exposure-based protocol to address panic attacks. During the eighth session, they talked about the manner in which Ms. Nieves challenged herself by going out in public and increasingly ventured outside her home comfortably. Dr. Marion recalled how they had initially planned to meet in person but elected to proceed with CVT to the home secondary to her anxiety. They discussed the manner in which CVT would provide an interim step to in-person care. Ms. Nieves recalled this agreement and commented that she was worried that in-person care would still be required. Although she felt she could return to meeting in person and understood how that might be helpful, she preferred the CVT modality because of its convenience.

They agreed to meet in person for her next appointment and, depending on how that went, to determine how to proceed. Ms. Nieves attended this session in person as planned. Visiting the CBOC this time was much easier than the last time they met in person. They discussed the benefit of confronting anxiety and how to balance that with the convenience of meeting via CVT at home. Ms. Nieves indicated that her preference for telehealth was related more to convenience than anxiety at this point. For clients who declined in-person care due to anxiety and avoidance, Dr. Nieves rarely offered care beyond three to five sessions. Dr. Marion agreed to resume home-based telehealth with several conditions. First, Ms. Nieves would continue to attend some meetings in person with Dr. Marion. Also, Dr. Marion requested that Ms. Nieves not avoid appointments with other providers at the CBOC where she received medical care. Finally, he requested that she continue the vigorous exposure work they had been pursuing as Ms. Nieves confronted problems in other areas of her life. Ms. Nieves was happy to resume care via CVT.

After the treatment protocol was completed, Ms. Nieves reported living without panic attacks for over a month. She was appreciative of the care she received and reiterated how much she enjoyed being able to meet from her home, particularly as treatment was getting started. Dr. Marion and Ms. Nieves mutually agreed to terminate care without referral. Dr. Marion told Ms. Nieves that she could contact him in the future should she have any future interest in mental health services.

OPTIONS AVAILABLE TO THE PSYCHOLOGIST

Dr. Marion could have required in-person treatment so as not to reinforce anxiety-related avoidance. He proceeded with CVT because the veteran would likely not engage in treatment if in-person care had been the only option at that time. When Ms. Nieves reported decreased anxiety later in the course of treatment, Dr. Marion could have again required a return to in-person care to facilitate confronting avoidance. He did not because he judged the client's interest in receiving care via CVT at that point more of a matter of preference than avoidance. Although behaviorally it is not ideal to reinforce avoidance by enabling a client to receive care from home, there is research that suggests this concern may not be an issue in practice (e.g., Bouchard et al., 2004).

Key Points From the Chapter to Remember

- Psychologists must seek out appropriate training experiences to develop and maintain competence in delivering telepsychology services.
- Competence includes being able to communicate the benefits and limitations of the technology being used in a manner that the patient or client can understand.
- The ongoing appropriateness of telepsychology needs to be assessed and documented periodically.
- Telesupervision provides an opportunity for the supervisor to model acceptance, openness, and boundary-governed rapport over CVT. It allows a trainee to experience the CVT milieu firsthand and engage in a process-oriented discourse over the modality.
- Supervisor and supervisee should establish a contract that clearly outlines the responsibilities and contingencies for the telesupervision.
- Similarly, it is important to collaboratively establish and document an emergency plan that includes a procedure to follow, local resources and contact information, and a discharge plan.

References

American Psychological Association. (2014). *Guidelines for clinical supervision in health service psychology.* Retrieved from http://www.apa.org/about/policy/guidelines-supervision.pdf

American Psychological Association. (2017). *Ethical principles of psychologists and code of conduct* (2002, Amended June 1, 2010 and January 1, 2017). Retrieved from http://www.apa.org/ethics/code/index.aspx

American Psychological Association Commission on Accreditation. (2014). *Policy statements and implementing regulations.* Retrieved from https://www.apa.org/ed/accreditation/about/policies/implementing-regs.pdf

Bouchard, S., Paquin, B., Payeur, R., Allard, M., Rivard, V., Fournier, T., . . . Lapierre, J. (2004). Delivering cognitive-behavior therapy for panic disorder with agoraphobia in videoconference. *Telemedicine Journal and e-Health, 10,* 13–25. http://dx.doi.org/10.1089/153056204773644535

Dwight-Johnson, M., Aisenberg, E., Golinelli, D., Hong, S., O'Brien, M., & Ludman, E. (2011). Telephone-based cognitive-behavioral therapy for Latino patients living in rural areas: A randomized pilot study. *Psychiatric Services, 62,* 936–942. http://dx.doi.org/10.1176/ps.62.8.pss6208_0936

Falender, C. A., & Shafranske, E. P. (Eds.). (2008). *Casebook for clinical supervision: A competency-based approach.* http://dx.doi.org/10.1037/11792-000

Glueck, D. A. (2011). Telepsychiatry in private practice. *Child and Adolescent Psychiatric Clinics of North America, 20,* 1–11. http://dx.doi.org/10.1016/j.chc.2010.08.006

Glueck, D. A. (2013). Establishing therapeutic rapport in telemental health. In K. Myers & C. L. Turvey (Eds.), *Telemental health: Clinical, technical and administrative foundations for evidence-based practice* (pp. 29–46). http://dx.doi.org/10.1016/B978-0-12-416048-4.00003-8

Grady, B., Myers, K. M., Nelson, E.-L., Belz, N., Bennett, L., Carnahan, L., . . . Voyles, D. (2011). Evidence-based practice for telemental health. *Telemedicine Journal and e-Health, 17,* 131–148. http://dx.doi.org/10.1089/tmj.2010.0158

Gros, D. F., Veronee, K., Strachan, M., Ruggiero, K. J., & Acierno, R. (2011). Managing suicidality in home-based telehealth. *Journal of Telemedicine and Telecare, 17,* 332–335. http://dx.doi.org/10.1258/jtt.2011.101207

Hilty, D. M., Ferrer, D. C., Parish, M. B., Johnston, B., Callahan, E. J., & Yellowlees, P. M. (2013). The effectiveness of telemental health: A 2013 review. *Telemedicine Journal and e-Health, 19,* 444–454. http://dx.doi.org/10.1089/tmj.2013.0075

Human Resources and Services Administration. (2015). *What are the reimbursement issues for telehealth?* Retrieved from http://www.hrsa.gov/healthit/toolbox/RuralHealthITtoolbox/Telehealth/whatarethereimbursement.html

Joint Task Force for the Development of Telepsychology Guidelines for Psychologists. (2013). Guidelines for the practice of telepsychology. *American Psychologist, 68,* 791–800. Retrieved from https://www.apa.org/pubs/journals/features/amp-a0035001.pdf

Leach, L. S., & Christensen, H. (2006). A systematic review of telephone-based interventions for mental disorders. *Journal of Telemedicine and Telecare, 12,* 122–129. http://dx.doi.org/10.1258/135763306776738558

Luxton, D. D., Mishkind, M. C., Crumpton, R. M., Ayers, T. D., & Mysliwiec, V. (2012). Usability and feasibility of smartphone video capabilities for telehealth care in the U.S. military. *Telemedicine Journal and e-Health, 18,* 409–412. http://dx.doi.org/10.1089/tmj.2011.0219

Luxton, D. D., O'Brien, K., McCann, R. A., & Mishkind, M. C. (2012). Home-based telemental healthcare safety planning: What you need to know. *Telemedicine Journal and e-Health, 18,* 629–633. http://dx.doi.org/10.1089/tmj.2012.0004

Pruitt, L. D., Luxton, D. D., & Shore, P. (2014). Additional clinical benefits of home-based telemental health treatments. *Professional Psychology: Research and Practice, 45,* 340–346. http://dx.doi.org/10.1037/a0035461

Shore, P. (2011). *The Assessment of Suitability for Home Based Telemental Health (ASH–25).* Unpublished manuscript, U.S. Department of Veterans Affairs, Portland, OR.

Sloan, D. M., Gallagher, M. W., Feinstein, B. A., Lee, D. J., & Pruneau, G. M. (2011). Efficacy of telehealth treatments for posttraumatic stress-related symptoms: A meta-analysis. *Cognitive Behaviour Therapy, 40,* 111–125. http://dx.doi.org/10.1080/16506073.2010.550058

Tolbert, C. J., & Mossberger, K. (2006). The effects of e-government on trust and confidence in government. *Public Administration Review, 66,* 354–369.

Turvey, C. L., Coleman, M., Dennison, O., Drude, K., Goldenson, M., Hirsch, P., . . . Bernard, J. (2013). ATA practice guidelines for video-based online mental health services. *Telemedicine Journal and e-Health, 19,* 722–730. http://dx.doi.org/10.1089/tmj.2013.9989

Yellowlees, P., Marks, S., Hilty, D., & Shore, J. (2008). Using e-health to enable culturally appropriate mental healthcare in rural areas. *Telemedicine and eHealth, 14,* 486–492.

Yuen, E. K., Gros, D. F., Price, M., Zeigler, S., Tuerk, P. W., Foa, E. B., & Acierno, R. (2015). Randomized controlled trial of home-based telehealth versus in-person prolonged exposure for combat-related PTSD in veterans: Preliminary results. *Journal of Clinical Psychology, 71,* 500–512. http://dx.doi.org/10.1002/jclp.22168

Ronald S. Palomares

Standards of Care in the Delivery of Telepsychology Services

2

Psychologists make every effort to ensure that ethical and professional standards of care and practice are met at the outset and throughout the duration of the telepsychology services they provide.

—Guideline 2, *Guidelines for the Practice of Telepsychology*

Rationale

Psychologists delivering telepsychology services apply the same ethical and professional standards of care and professional practice that are required when providing in-person psychological services. The use of telecommunication technologies in the delivery of psychological services is a relatively new and rapidly evolving area, and, therefore, psychologists are encouraged to take particular care to evaluate and assess the appropriateness of utilizing these technologies prior to engaging in, and throughout the duration of, telepsychology practices to determine if the modality of service is appropriate, efficacious, and safe.

Telepsychology encompasses a breadth of different psychological services using a variety of technologies (e.g., interactive videoconferencing, telephone, text, e-mail, Web services, and mobile applications). The burgeoning research in telepsychology suggests that certain types of interactive telepsychology interventions are equal in effectiveness to their in-person counterparts (specific therapies delivered over video teleconferencing and telephone). Therefore, before psychologists engage in providing telepsychology services, they are urged to conduct

http://dx.doi.org/10.1037/0000046-003
A Telepsychology Casebook: Using Technology Ethically and Effectively in Your Professional Practice, L. F. Campbell, F. Millán, and J. N. Martin (Editors)

> an initial assessment to determine the appropriateness of the telepsychology services to be provided for the client/patient. Such an assessment may include the examination of the potential risks and benefits of providing telepsychology services for the client's/patient's particular needs, the multicultural and ethical issues that may arise, and a review of the most appropriate medium (video teleconferences, text, e-mail, etc.) or best option available for the service delivery. It may also include considering whether comparable in-person services are available and why services delivered via telepsychology are equivalent or preferable to such services. In addition, it is incumbent on the psychologist to engage in a continual assessment of the appropriateness of providing telepsychology services throughout the duration of the services delivery. (Joint Task Force for the Development of Telepsychology Guidelines for Psychologists, 2013, pp. 794–795)

Psychologists are called on to use professional judgment in determining standards of care in any given decision scenario. The American Psychological Association's (APA; 2017) *Ethical Principles of Psychologists and Code of Conduct* provides standards against which decisions about professional conduct are made; however, most professional decisions are made through the judgment of psychologists about what is and is not a reasonable standard of care. A standard of care means "the prevailing professional judgment of psychologists engaged in similar activities in similar circumstances, given the knowledge the psychologist had or should have had at the time" (APA, 2017, p. 2). The standards of care call on psychologists to use reasonable judgment expected of competent psychologists to determine the appropriateness and safety of telepsychology services for each client who is offered services (Clough & Casey, 2015). How should psychologists determine appropriateness, and what factors should be considered in that determination?

Appropriateness includes consideration primarily of client variables such as diagnostic impression, cultural values and ethnic status, presenting problem, therapeutic needs, treatment plan, mental stability, and substance use. These factors then lead to the consideration of the risks and benefits of technology given the specific client variables (e.g., geographic barriers) and the client's technological competence. Psychologists then decide on the appropriateness of telepsychology services for any given client (Luxton, 2013). Psychologists should be able to justify that telepsychology services are at least equivalent to face-to-face services before making a determination. The interest of either the client or the psychologist in adopting telepsychology as the medium for services is certainly a factor but is subordinate to the client variables as a decision factor. Video teleconferencing or Clinical Video Technology (CVT) is the gold standard in that it simulates face-to-face presence most closely. However, this venue, as well as others, must also be evaluated for appropriateness, privacy, and security, among other concerns. Psychologists must weigh the risks and benefits of synchronous versus asynchronous audio (e.g., telephone) and synchronous versus asynchronous venues that are neither video nor audio (e.g., texting, e-mail) in light of the client variables. The client's competence to participate, even during in-person services, must be assessed to ensure his or her ability to engage in the discourse. Telepsychology presents additional responsibility for psychologists in that they must ensure their own technological competence and clinical competence to be effective with clients electronically. They must also determine that the client can use the technology effectively. In weighing telepsychology services for a given client, clinicians should review the existing literature on the evidence-based use of the approach with similar clients and using a similar level of technology.

Assessment for appropriateness is a process, not an event at the beginning of services. The effectiveness of telepsychology services can change across time, just as face-to-face effectiveness can change. Hence psychologists must continuously assess technology effectiveness and seek out reasons for any changes.

Case Study 1: Factors of the Remote Environment

RELEVANT EXCERPT FROM THE GUIDELINE

> Psychologists make every effort to ensure that . . . professional standards of care and practice are met at the outset. (Joint Task Force, 2013, p. 794)

SETTING: INDEPENDENT PRACTICE

Dr. Nepal, a licensed psychologist, has her own small private practice and recently began considering the incorporation of some telepsychology services into her clinical practice. She has been in practice for 18 years and has always considered new research-based, empirically supported therapeutic approaches to improve her practice. The predominant symptoms with which her clients present are anxiety based, and she understands that current research supports the use of telepsychology with certain therapeutic approaches and the diagnostic classification of anxiety.

SCENARIO

Following the *Guidelines for the Practice of Telepsychology* (Joint Task Force, 2013), state psychology board rules, regulations and guidance, and information gleaned from the current literature on the application of telepsychology in clinical practice, Dr. Nepal identifies a current client whom she believes could benefit from a treatment approach that uses telepsychology. Specifically, Dr. Nepal believes that this 43-year-old female client with a social anxiety disorder will be better able to participate in their therapeutic interactions and focus on current issues using CVT rather than traditional in-person treatment in Dr. Nepal's office. The client relates that she gets very anxious just thinking about the process of leaving home and being out in public while traveling to Dr. Nepal's office. In fact, she relates that the anxiety she feels is what has caused her to cancel numerous appointments, which Dr. Nepal suspected and which provides additional support to her decision to use telepsychology with this client.

Dr. Nepal thoughtfully reviews the client's situation and treatment plan to ensure there are no additional multicultural or ethical issues to be considered in light of adding the telepsychology component. Finding none, she feels confident in moving forward and introducing this option to the client.

Dr. Nepal plans to continue to use the same therapeutic approach she has been using with her client in in-person sessions but change the setting so that her client will be at home. Her next step is to select a Health Insurance Portability and Accountability Act (HIPAA; 1996)–compliant audiovisual program that will best allow the client to remain at home for their sessions while Dr. Nepal participates from her office. In the initial discussion about this new approach, the client is ecstatic and relieved to hear she can remain at home for their sessions.

During several of their scheduled in-person sessions, Dr. Nepal goes over all the instructions of how to use the HIPAA-compliant CVT program: She first ensures that the client's home computer is compatible with the selected program and that the client has a camera; they practice with two computers in the office, and Dr. Nepal ensures that the client understands all aspects of the installation, use, and how to troubleshoot this particular program. She further ensures that the client's home computer is compatible with the office computer in all features. Dr. Nepal also goes over an addition to their original consent form that focuses specifically on concerns with the use of this new technology, such as privacy and confidentiality. After listening carefully and asking several questions, the client signs this addendum to their original confidentiality agreement, and Dr. Nepal believes that the client is embarking on this new therapeutic approach with a full understanding of the issues regarding confidentiality.

During their first telepsychology session, the actual process of making the CVT connection and engaging in therapy moved forward smoothly and effortlessly. However, several issues of privacy in the home setting came up during the sessions; Dr. Nepal is reconsidering the current arrangement and even thinking about abandoning the process with this particular client.

The doubts and reevaluation are not based on the client's diagnosis or capabilities or on the actual medium itself. Rather, the client has a desktop computer that is located in an alcove of the family kitchen. With several children at home, her mother-in-law who lives with them, and assorted guests and friends, the kitchen (and the whole house) is rather chaotic. It is the beginning of summer, and the children will be home for the next 2 to 3 months; thus, the client cannot create a private, undisturbed area for her sessions. The client's mother-in-law usually watched the children when the client would go to her sessions, but she is unable to keep them from going into the kitchen, a main thoroughfare of the house, while the client uses the computer.

KEY ELEMENTS, CHALLENGES, AND DECISION FACTORS

Dr. Nepal engaged in numerous positive and appropriate steps. She researched the literature about the appropriateness of the technological modality she was considering and matched it with the client. Her determination of the appropriateness of the telepsychology service for this client included an examination of potential risks and benefits, any multicultural or ethical issues that might arise, and a review of the most appropriate medium (e.g., video teleconference, text, e-mail) and best options available for the service delivery. She felt that telepsychology was warranted by the specific circumstances related to both the diagnosis and the client. Before the actual use of the new telepsychology component, Dr. Nepal reintroduced confidentiality with the client, ensuring she was making an informed decision to move forward with the technology, while also being aware of the increased potential for loss of confidentiality and security. Additionally, Dr. Nepal had the client practice with the CVT program in her office to answer any questions she might have and ensure she was competent in using the technology.

So what went wrong? Dr. Nepal failed to evaluate the client's environment to determine the suitability of using her home and computer for the sessions. Although she discussed confidentiality and privacy with the client, she did so in a general way, focusing on the Internet not being a totally secure environment and discussing how the technology might fail. What is also critically important here is the setting where the client will be during a telepsychology session. With the client's computer placed in a high-traffic area of her house, the client could not maintain confidentiality—or actually focus on the session—because she was interrupted and distracted by the noises and activity in her home.

The element of standards of care that Dr. Nepal failed to consider is the importance of assessing the remote environment for privacy breaches and risk of distractions. The psychologist and the client shared the responsibility to consider the factors that create a conducive space for services just as the face-to-face space is controlled for intervening disruptions.

OPTIONS AVAILABLE TO THE PSYCHOLOGIST

Dr. Nepal had the client come to her office for their next scheduled appointment and presented her with several options. Before discussing options, however, Dr. Nepal asked what the client thought about their first CVT session. The client expressed concern and frustration similar to what Dr. Nepal experienced. At this point, Dr. Nepal raised some options to consider. First, she said that they could discontinue using telepsychology and return to face-to-face sessions. An alternative was to have the family members leave the house during the sessions. A third option was to use a portable computer or tablet, allowing the client to move to a quiet, nondistracting location within the house for their sessions. While they brainstormed options, the client volunteered the potential for her to use a friend's home, at least during the summer while her own kids were out of school and at home. The friend lives within walking distance of her home, and the client often waters the plants and feeds a cat for her friend when she travels. This would allow a quiet place for their sessions. They discussed the pros and cons of all options, considered others, and then decided on one that both felt would best fit the needs of the client and the therapeutic process.

THE BEST DECISION POSSIBLE

The first decision to be made is whether the client wants to continue her therapy through telepsychology or switch to in-person treatment. If the client prefers in person, Dr. Nepal should either accept those conditions or refer her to a colleague, not try to talk the client out of in-person therapy. The client variable of preference is an important aspect of evidence-based practice and should be respected. Dr. Nepal and her client determined that, particularly for the short term, the availability of the friend's home was a good option.

If the client opts to continue telepsychology, continuing from her friend's home could be the best temporary solution. Because the client already made visits to the home for tasks and chores, no new agreement with the neighbor or negotiated access or responsibility for use of the home was needed, so the client had time to come up with a longer term solution when the neighbor returned to her home. Trying to change the family's use of the house at any given time is fraught with problems and would not typically be considered a viable solution. For a longer term solution, the client could begin creating a space in her house that is conducive to her treatment sessions and begin orienting family members to the designated use and privacy of that space. This process should begin right away so that when the client can no longer use the neighbor's house, the space in her own home would be operational.

Case Study 2: Accuracy of Student Reporting in Remote Supervisory Environment

RELEVANT EXCERPT FROM THE GUIDELINE

> Psychologists make every effort to ensure that ethical and professional standards of care and practice are met . . . throughout the duration of the telepsychology services they provide. (Joint Task Force, 2013, p. 794)

SETTING: REMOTE TRAINING AND SUPERVISION

Dr. Fernandez was recently assigned the position of university-based practicum supervisor for doctoral students in his university's training program. Having several years' experience in providing direct services as well as training on providing supervision, he was excited about the new opportunities and experiences this would provide.

As the new semester began, Dr. Fernandez found out that one student was completing a practicum at an off-site training facility, located in a town that is a 3-hour drive from the campus. Although there was an on-site supervisor at the student's practicum location, Dr. Fernandez was responsible for providing supervision as well. To further complicate the situation, Dr. Fernandez found that he was teaching classes during the times the practicum student was on campus, making it extremely difficult to arrange for a time to meet for their direct face-to-face supervision on a weekly basis. Thus, to ensure he maintained weekly supervision, Dr. Fernandez arranged to use CVT and a HIPAA-compliant software program to allow supervision of the student remotely, with Dr. Fernandez in his office and the student at the practicum site.

SCENARIO

Dr. Fernandez selected a HIPAA-compliant CVT program to be used on his university-issued computer and the student's personal laptop for their supervision sessions. Although the student was using a personal laptop, the software program was obtained by the university because this was a university-sanctioned activity, requiring the university's information technology department to install the software on the student's laptop and ensure an appropriate level of security and encryption was met. After extensive research, consultation with peers, and review of the state and university laws and policies and the *Guidelines for the Practice of Telepsychology* (Joint Task Force, 2013), Dr. Fernandez conducted his own examination of the potential risks and benefits of providing telepsychology supervision to a student. He evaluated the multicultural and ethical issues that could arise and reviewed the most appropriate medium (e.g., video teleconference, text, e-mail) for the service delivery. After his review, Dr. Fernandez decided that CVT was the most appropriate approach. He then discussed the potential risks and benefits with the student and reviewed specific procedures to follow when there were connection difficulties, emergencies, or other unforeseen circumstances, including the potential loss of confidentiality and security of their supervision sessions.

Dr. Fernandez and the student then found a convenient day and time for them to connect online and hold their weekly supervision sessions. Before the start of classes, the supervisor and the student met in his office and conducted a trial connection between their computers, ensuring they both had the appropriate equipment and configurations for the selected program. Additionally, they were then able to ensure that both knew how to correctly use the program, and at the end of this meeting, both agreed that they felt confident and comfortable using this software for their supervision sessions.

The first week of classes found the two of them connecting and holding their first remote supervisory session. At the end of this first session, Dr. Fernandez ensured that they had 5 minutes to talk about the use of this technology and see whether there were any questions, concerns, or potential improvements that could be made with the process. Both agreed that all had gone well with the connection and the content of the supervision session; neither saw any need for change at this point.

The first 6 weeks went by, and both the student and Dr. Fernandez considered the weekly CVT telepsychology supervision sessions a success. Every few weeks, Dr. Fernandez would save the last 5 minutes of the session for an evaluation of the technology component to see if there was a need to change the process in any way. No changes had been made; both participants stated that this method was meeting their needs, and each felt it to be a smooth, easy process. However, it should be noted that there were periodic connectivity issues, seeming to develop from the low Wi-Fi signal the student had when meeting in an enclosed office space. They handled this by switching to an audio-only component when the weak signal did not allow for visual transmission. When the student first logged into the program and received a note that the visual component might not be available due to a poor Internet connection, they would then connect using the audio-only part of the program. This seemed to happen more often as the semester progressed, but both thought that they could continue with remote sessions because the audio content continued to meet their needs.

With 3 weeks remaining in the semester, Dr. Fernandez began hearing rumors among the other students that his student was having some problems integrating into the practicum site, both in collaboration and interaction with peers and in adapting to the practices of the site. For example, the student was reported to have had several verbal confrontations with another practicum student at the site over sharing testing kits and to have argued with clinic administrative staff over records access. Dr. Fernandez was surprised to hear the rumors—and very concerned about whether they were true—because he had not been aware of any of the problems raised. In fact, whenever asked about how his adaptation and integration into the site and with other students and professionals was going, the student reported that all was going smoothly, that he got along well with the staff and clients, and that he thought he had integrated into the system easily. Satisfied with these reports, Dr. Fernandez then allowed their supervision sessions to focus on case conceptualizations, treatment options, and logistics.

As is appropriate in the supervisor's role, Dr. Fernandez raised the matter of the rumors with the student during their next supervision session. The student appeared surprised by the questions Dr. Fernandez was asking, and the session then switched to audio only because the student said the connection became weak. Conducting the rest of this supervision session through only an audio medium, Dr. Fernandez heard anxiety and evasiveness in the student's voice and was unable to have the student clearly respond to the concerns he raised.

At this point, Dr. Fernandez began to question all the information he had received from the student during their supervision sessions, wondering whether the student had glossed over problems with his integration into the actual practicum location. Upon further evaluation, Dr. Fernandez began to wonder about the "poor connection" issue and whether the student felt that by removing the visual component of the session, he would be less likely to notice visual clues to his problems. He even wondered whether the student was actually at the practicum location during their supervision sessions or if perhaps they were connecting somewhere else and the loss of the video portion masked the student's actual location. Many things began to flow through Dr. Fernandez's mind as to the possible level of deceitfulness in which the student could have engaged during their supervision sessions.

KEY ELEMENTS, CHALLENGES, AND DECISION FACTORS

It should be noted that Dr. Fernandez went about the process of developing the remote audiovisual supervision sessions in a conscientious manner. He conducted a comprehensive literature review on using CVT technology in supervision, consulted with colleagues, and reviewed national guidelines and local laws and university policies to help make the decision to engage in this process with the student. Dr. Fernandez also conducted a simulation, with both computers and individuals present, to ensure that they could connect and see if there were any problems with either the technology being used or their ability to use it. Finally, Dr. Fernandez would periodically check in with the student to discuss the process of conducting supervision through a CVT medium to see whether any changes were necessary.

Dr. Fernandez appears to have made the assumption that he could continually engage in the supervision process when there was only an audio component, relying on hearing what was being said and not having the visual component available. He failed to ensure that the information being provided to him from the student was accurate and true and to check regularly with the on-site practicum staff. On the basis of the information the student gave him, Dr. Fernandez elected to focus on the clinical issues and paid less attention to the student's interpersonal and professional competency issues.

OPTIONS AVAILABLE TO THE PSYCHOLOGIST

As the student's university-based practicum supervisor, Dr. Fernandez was responsible for the student and the connection between the university and the practicum setting. His first action was to discuss the issues with the student to obtain his perspectives and responses. He then contacted the student's on-site practicum supervisor to see whether there were any issues or concerns she had with the student, focusing on the issues that began to develop when the student was confronted. Information obtained from the practicum-based supervisor confirmed there were some concerns about the student's ability to integrate with the site, both interpersonally and collaboratively. However, because the student was completing his caseload requirements and the on-site supervisor thought the student's clinical skills were developing well, she did not see a need to contact Dr. Fernandez. Dr. Fernandez discussed the professional development of the student, in addition to his clinical skills development, and asked for more information. With the new information and insight, he then requested a direct face-to-face meeting with the student on campus. Although it was inconvenient for both of them, they were able to arrange a very early morning meeting where the supervisor raised these issues with the student.

The student realized he was not relating to other students or working well within the practicum site policies and procedures, but he had not raised these issues because he believed he was managing and treating his caseload effectively. He realized after the discussion that it was in the interest of his professional development that he resolve these problems before going further with his training. Dr. Fernandez realized that he had rationalized the failure to maintain video connection as a technology problem and had relied too heavily on the student's report. He may have been able to discern signs of difficulties had he been in video contact with the student. Furthermore, he had decided to focus on clinical rather than professional skills and thus missed the student's evasive body language and unease with supervision as well as his deficient interpersonal skills. The failure of standards of care in this case was that Dr. Fernandez established criteria for remote supervision at the outset of training but did not maintain those criteria (i.e., visual access during supervision) throughout supervision.

THE BEST DECISION POSSIBLE

Dr. Fernandez did implement the technology requirements, including technology competence for the initiation of therapy, but overlooked the important variables of both in-person and remote therapy. The visual aspect of supervision for training, more so than for consultation, is important for the reasons he later discovered. Even more significant, supervision is about not only technical skills but also the working alliance and the ability to assess students' interpersonal skills with clients, other students, and faculty.

Regardless of the use of technology during supervision, Dr. Fernandez realized that he should always seek input from the on-site supervisor regarding all aspects of the supervisee's work, including professional and clinical development. He further realized that in the future he would only engage in limited audio-only telepsychology supervision and only when remote conditions or other emergency situations prevailed. He determined that going forward he would make physical site visits when engaged in telepsychology supervision.

Case Study 3: Putting Technology Enthusiasm Before Research

RELEVANT EXCERPT FROM THE GUIDELINE

> Psychologists make every effort to ensure that ethical . . . standards of care and practice are met at the outset. (Joint Task Force, 2013, p. 794)

SETTING: INTERNSHIP SUPERVISION AT A PUBLIC SECTOR SITE

Mary Lou is a psychology doctoral intern working at a local mental health clinic in a large urban city. She considers herself to be skilled with technology, and, after reading about the incorporation of telepsychology services into clinical practice, she is excited to try it out herself.

SCENARIO

After the first month of her internship, Mary Lou asked her clinical supervisor numerous times if she could try to incorporate some telepsychology services using an audiovisual component with a client. This would allow the client to remain at home and not take city buses or walk long distances, while Mary Lou would be housed in her office at the clinic. Additionally, this particular client has had a history of being late to sessions, blaming the public transportation system for her tardiness. The supervisor agreed, but only after Mary Lou first explained exactly what she was planning to do and how it would work.

Ecstatic, Mary Lou began using the Google search function to find an app that would allow her to have psychotherapy sessions with the participants in two locations.

While reading reviews for various programs, she learned that some were free but others could become very expensive. Knowing the center had a limited budget, Mary Lou narrowed her search on the Internet for free apps. She finally found a free program with numerous five-star (out of five) reviews, all touting ease of use, great technical support, and colorful design.

Mary Lou tried the program at home with her roommate on a second computer, and it worked exactly as described. They had a wonderful conversation from two rooms in the apartment, and both said how much they liked the design and smooth process for setting it up and connecting. Mary Lou was now ready for a demonstration with her supervisor and then to begin using the program with clients.

At her next supervision session, Mary Lou began talking rapidly about the program. She described what it did and how it would change the life of her client because she would not have to hazard the various transportation issues and her on-time attendance difficulties would be resolved; instead, she could connect easily at home and have her sessions. At this point, the supervisor, who had read the *Guidelines for the Practice of Telepsychology* (Joint Task Force, 2013) began to ask Mary Lou several questions, the first being, "Why this technology with this client?" Mary Lou explained that she selected the client because not having the long commute would help her focus on their therapeutic sessions and not worry about transportation issues, which often contributed to her being late for sessions, resulting in limited therapeutic time.

The supervisor then asked Mary Lou what research was available on using telepsychology services in clinical practice. Mary Lou explained that she searched the Internet for the best audiovisual technology program she could find that was free and then read the numerous online reviews. The supervisor patiently reframed the original question and asked, "Yes, evaluating the program for use is important, but what does our professional research tell us about using telepsychology services in clinical practice?"

Mary Lou seemed a little perplexed. She asked, "Has there been research done on this?" At this point, the supervisor gave Mary Lou a copy of the *Guidelines for the Practice of Telepsychology* (Joint Task Force, 2013) and said, "Please read this first and then use a professional search engine to read the current research results and their guidance for use of these services in clinical practice. We will talk about this next week before we proceed further."

KEY ELEMENTS, CHALLENGES, AND DECISION FACTORS

As with the use of any new therapeutic technique, the individual must carefully review the professional literature base to determine what research findings suggest with regard to the identified technique. In this case, Mary Lou, driven by her desire to both help the client with transportation issues and her own desire to jump into technology in clinical practice, ended up far astray from using sound clinical judgment.

In asking Mary Lou "Why this technology with this client?" her supervisor modeled the starting point when considering using technology in clinical practice. The question actually has two parts: the identified technology and the client. Technology should never be incorporated into clinical practice solely because the psychologist wants to use technology. The psychologist should carefully consider the various options, including not using any form of technology, while considering each individual client to determine how appropriate the identified technology is for the client's diagnostic impression and access to technology. Furthermore, Mary Lou overlooked the importance of ensuring her ability to conduct services with the proposed system, her client's ability to navigate the technology, and her thorough knowledge of managing the technical aspects of telecommunications. Mary Lou, thus far, had not considered the importance of emergency remote services and the importance of security features on her equipment.

The research base on the use of that technology with clients presenting with specific clinical features also needs to be considered. Additionally, the psychologist should always identify multicultural and ethical issues that could arise when adding a telepsychology component to ensure that concerns can be addressed appropriately.

OPTIONS AVAILABLE TO THE PSYCHOLOGIST

Mary Lou returned the next week with enthusiasm as she described to her supervisor all she had learned. She told her supervisor that she spent every spare minute of her free time searching the professional literature base for anything she could find on telepsychology practice. She said, "I am amazed by how much I didn't know or even consider before embarking on this endeavor! Did you know that . . ." and she began sharing numerous issues that had to be considered and addressed at the beginning of the process.

Although disappointed that she wasn't going to be able to start CVT services with her client right away, Mary Lou said she would be back with a plan to share with her supervisor. They both agreed that once she had a plan, including research-based information and guidance, they would meet again to discuss next steps.

Meanwhile, the supervisor also stated that he would begin his own review of telepsychology and its incorporation in therapy to advance his knowledge and skills with this new adjunct to therapy. The failure of standards of care here is the failure to observe APA Ethical Standard 2.04 (APA, 2017) in which psychologists base their work on established scientific and professional knowledge of the discipline.

THE BEST DECISION POSSIBLE

Mary Lou realized that she had let her enthusiasm get ahead of her consideration of the many factors in initiating a new delivery method for psychotherapy. She decided to step back and assess (a) her knowledge and understanding of the technology and her responsibility for the client's competence in electronic communication; (b) the appropriateness of her chosen treatment plan and commensurate research supporting the approach; and (c) the diagnostic impression, mental status, medical conditions, and other factors of the presenting case. Mary Lou began to realize that the choice of using telepsychology should be based on many factors rather than simply her personal interest. Exploring in depth the preferences of the client, the ability of the client to participate, and both parties' understanding of the conditions of telepsychology that are not applicable for in-person services is of critical importance. If telepsychology services are initiated at some point, Mary Lou will be particularly vigilant in committing to an ongoing assessment of the process, outcome, and, importantly, the evaluation of the client.

Case Study 4: Failure to Consider Client Variables

RELEVANT EXCERPT FROM THE GUIDELINE

> Psychologists make every effort to ensure that . . . professional standards of care and practice are met at the outset. (Joint Task Force, 2013, p. 794)

SETTING: PUBLIC SECTOR AGENCY

Psychologist Dr. Adamson had been in practice for 3 years, working in a small community agency, where she saw a variety of clients from different socioeconomic backgrounds with a wide range of presenting issues. As an early-career psychologist, Dr. Adamson began following telepsychology research. Once hired by her agency, she began the process of developing rules and procedures for incorporating telepsychology services with the agency's clients when appropriate. Dr. Adamson had attended several continuing education programs and continued to read the most current research-based literature about the use of telepsychology services in clinical practice, and she joined a group of colleagues who were at various stages of incorporating telepsychology into their practice settings.

SCENARIO

For 2 years now, many of Dr. Adamson's clients have received psychotherapy via telepsychology services. Having reviewed all current laws and regulatory rules related to telepsychology, and using the *Guidelines for the Practice of Telepsychology* (Joint Task Force, 2013) as her starting point, Dr. Adamson put together what appeared to be a successful add-on benefit to the services her clients received at the clinic. Many of her clients engaged in psychotherapy using a HIPAA-compliant CVT system, allowing them to remain at home during their sessions.

Her colleagues considered Dr. Adamson's program very successful. In fact, she had been asked to speak with psychologists from other clinics to explain how she developed her program, the processes she had in place, and to give them suggestions on how to adapt telepsychology to their own clinical settings. Dr. Adamson was constantly looking at alternatives and ways to improve her program.

Meanwhile, Dr. Adamson found that one of her telepsychology-based clients seemed to continue to struggle and did not seem to be making progress over the previous 2 months. Dr. Adamson was not sure why the client's progress had reached a point of stagnation and decided to consult with a colleague who had been engaged in providing telepsychology services for more than 5 years now about her concerns.

Her colleague, Dr. Cinatl, who has practiced extensively in both face-to-face and telepsychology venues, initially listened to Dr. Adamson describe the case, the presenting issues, and the progress thus far in the therapeutic process. Then Dr. Cinatl asked Dr. Adamson what barriers she could think of that might be keeping this client from moving forward. As they talked about what might be contributing to the client's stagnation, Dr. Cinatl asked Dr. Adamson what impact the telepsychology component of service delivery may have had on this particular case. Surprised, Dr. Adamson asked her colleague why she would ask that question. Dr. Cinatl explained that it was possible that the method of services—in this case, the CVT delivery—could affect the therapeutic relationship in some manner because it added new elements that might not be present in a direct services, face-to-face approach. When probed for more information, Dr. Cinatl explained that seeing someone on a computer screen is different from seeing someone in person. She wondered if Dr. Adamson was missing some visual cues that are more readily apparent when sitting down with a client across from her versus seeing the same person on a computer screen. Or perhaps Dr. Adamson was presenting with her own distracting or unintended visual cues that were affecting the client and the therapeutic process.

KEY ELEMENTS, CHALLENGES, AND DECISION FACTORS

Dr. Adamson had developed and implemented what appeared to be a successful telepsychology service component of her practice. She engaged in many of the steps recommended by the literature and the guidance provided by APA and other organizations. In addition, she attempted to stay current on the research literature in the area and was constantly evaluating and looking for ways to improve her program and the services she provided. Another important positive step Dr. Adamson took was sharing her program and her work with other professionals, resulting in a continual learning process for her.

However, and despite her best efforts, Dr. Adamson forgot to consider how the specific modality—the CVT process—affected the client on both a personal and a therapeutic level. To her credit, when she realized that she could not determine on her own why her client was not making progress, Dr. Adamson consulted a colleague. As many good consultations go, her colleague helped her to see a different perspective to the case. With the new information, Dr. Adamson could then develop new ways to help her client begin to move forward.

The failure of standards of care in this case was the oversight of Dr. Adamson in comprehensively and frequently assessing the appropriateness of telepsychology services for this client given the client variables, specifically diagnostic impression, therapeutic needs, and emotional stability.

OPTIONS AVAILABLE TO THE PSYCHOLOGIST

As the two psychologists discussed the case in light of this new insight, Dr. Adamson questioned whether her client's struggling to move forward at this point was actually due in part to the delivery mode. They asked each other what potential issues could arise from a CVT telepsychology service delivery method. They discussed the two-dimensional aspect that a computer screen provides versus real-life, face-to-face therapy. Dr. Adamson thought of the presenting problems and the subsequent diagnosis of depression. The client had presented with abandonment issues, broken relationships with parents and significant others, and trust issues. She began to realize that because of the client variables of greatest importance in this case, the client might need a face-to-face venue based on diagnosis, relational fragmentation, and inability to connect that might be further exacerbated by the technological delivery of services.

THE BEST DECISION POSSIBLE

After their brainstorming process concluded with several potential solutions to consider, Dr. Adamson met with her client for their next scheduled session. However, rather than proceeding as she had before, Dr. Adamson began to look at the entire process in a new light, as well as what her client was presenting in terms of the therapeutic relationship factors. Based on the information gleaned from both her consultation and a critical eye toward a reevaluation and reassessment of the case, Dr. Adamson then began to work on a plan to move beyond those barriers and find a way to help the client make progress towards her therapeutic goals.

Dr. Adamson had begun treating the medium of telepsychology as a default standard of treatment and did not even consider in-person services in her practice. Partly because she was receiving recognition for her telepractice program, she unintentionally subjugated the client variables and therefore the treatment needs of the client based on presenting problems, diagnostic impressions, and client preferences.

Upon realizing this perspective, Dr. Adamson began being deliberate about her assessment of clinical intake, presenting problem, and other client variables when accepting new clients. She thought further about her diagnostic impressions, coping skills, defense mechanisms of clients, and other variables that might affect her decisions not only about an in-person versus a telecommunication medium but also her chosen treatment plan and its application to the conditions of practice in light of standards of care.

Case Study 5: Social Media and Psychological Services

RELEVANT EXCERPT FROM THE GUIDELINE

> Psychologists make every effort to ensure that . . . professional standards of care and practice are met at the outset and throughout the duration of the telepsychology services they provide. (Joint Task Force, 2013, p. 794)

SETTING: INDEPENDENT PRACTICE

Dr. Sudan maintained a psychological practice in a large city and saw a variety of adult clients, mostly dealing with self-esteem, confidence, and relationship issues, for more than 20 years. She did not engage in any telepsychology services directly with clients (e.g., no CVT services of any type). However, Dr. Sudan did write a therapeutic blog, maintained on her clinic's website and only accessible to her clients who were currently receiving services at her practice. Her blog consisted of postings on various issues that she found were important to many of the clients she saw. For example, her most recent posting was focused on identifying various behaviors someone engages in when they are enabling or supporting a partner's emotionally abusive behaviors.

SCENARIO

Throughout Dr. Sudan's career, she had enjoyed writing professional documents covering a variety of topics, often based on current trends, issues, and highlights related to areas in which she was well-versed through her practice, a review of current research, and general knowledge. Approximately 10 years ago, Dr. Sudan began writing short papers that focused on a specific issue that was relevant to one or more clients. She would give a copy of the paper to a client near the end of a session, discussing the purpose and intent of the article, as well as how they would follow up on the information it contained in future therapeutic sessions.

As Dr. Sudan's practice flourished, the number of these types of papers grew. About 3 years ago, Dr. Sudan made the decision to go digital, and after initially e-mailing the papers to her clients, she decided to publish them on her website in the form of blog entries. However, Dr. Sudan was not sure how to technically create a blog space; what level of security the blogs would need, including how to allow her clients access but not the general public; and what liabilities or level of risk she was being placed in by publishing these blogs.

The first step she took was to decide how to share the information with her clients. She considered a number of questions. Would all her clients be able to access all of the posted blogs, or only specific ones? Would she need to password protect each blog post individually, or just the site where they were located? What was her clinical intention for the use of these blogs? Were they to be considered as external readings, available to any and all clients, with no specific therapeutic context? Or would clients only be given access to specific blogs that would then be discussed in upcoming therapy sessions?

Because she wasn't sure what would be the most appropriate approach for her clients' well-being as the priority, Dr. Sudan felt she needed consultation and support from a colleague who was more experienced in the use of blogs. However, she was not able to locate a colleague who used blogs in a therapeutic setting, so she ended up talking with several colleagues to brainstorm the best approach. On the basis of these various consultations and after much thought, Dr. Sudan decided that she would use the blog posts as she originally intended them to be used, as an adjunct to specific therapy sessions. With that decision made, she was then able to determine that she would need to limit access to the blog postings to specific clients at specific points in their therapy process, when the two of them could process the information during a therapeutic session. This required specific passwords and links that could be given to a client when Dr. Sudan was ready for them to access the information contained in the blog.

After resolving these questions, Dr. Sudan's next step was to contact her malpractice insurance carrier to ask for a consultation of risk when sharing this type of information with clients via a blog space. Given her intended use of the blogs and the password protection, as well as inclusion of the information contained in the blog in upcoming therapy sessions, she was told her plan contained minimal risk to the clients and herself.

Dr. Sudan then began working with her site's webmaster to begin the programming process to upload and password protect the various blogs. She also continued to write and revise her previous work, ensuring that the information was up-to-date with the latest research and was appropriate for her clients. She also established a calendar setting to remind her to review each blog every 3 months and update the information or remove it, as appropriate. She continued to write new blogs and incorporate them into her therapy sessions as needed.

KEY ELEMENTS, CHALLENGES, AND DECISION FACTORS

Dr. Sudan created a new process in her practice to disseminate information that was used in her therapeutic sessions. However, she quickly reached a key decision point: what the actual process would be in using these blog postings. Would they be general postings available to anyone on the Internet, limited postings to clients on her website, or extremely limited with her determining who and when a client had access to the blog? She ultimately decided to go with the most restrictive approach when she revisited her reason for the development of the information. She originally wrote the papers with the purpose of using them in conjunction with therapy, not as a general sharing of information to a general public. Deciding that she would remain with her original purpose, Dr. Sudan was then able to make several follow-up decisions, such as how clients would access the information and how she could facilitate the ease of the access.

Working with her webmaster, Dr. Sudan was able to create a process in which she could share a link with a client on a specific blog and provide instructions on what was expected from the client and how the information would be raised in future therapeutic sessions. Another challenge Dr. Sudan faced was ensuring the information in each blog remained current. Previously, before handing a copy to the client, she would review the document, make updates to it, and then print a copy. Now she established a calendar reminder system that would alert her when a blog posting was more than 3 months old, reminding her to review and update as needed.

OPTIONS AVAILABLE TO THE PSYCHOLOGIST

Dr. Sudan initially attempted to consult with another psychologist on how best to proceed with developing a set of blog postings on her clinical website. However, she could not find a colleague who had engaged in this type of practice, so she consulted with several colleagues to discuss her plans and request their input on how she might proceed. Dr. Sudan faced several choices. She could develop educational and informative blog material that was applicable to all clients given the generalized nature of the material. This process would be time- and effort-efficient because the material would apply generically to all clients. Further, the processes of preparing the blogs would be minimal. As Dr. Sudan considered this choice, she realized that what she had wanted to do all along was to individualize her blog messages to specific clients so that the messages would be applicable at any given time or under any circumstance, depending on the work of the client. She realized that this option would be much more time consuming and take much more care in thinking about the needs of each client at any given time.

THE BEST DECISION POSSIBLE

Through these various discussions, what Dr. Sudan intended became more clear to her and ultimately allowed her to answer her own questions, thereby giving her the direction she should take. She realized that the concept of incorporating the blogs into her professional practice was and should be seen as an adjunct to the purpose and effectiveness of her work with clients and that the blogs should enhance the experience of the clients in their respective treatment plans. As a result, Dr. Sudan realized the importance of the blogging being very specifically developed for individual clients. She determined that general informational material that is educational and that enhances self-reflection is qualitatively different from material arising from her intention to individually enhance her clients' therapeutic experience. Dr. Sudan then contacted her malpractice insurance carrier to obtain guidance on the level of risk she was taking when using these blog posts within her practice.

After discussions with her malpractice carrier, she considered several other factors: (a) When considering using technology, Dr. Sudan would first carefully consider the reason and have an appropriate justification for adding the technology into the practice; (b) seeking consultation from colleagues, even when none of them had used the technology in the way the Dr. Sudan intended, helped clarify the rationale and purpose; (c) information posted on a blog could have a variety of settings allowing others access, including general or open to the public, limited to those with access to a specific website, or extremely limited to only individuals the posting person wants to have access; and (d) information posted on a website should always have a set time for the individual responsible for it to review or revise to ensure it is current.

Key Points From the Chapter to Remember

- Develop a plan for using telepsychology and technology with clients that outlines the rationale and process. Discuss the reason for introducing the telepsychology component with the client and obtain consent.

- Review the available literature to support the use of telepsychology with each client's specific diagnosis and conduct ongoing monitoring to ensure that telepsychology continues to meet the intended therapeutic purpose.
- Make a determination of technology use primarily based on appropriateness for the individual client. The primary determinants of appropriateness are client variables, which should include the following:
  - Evaluate and address multicultural and ethical issues that arise when first introducing the telepsychology component. Also, periodically confer with the client on any multicultural or ethical issues that could have arisen during therapy.
  - Consider factors such as mental health status, diagnostic impression, medical conditions, treatment history and needs, therapeutic needs, and emotional stability of the client as well as relative significance of the working alliance. Furthermore, assess and determine emergency access.
- Use of telepsychology services should be deemed at least as effective as face-to-face services and should be determined by evidence-based findings regarding client variables and application of the techniques or theoretical approaches employed.
- Discuss and address new issues of confidentiality and security that arise with the introduction of the telepsychology component in therapy, including securing the area where the patient will be during the telepsychology sessions.
- Technology competence should be ensured both for the psychologist and the client. When evaluating the progress of a client, the psychologist should also evaluate the use of technology. When beginning the development of a new competency, such as using telepsychology, the psychologist should attend professional development activities focused on this new skill and seek consultation from others experienced with using technology.
- Practice using the equipment and software to ensure the patient is comfortable with and capable of engaging in telepsychology.
- The remote setting is a major factor in successful telepsychology use and should be evaluated before services begin. The Standards of Care Guideline includes expectations of meeting the APA (2017) *Ethical Principles of Psychologists and Code of Conduct* that includes basing practice on sound research and scientific knowledge.
- The psychologist should review current laws, state and national, as well as regulatory rules to ensure that the psychologist is engaged in appropriate and legal practice.
- Join or create an ongoing, standing group of other psychologists who use technology in their work to provide continual consultation and support.

References

American Psychological Association. (2017). *Ethical principles of psychologists and code of conduct* (2002, Amended June 1, 2010 and January 1, 2017). Retrieved from http://www.apa.org/ethics/code/index.aspx

Clough, B. A., & Casey, L. M. (2015). Smart designs for smart technologies: Research challenges and emerging solutions for scientist-practitioners within e-mental health. *Professional Psychology: Research and Practice, 46,* 429–436. http://dx.doi.org/10.1037/pro0000053

Health Insurance Portability and Accountability Act, Pub. L. No. 104-191, 110 Stat. 1936 (1996).

Joint Task Force for the Development of Telepsychology Guidelines for Psychologists. (2013). Guidelines for the practice of telepsychology. *American Psychologist, 68,* 791–800. Retrieved from https://www.apa.org/pubs/journals/features/amp-a0035001.pdf

Luxton, D. (2013, August). Considerations for planning and evaluating economic analyses of telemental health [Special issue: Advances in Telehealth and Telepsychology]. *Psychological Services, 10,* 276–282. http://dx.doi.org/10.1037/a0030658

Margo Adams Larsen and Cindy Juntunen

Informed Consent 3

Psychologists strive to obtain and document informed consent that specifically addresses the unique concerns related to the telepsychology services they provide. When doing so, psychologists are cognizant of the applicable laws and regulations, as well as organizational requirements, that govern informed consent in this area.

—Guideline 3, *Guidelines for the Practice of Telepsychology*

Rationale

The process of explaining and obtaining informed consent, by whatever means, sets the stage for the relationship between the psychologist and the client/patient. Psychologists make reasonable efforts to offer a complete and clear description of the telepsychology services they provide, and they seek to obtain and document informed consent when providing professional services (APA *Ethical Principles of Psychologists and Code of Conduct,* Standard 3.10 [American Psychological Association, 2017]). In addition, they attempt to develop and share the policies and procedures that will explain to their clients/patients how they will interact with them using the specific telecommunication technologies involved. It may be more difficult to obtain and document informed consent in situations where psychologists provide telepsychology services to their clients/patients who are not in the same physical location or with whom they do not have in-person interactions. Moreover, there may be differences with respect to informed consent

http://dx.doi.org/10.1037/0000046-004
A Telepsychology Casebook: Using Technology Ethically and Effectively in Your Professional Practice, L. F. Campbell, F. Millán, and J. N. Martin (Editors)

> between the laws and regulations in the jurisdictions where a psychologist who is providing telepsychology services is located and those in the jurisdiction in which this psychologist's client/patient resides. Furthermore, psychologists may need to be aware of the manner in which cultural, linguistic, and socioeconomic characteristics and organizational considerations may impact a client's/patient's understanding of, and the special considerations required for, obtaining informed consent (such as when securing informed consent remotely from a parent/guardian when providing telepsychology services to a minor).
>
> Telepsychology services may require different considerations for and safeguards against potential risks to confidentiality, information security, and comparability of traditional in-person services. Psychologists are thus encouraged to consider appropriate policies and procedures to address the potential threats to the security of client/patient data and information when using specific telecommunication technologies and to appropriately inform their clients/patients about them. For example, psychologists who provide telepsychology services should consider addressing with their clients/patients what client/patient data and information will be stored, how the data and information will be stored, how it will be accessed, how secure the information communicated using a given technology is, and any technology-related vulnerability to their confidentiality and security that is incurred by creating and storing electronic client/patient data and information. (Joint Task Force for the Development of Telepsychology Guidelines for Psychologists, 2013, pp. 795–796)

Informed consent is among the most fundamental of ethics concepts that guide psychologists. It provides information that may affect the client's decision to engage in the services offered, including about the treatment itself or the outcome of treatment, that is critically important in respecting the rights of the clients. When applying informed consent beyond in-person practice to telepsychology, several new factors are introduced.

Psychologists ensure their competencies in their areas of practice and are apprised of continuing education, lifelong learning, and other means to maintain their clinical competence. Telepsychology introduces technical competence as a requirement for practice and ensures that clinical competence will be sustained in this new medium of communication. Psychologists are responsible for ensuring that clients are also technologically competent to practice electronically. Language, culture, ethnicity, and other diversity factors are important in all venues including in telepsychology practice. When technical competence for both psychologists and clients are necessary and diversity competence is necessary for psychologists, these factors become critically important areas to be communicated in informed consent so that misinterpretations and miscommunications are minimized.

Psychologists will want to clearly identify the boundaries of practice that include if and when the psychologist is available to communicate through texting or e-mail and how the interactions are treated (e.g., prohibition against forwarding psychologists' communication, storing therapeutic material), as well as other out-of-session interactions. Confidentiality is an important inclusion for informed consent because there are now many inherent risks to confidentiality through technology breakdowns, human error, and equipment failure that do not apply in person and for which the client may not be aware without explicit discussion.

Fee structure, billing, and treatment of interruptions are significantly affected when applied to telecommunications. Various forms of contact (e.g., video chat, texting, telephone, e-mail) will need to be clearly delineated, in addition to the actual session interaction. Failures of equipment, human error during telecontact, and other variations that are not as prolific in in-person practice need to be agreed on before services begin.

Given these few examples, it becomes evident that informed consent is a key factor in general practice but also in bridging ways of thinking about in-person practice to telepsychology practice. Psychologists may meet all of the standards of practice for telepsychology, but if the client is not apprised adequately through informed consent, then psychologists are, in fact, not meeting standards of practice.

The four case studies in this chapter highlight various setting considerations when developing informed consent procedures related to telepsychology: informed consent that includes some common "think-ahead" considerations to assist in the progressive development of procedures for when clinical situations are significantly risky, when care is provided in a training setting, when children are direct service recipients, and when services are consultative to an organization but involve many employees. Each case study is designed to provide positive strategies and prompt the reader to critically consider difficult situations before they become lessons learned.

Case Study 1: Risky Clinical Situations

RELEVANT EXCERPT FROM THE GUIDELINE

> Psychologists strive to obtain and document informed consent that specifically addresses the unique concerns related to the telepsychology services they provide. When doing so psychologists are cognizant of the applicable laws and regulations, as well as organizational requirements that govern informed consent in this area. (Joint Task Force, 2013, p. 795)

SETTING: INDEPENDENT PRACTICE

Dr. Thomas Gray was a psychologist in independent practice. He offered assessment and therapy services to adult clients with diverse clinical concerns. Dr. Gray's clientele comprised a relatively diverse population spanning remote service areas. His specialty was working with difficult clients, and he was often requested by the court to provide ongoing therapy to some of the most challenging cases. Dr. Gray was eager to explore the world of telepractice, identifying the telephone as an extremely valuable tool that had augmented dialectical behavior therapy (DBT) for borderline personality disorder for many years. He had a group of colleagues throughout the state with whom he could share an emergency on-call response schedule. These psychologists had developed a call-in network for crisis calls for their patients with borderline and personality disorders within the jurisdiction, as was customary of the empirically validated DBT treatment model they all practiced. As Dr. Gray's practice expanded and technology advanced, he saw the potential for using videoconferencing to reach more remote clients and to reduce the rate of no-shows within his practice. He was familiar with the *Guidelines for the Practice of Telepsychology* (Joint Task Force, 2013), developed by the APA, the Association of State and Provincial Psychology Boards, and The Trust. He attended several telepsychology workshops online and through his state psychological association. He had routine teleconsultation calls on a weekly basis with his DBT colleagues to discuss ongoing case management and sought information from the APA.

Dr. Gray was thoughtful in his selection and application of technology products to manage his clinical work. At the outset of his practice, he developed a specific and detailed set of informed consent procedures that clearly outlined various aspects of his clinical services, the nature of the crisis call team, and his rules and requirements with regard to videoconferencing services, when in-person office services would be required for care, and requirements for confidentiality and commitment to more intensive care. In creating the informed consent, Dr. Gray reviewed a risk analysis and task checklist related to telepsychology care (see the Self-Assessment Checklist in Exhibit 3.1). Dr. Gray had reviewed his state-specific mandatory reporting laws and commitment laws, and he reviewed and documented these with each potential client before the beginning of services. Given the difficult population with whom Dr. Gray primarily worked, he required the initial visit be completed in his office to review the detailed informed consent for services, obtain consent signatures, and provide copies of these documents to his patients for their future review to engage in videoconferencing services.

As part of this consent process, Dr. Gray required his patients to bring the device they would use for their videoconferencing services to the initial appointment so he could review with them the security and privacy settings and discuss detailed guidelines and recommendations with regard to online and digital information sharing. Although not an information technologies expert, Dr. Gray had found that taking the time to identify some of the user-controlled aspects of device privacy and security helped eliminate time spent on this in future sessions. Dr. Gray explicitly indicated that he would only read and respond to digital information that was sent through his encrypted e-mail portal that was part of his electronic medical record (EMR) system, a system his patients used for scheduling and that he used for records management and billing. Dr. Gray reviewed his strict requirements regarding the use of videoconferencing for DBT, and his informed consent form included specific information for court-referred/court-ordered therapy services. Finally, he reviewed the consenting procedures for the crisis call team in which he and his colleagues participated and how this information, as well as process, worked. Detailed consent and release forms had been developed for this purpose, and Dr. Gray required this of all his patients in DBT care, including the authentication processes.

Dr. Gray's practice grew steadily, and the consultation team in which he participated provided significant professional support as well as opportunities to have brief contacts with other clinicians' cases. Dr. Gray knew that all providers on the five-person consultation team used the same consenting documentation and paperwork

EXHIBIT 3.1

Informed Consent Self-Assessment Checklist

- Did I inform patients/clients/consultees how I will communicate with them using technology, what type of information is appropriate to share over this modality, and the time frame they may expect a response?
- Did I have a plan for how I will react if I receive sensitive information (e.g., grounds for mandated reporting) from a patient/client/consultee through technological communications?
- Did I screen patients/clients/consultees for appropriateness with technology-based services (e.g., clinical, technological, language)?
- Have I identified any particular risks related to interventions that have or have not been tested in a technology-based service delivery? Have I made these risks clear to the patients/clients/consultees so that they are able to make an informed decision about initiating or continuing with services?
- Did I obtain documented informed consent with all patients/service recipients or their guardians at the outset of services?
- Does my informed consent include information about my privacy, security, and data storage, transmission, and disposal policies?
- Have I clearly indicated who will have access to the client's or participant's information, including supervisors or treatment teams within my agency or training clinic, or employers and managers in an organization?
- Did I assess how secure my patient's or consultee's technological equipment is and how my client will access my remote clinical services (e.g., secured land line, secured website)?
- Did I establish a fee schedule related to telecommunications-based services that specifies issues related to technology disruptions?
- Was I knowledgeable about emergency, professional, and consultative local resources for the person I plan to serve remotely?
- At the outset of a remote service, did I obtain a contact number for my client in case of technological failure or clinical emergency?
- Did I have a clearly articulated plan for transferring clients in the event that the initial clinician or trainee cannot provide necessary or recommended services?
- Did I review available resources for informed consent on a yearly basis (i.e., American Psychological Association [APA] records management guidelines, *Guidelines for the Practice of Telepsychology* [Joint Task Force, 2013], risk management documents, new laws, and seek consultation regarding current practices)?
- Did I understand how jurisdictional (including international) law differences can influence the strategies I used to collect, store, and share information gathered by electronic means, and have I clearly communicated the implications of these differences to patients/clients/consultees in language they can understand?

that he had shared with them as a template for participation on the team and that all providers were completing release of information forms for patients accessing the crisis team line. Furthermore, at the beginning of an emergency call, providers used a standard procedure of requesting patient identifying authentication information that providers could review with an up-to-date listing, as well as the patient's first name, geographic location and address, method of calling (e.g., cell phone, VoIP from computer, landline), and ongoing provider for the purposes of timely crisis management as well as documentation and billing purposes (including routing the primary provider a copy of the call notation via encrypted EMR).

Dr. Gray was familiar with the 18 health information identifiers protected by the Health Insurance Portability and Accountability Act (HIPAA; 1996), and the crisis call team had worked out a sophisticated system in which an authentication code was required by patients to access the services, which only they and the care team knew. This provided for a HIPAA-compliant approach to multiprovider services in a teletherapy situation. In addition, the explicit informed consent process that patients were required to complete to participate in this DBT treatment approach had been well thought out with regard to informing the patients in an appropriate manner, providing detailed information so that providers could implement consistent policies and procedures; this allowed for videoconferencing as an augmentation to care, improving the treatment outcomes for many. The team of colleagues had given much consideration to and documented within the informed consent documents specific requirements for when clinical needs intensified and telepsychology was no longer the best practice delivery system.

SCENARIO

Recently, Dr. Gray was on call and responded to a colleague's patients who utilized the service during increased distress and dysregulation. He requested the authentication code, which the patient provided along with noting his stated geographic location (i.e., where he was calling from on his cell phone) and that Dr. Wo was his primary psychologist, per procedures of all crisis calls and informed consent policy. Dr. Gray also briefly reminded the patient of the informed consent and exception requirements and obtained patient verbal consent to remain on the call. Although Dr. Gray could verify the patient's authentication code with the team's call list, the veracity of the patient's location was questionable because he was calling from a cell phone. Dr. Gray documented all the information shared by the caller, including the client's expression of recurrent suicidal ideation through which he had developed a specific plan. In addition, he noted other auditory observations, including the timing of what sounded like a public alert warning siren, although it was 1 p.m. on a Wednesday afternoon. Dr. Gray talked with the patient and followed the DBT crisis call procedures outlined in the manual, the consent paperwork, and the call-team policy manual, including documenting the call. Despite the call ending with the patient stating he felt positive about the safety plan they discussed and that his significant distress had passed after talking through the details on the call, Dr. Gray still had a gnawing feeling about missing something. He attempted to recontact the patient at the stated number, left a message per the protocol, and requested the patient return his call within a half hour or he would seek further safety assurances for the patient. He knew Dr. Wo was out of town, and he could not connect with him to consult. When the client had not returned the message on the half hour, Dr. Gray called the patient again. His concern was growing given the discussion on the call, and he clinically noted that if everything were as the patient described, he would have received a return call by now.

KEY ELEMENTS, CHALLENGES, AND DECISION FACTORS

There are significant risk factors at play for Dr. Gray in considering what to do next. The preparation and planning of the crisis team resulted in having a specific policy, consenting with patients at the onset of care as well as the onset of crisis calls, and excellent documentation, all of which played a role in the outcome of this case. Dr. Gray did not hesitate to contact one of his call-team colleagues to immediately review the crisis call, as well as the nagging feeling he was having. In talking through the situation with his colleague, Dr. Gallo, he reviewed the elements of the informed consent documents, that consent had been reviewed on the call, and that the team policy was to ensure patient safety through breach of confidentiality should there ever be reasonable concern. Although the nagging feeling wasn't enough to be considered "reasonable concern," the nonreturn of a follow-up call was increasingly worrisome. Dr. Gray and Dr. Gallo reviewed their jurisdiction's laws with regard to mandated reporting and documented this as well, confirming that suspicion of harm to self was supported by law as a reason to waive confidential information to a public protection authority (in this case, the county sheriff's office). Dr. Gray proceeded to contact public safety authorities to complete a safety check. When the initial information was insufficient to find the patient, further details related to the safety situation were released to the authorities. Dr. Gallo and Dr. Gray reviewed the risks and benefits of breaching the confidentiality, the informed consent procedures, as well as the risks related to the population the team served.

Fortunately, Dr. Gray had documented his concerns and his steps in contacting local public safety authorities in the area where the patient stated he was located at the time of the call. He reviewed the concerns for the client's safety with law enforcement and requested that they conduct a safety check on the individual. Law enforcement found no sign that the individual was or had been at the geographic location he had indicated, further raising Dr. Gray's concerns. Dr. Gray revealed additional information to the officer, including the cell number, time of the call, observation of the public alert at 1 p.m., and that the client had indicated he had access to a gun. With this information, the officers were able to narrow down a potential location for the patient and found him unconscious in his car smelling of marijuana and with a gun at his side. He was transported to the local emergency department. Dr. Gray documented this call and follow-up in the encrypted EMR call record. Dr. Wo was alerted as soon as he returned to practice and reviewed the situation with Dr. Gray before visiting with his client at the county psychiatric facility.

OPTIONS AVAILABLE TO THE PSYCHOLOGIST

After this call, Dr. Gray again consulted with the crisis call team to review the procedures for the group, the DBT process, and the methods with which the policies and informed consent were developed and put into place. The team felt the steps had been preventive in being able to assist Dr. Gray in following up in this circumstance. Further discussion focused on specific time management and using increased technological processes in authenticating patient locations. The team reviewed the potential for adding video consultation to these calls, having recently learned of an application for medical providers that reportedly was HIPAA compliant and could provide short-term, urgent, clinic-style consultation for patients seeking medical care for more routine type issues. Although the team determined the increased observational data available from visual analysis and assessment of the patient and their surroundings would be helpful, they reviewed that the psychologists often took crisis calls from their homes on weekends and when out in the community, which would place an increased burden on the team with regard to finding and ensuring a HIPAA-compliant mobile process for a videoconferencing. Given the basis of these calls was for crisis management, the team felt that the degree to which confidentiality could not be ensured on their personal devices outweighed the benefits they would gain from more information. The team opted to continue telephone crisis care.

The team was also interested in following up on GPS apps that could provide a positive location for callers to their EMR and were hoping the cost would not be prohibitive. Legal consultation was their next step in determining whether this service could further augment their crisis call process regarding (a) guidelines for informed consent, (b) malpractice carrier consultation, (c) health care attorney or information technology (IT) consultants, and (d) colleague and consultation group continued discussion.

THE BEST DECISION POSSIBLE

Dr. Gray and his colleagues had consulted early, planned strategically, and used many resources as guides for developing their telepractice informed consent and model of crisis care. The Self-Assessment Checklist (see Exhibit 3.1) was helpful as they considered various situations and procedures that would need to be addressed by their informed consent and clinical processes. In addition, as situations arose, Dr. Gray and the crisis call team reviewed and revised their procedures as was appropriate for their new knowledge, new technology available, and relative comfort with high-risk clients.

Case Study 2: University Training Clinic

Within the training clinic context, informed consent includes specific information about the role and competency level of the trainee clinician (hereafter called *clinician*), the supervision received, and the identification of supervisors and peers who may be able to observe the services being provided by the trainee clinician. In addition, because clinicians in training often rotate through various practicum settings, their work with clients is often artificially time-limited. For clients receiving telepsychology services, who are perhaps not as familiar with the staffing procedures of the training clinic, this can add to confusion. Appropriate informed consent at the beginning of the process can alleviate stress and support the continuity of therapeutic relationships among multiple clinicians for the long-distance client.

RELEVANT EXCERPT FROM THE GUIDELINE

> In addition, [psychologists] attempt to develop and share the policies and procedures that will explain to their clients/patients how they will interact with them using the specific telecommunication technologies involved. It may be more difficult to obtain and document informed consent in situations where psychologists provide telepsychology services to their clients/patients who are not in the same physical location, or with whom they do not have in-person interactions. (Joint Task Force, 2013 p. 795)

SETTING: UNIVERSITY TRAINING CLINIC

As part of its mission, the Counseling and Psychological Services Training Clinic (TC), a university-based training clinic in a public state institution, serves the needs of the rural state in which it is located. In response to severe mental health professional shortages throughout the region, the TC staff and its home department have been encouraged to deliver telepsychology services to residents in rural areas throughout the state. The TC bills clients on a sliding-scale fee structure, does not bill to third-party payers, and is one of the few clinics in the state that can see very poor and uninsured clients. Graduate students pursuing master's degrees in counseling and doctorates in psychology provide services at TC, and licensed clinicians supervise all services. None of the supervisors were telepsychology providers before their involvement in TC, but all have now completed some training in telepsychology service provision and ethics and identify themselves as "becoming competent" in this area. All trainee clinicians are required to complete training in ethics and using telepsychology equipment before being assigned clients. Services are provided through a HIPAA-compliant videoconferencing system that is provided by the state university system and maintained by university IT personnel.

SCENARIO

A social worker from a rural county in the jurisdiction contacted the TC director, Dr. Johnson, seeking services for a child in foster care who was awaiting adoption by foster parents. The social worker sought telepsychology services because the nearest mental health professional was a 2-hour drive from the foster home, and the parents could not afford to take a day from work to manage the necessary travel. The client was a 9-year-old girl (Allie) with one male sibling, and both were placed with the same foster family and looking forward to being adopted by them. The children's birth parents had released all custodial rights, and the client and her brother had been living happily with the foster parents for several months. However, Allie was also demonstrating some disruptive behavior and reported feelings of sadness at "never seeing" her biological mother again. The goal of therapy, as presented by the social worker, was to help Allie deal effectively with the termination of her relationship with her biological mother and ease the transition into her adoptive family.

Dr. Johnson learned that Allie had never had any previous counseling or any kind of mental health services. In addition, the social worker revealed that Allie and her brother had been removed from the parental home after several incidents of neglect and physical abuse, which occurred while both parents were intoxicated. In a follow-up conversation with the foster parents, Dr. Johnson learned that Allie had some difficulty trusting adults and that she was having a hard time forming relationships with the teachers at her new school. Her younger brother did not have these concerns, and the foster parents speculated that Allie may have "protected" her younger brother from some of the adults who visited their family home.

In deciding whether to accept this referral, Dr. Johnson consulted with the TC supervision team. The first decision the team made was that it would be important for the clinician and primary supervisor to meet with Allie, at least one foster parent, and the guardian in person for a first meeting to ensure that all involved parties understood how the telepsychology system worked and how the TC was staffed. In addition, the team felt it was important for Allie to meet her clinician in person before beginning the interaction via video so that she would have the chance to build some trust and also to ensure she recognized the clinician as a real person, and not just a face on a monitor.

That first meeting occurred at the school Allie attended and where her foster mother was a teacher, to which Dr. Johnson and the assigned clinician (Jon Webster) traveled. The social worker and foster mother had suggested the school as a meeting site because they believed it would be a good location for telepsychology services. The school had more a reliable Internet connection than their home, and having the session at the end of the school day was convenient for all of them. The school counselor agreed that Allie could use a quiet and secure room at the school for counseling sessions, which allowed the team to ensure that the computer access was suitable and the surroundings were safe for Allie. Dr. Johnson and Mr. Webster confirmed that the room was accessible only by the school counselor and principal. Its primary use was for the counselor to meet privately with students and maintain necessary paperwork, which was secured in locked cabinets and would not be available for Allie to view, even if in the room alone. The room was located on the same hallway as the school nurse and another administrative office, in a relatively quiet and private space of the building. Together, Allie, her foster mother, and the school counselor agreed that the school counselor would help Allie get started in the session and would then leave the room but remain nearby in case Allie needed any help. Sessions were scheduled to occur at the end of the school day on Tuesdays, when the foster mother stayed late at the school to prepare lessons and the school counselor was able to stay and work on program evaluation activities in the office next door. Using this schedule, Allie was able to avoid missing any class time.

This first meeting also allowed the TC team to go carefully through all aspects of informed consent with both the social worker and foster mother, as well as explain to Allie how the telepsychology sessions would work and how her image and the words she spoke into the computer microphone would be protected. Mr. Webster and Dr. Johnson explained that all of the sessions would be recorded and that the recordings would be saved and stored in the TC computers and not in the school. The recordings were accessible only by Mr. Webster, Dr. Johnson, and by another faculty supervisor, Dr. Young. Because Dr. Young could not travel with them to attend the meeting, he did join briefly via videoconferencing to greet Allie and her foster mother. This allowed Allie to see how Mr. Webster would appear on the screen and how the video sessions would look and sound. In addition, Mr. Webster explained that Dr. Johnson, Dr. Young, and other clinicians at the TC would be able to watch their sessions and described that the other clinicians were also students working on their graduate degrees just as he was. Allie asked if she could meet the other students who would be watching their sessions, and both Mr. Webster and Dr. Johnson indicated that she could see them via videoconferencing if she wanted to, although those students would not be able to travel to her school. Mr. Webster also told Allie that he would be able to work with her "all spring" if she wanted, because he would be graduating in May. Dr. Johnson explained to both the social worker and foster mother that only enrolled students can see clients at the TC and that once Mr. Webster graduated, he would not be able to see Allie but that they could refer her to another clinician in the agency. All of this information was also conveyed in the written informed consent and assent forms. Once Allie asked her questions and Mr. Webster and Dr. Johnson checked in with her foster mother and the guardian social worker to ensure that everyone felt comfortable with the videoconferencing system and the TC supervision process, all of the parties signed the informed consent and assent forms.

Mr. Webster began providing services to Allie the following week, which was in January. He continued to see her weekly, and she demonstrated a positive response to counseling; her foster parents reported decreased acting-out behaviors and increased engagement in family activities. Allie's behavior at school continued to present some concerns, however, and in March, she revealed that she did not like one of her teachers because she reminded her of the "bad people" who had visited her parents. This revelation triggered a period of disruption for Allie, and it became apparent that during her school days, she was remembering past abuse. Together, Dr. Johnson and the TC supervision team decided Allie would benefit from trauma-focused cognitive behavior therapy (TF-CBT; Cohen, Mannarino, & Deblinger, 2006), which Mr. Webster was trained to provide. However, he was going to graduate in May (in approximately 6 weeks) and would not be able to continue working with Allie past that point. The decision the TC team faced was whether to continue working with Allie and, if so, whether to transfer her to a different clinician or have Mr. Webster work with her until graduation.

KEY ELEMENTS, CHALLENGES, AND DECISION FACTORS

The informed consent forms of the TC clinic that were reviewed and signed by both of Allie's guardians and the assent form reviewed and signed by Allie clearly stated that clinicians were students who would be rotating through the TC and could not continue seeing clients after graduation. However, in Mr. Webster's conversation with Allie, he discussed being able to see her "all spring," and the current situation could potentially shorten their work together. This brings up two important considerations for the client. First, Allie has established a trusting relationship with Mr. Webster, and a change in the treatment plan must be carefully addressed to maintain that trust with a new counselor. Second, because their interaction is limited to video communication, Allie and her foster parents may be less cognizant of the workings of the TC clinic than many clients would be, and so a periodic review of informed consent and assent, with both Allie and at least one guardian, would be more important.

Given the team's belief that TF-CBT is the most appropriate treatment strategy for Allie, they need to assess whether this service falls within the scope of services covered in the informed consent. They also need to determine whether there is any evidence that TF-CBT has been successfully conducted via telepsychology and if any risks to such an intervention have been identified. This evidence and potential risks need to be shared with Allie, her foster parents, and the guardian social worker, along with the rationale for making changes to the treatment plan. In addition, the foster parents need to be fully informed about the expectations for their involvement in TF-CBT, which includes parental skills development. This information can be shared with the foster parents and Allie via telepsychology. However, it may also be important to have another face-to-face meeting with both foster parents present to go over the parents' role if there is any confusion or concern about the expectations.

Another key decision Dr. Johnson and the supervisory team needs to make is whether to have Mr. Webster continue working with Allie as he has been, have him initiate TF-CBT with Allie, or transfer her now to a new counselor who can begin with TF-CBT. In addition to consulting with Mr. Webster and relying on their own supervision notes, they will need to gather information from local sources, including foster parents, the family's social worker, and school personnel to better understand Allie's daily functioning and the potential urgency of changing the treatment plan. They will also need to gather information about where services will be provided if they continue past the end of the school year at Allie's school. For example, if the school building would be available for use by the foster mother who teaches there, would that be a safe situation? Or would it be better to prepare for telepsychology services at home? If at home, it may be necessary for another face-to-face visit to ensure that there would be adequate security and privacy measures in place in the home. If the decision is made to transfer Allie to a different clinician, they will need to ensure that that student is trained in telepsychology as well as TF-CBT and that the student has appropriate understanding of the communication strategies that Mr. Webster and Allie have established to facilitate telepsychology interventions. Also, because they do have a training mission, they will need to assess the extent to which this assignment will be appropriate for someone who is currently learning these skills. In addition, they will need to inform Allie, her foster parents, and the social worker of the new clinician's credentials and supervisor information and ensure that the new clinician reviews all aspects of informed consent with the family. If the family is agreeable, videoconferencing could be used for these conversations, but the team will also need to assess whether another face-to-face visit is needed.

OPTIONS AVAILABLE TO THE PSYCHOLOGIST

The TC staff could make a decision to refer Allie to another provider outside of the TC. However, this would likely place a significant burden on the family, and they may be less likely to continue with services if they have to drive long distances for appropriate care. To minimize that risk, the TC staff decided how to best meet Allie's needs via telepsychology services. After verifying that telepsychology is not contraindicated for TF-CBT, they discussed the pros and cons of having Jon continue as Allie's provider, knowing that he will graduate before the TF-CBT intervention concludes.

They assessed the other students available with the appropriate skills and knowledge to work with Allie, and identified two students who would be in the clinic for at least another year. One of them has met Allie via videoconference because she was part of Mr. Webster's peer supervision group, and Allie asked to see them all early in her work with him. The other student was not in that supervision group and was not familiar with Allie's case. Neither student has worked with a client via telepsychology, but both have completed the required TC training protocol.

THE BEST DECISION POSSIBLE

Dr. Johnson and the TC supervision team decided that Mr. Webster would begin to transition Allie to the trainee clinician, Ms. Wolf, who was part of Mr. Webster's supervision team. They had him set up three transition sessions with Allie. In the first, he described the change to Allie and then invited her foster mother to join the session to let her know about the changed focus in treatment and the need to transition to a new clinician. In this process, he referred to the informed consent process from the first meeting, which had also been periodically reviewed as noted earlier, and described the ways in which this action is believed to be in Allie's best interest. He also described the potential risks and benefits of conducting TF-CBT via telepsychology. Dr. Johnson observed this session and was available for questions at the end. Allie and her foster mother asked about the new clinician, and Allie was relieved to hear it was someone she had already met. Allie's foster mother was glad that Dr. Johnson would continue to be the primary supervisor because she felt more comfortable with a known contact. In the second session, Mr. Webster and Ms. Wolf both met with Allie, and Allie was invited to ask Ms. Wolf questions and tell her about her work with Mr. Webster. During this session, both clinicians described what the next few sessions of TF-CBT would be like. They also spent a few minutes at the end of the session talking with Allie's foster mother. In the third session, Ms. Wolf led the session, and Mr. Webster joined briefly to end his work with Allie. He left after the first 10 minutes of the session, and Ms. Wolf continued with the session. Through this process, Mr. Webster, Ms. Wolf, and the TC supervision team were able to be reasonably sure that all parties understood the implications of the transfer and the risks and benefits of the new treatment protocol. In addition, they modeled transparency and helped engage the distant clients more fully into TC procedures and functions.

Case Study 3: Discrete Trial Distance Learning

RELEVANT EXCERPT FROM THE GUIDELINE

> Furthermore, psychologists may need to be aware of the manner in which cultural, linguistic, socioeconomic characteristics, and organizational considerations may impact a client's/patient's understanding of, and the special considerations required for, obtaining informed consent (such as when securing informed consent remotely from a parent/guardian when providing telepsychology services to a minor). (Joint Task Force, 2013, p. 795)

SETTING: EDUCATIONAL PRACTICE

Dr. Harry Ip is a well-known behavioral interventionist who has been working in the area of early intervention and intensive treatments for children with autistic disorder for almost two decades. He is a licensed psychologist trained in applied behavior analysis (ABA) who has devoted his practice to early intervention for children with autism. This treatment approach has been well established as an empirically validated intervention for improving communication and social skills in children with autism and pervasive developmental disorders and has its roots with Lovaas (1977) in the mid-60s. Dr. Ip is the owner and developer of an online training program for parents and behavioral tutors that organizes and analyzes ABA treatment protocols to assist with daily intervention determinations. The program Dr. Ip has created includes video-based training for clinicians, behavioral assessment tools for parents and therapists/tutors, and mechanisms for charting and tracking patient progress through Dr. Ip's entire early intervention program.

SCENARIO

Consistent forms and techniques are used in implementation of this intensive 40-hour per week therapy protocol, which has typically generated significant amounts of paperwork and data tracking for analysis related to a single patient. Dr. Ip is quite excited about the potential for the development of a mobile device application that could be used to set up the daily treatment protocols for tutors as well as allow them to collect data for these trials within the application on the same device. After the completion of a daily intervention session, the mobile device could upload the data to Dr. Ip's EMR, which is HIPAA compliant and certified to interact with the data collection software system (also HIPAA compliant) to provide tracking analysis and graph the child's progress. Dr. Ip is also interested in capturing video observation data from behavior therapy sessions to assist with his supervision of the behavior therapy team working with the child and to conduct live supervision via videoconferencing directly during therapy sessions occurring in patients' homes.

KEY ELEMENTS, CHALLENGES, AND DECISION FACTORS

Dr. Ip is interested in ensuring that all components of his online and mobile therapy program are HIPAA compliant and that all aspects of this process have been well-documented and reviewed in his informed consent paperwork and procedures with his patients. This is particularly challenging because the treatment receivers are children whose parents are requesting services provided by a team of trained and supervised individuals. For example, 2-year-old Lincoln's team includes his parents, his 16-year-old sibling, and treatment extension tutors (college age). Confidentiality policies as well as mandated reporting policies have been reviewed with all care providers and parents. Dr. Ip has consulted with his risk management provider as well as his attorney and IT consultant to ensure that all aspects required for review in informed consent are indeed present.

Additionally, Dr. Ip has been trained in the various aspects of these domains for his understanding of the process to explain to the families with whom he works in his practice. He decided that the mobile devices would be best managed through his business, and the tutors and families would not be permitted to use their own devices because they cannot be secured for data transfer purposes. In addition, the online portal requires password protection and authentication, so there are three levels of security to keep patients' confidential protected health information safe within the EMR. With this in mind, Lincoln's parents were educated on the process for signing in to complete assessments, choose therapy programs, and to download and upload the daily programming to and from the mobile device. Dr. Ip has been quite cautious about who has access to the data sets and has taken the steps necessary to obtain business associate agreements from the various support companies with whom he works (e.g., mobile device store, web host, technology partners). Lincoln's parents were informed of this as well. Dr. Ip's treatment targets children generally under age 3 years who are nonverbal and often noncompliant. Although it is unlikely he would be able to obtain a meaningful assent process from any of the children, Dr. Ip does briefly go through the same informed consent process with each of them to review the strategies for personal and mental health record safety. Parents are present during this process and also provide their consent. These procedures are documented within his session notes, and copies of the information reviewed are provided to the parents or guardians; these are also available on the devices provided for the intervention. Dr. Ip has considered various ways to authenticate those seeking online access to his program and EMR system. Given that treatment primarily occurs within a patient's home or community, the most consistent access that tutors and therapists (and patients) would have to the Internet would be public, either in the community (i.e., library free Wi-Fi) or the families' own Internet within their home. Dr. Ip wanted to make sure that, to the best of their ability, there could be some level of security and privacy with regard to digital communications and data exchanged between the mobile device and his online program.

OPTIONS AVAILABLE TO THE PSYCHOLOGIST

Well-thought-out and documented informed consent policies that are continually reviewed with staff and patients make the process for cutting-edge approaches to therapeutic intervention increasingly possible. Dr. Ip recognized the value in automating much of the behavioral intervention in a manner that used technology to make the data collection and processing procedures extremely efficient and allowed for immediate feedback to the tutor about how the child was doing. Treatments could become streamlined, and file cabinets of paper data would become obsolete. The amount of time required by therapists, supervisors, and parents to oversee the program was reduced by more than half, which increased the availability of therapists to implement therapy. Dr. Ip saw extreme potential in this program and reviewed the specific details with his technology development team, his legal consultant, his IT consultant, his professional ABA colleagues, psychologist colleagues, and malpractice insurance carrier. He had business associate agreements with all of these contacts.

Although not cheap, the price point that parents were already willing to pay for access to the online portion of his protocol had covered some of the basics for the development of his mobile application. Dr. Ip was clear that he would need to update his informed consent policy or at the very least have two that would address which aspects of the behavior therapy intervention the children were receiving, should parents opt not to use the digital components due to limited insurance coverage, fee-based services, and other concerns. In addition to all the business-related factors, Dr. Ip discovered a mechanism that allowed for a virtual private network (VPN, a secure connection between a device and a work network over public Internet) between his mobile devices and the office, allowing a private and secure approach to both his supervision model and the data management.

Dr. Ip used several resources in considering his informed consent processes and procedures. He spent time consulting with knowledgeable colleagues and also reviewed the APA records management guidelines and specific jurisdictional paperwork related to EMRs that APA provided to jurisdictions. He contacted his risk management company to review aspects of informed consent related to children and particularly vulnerable populations as well as general risk management considerations for mobile health applications. Dr. Ip considered carefully the APA Telepsychology Guidelines, which provided various aspects to consider related to the transmission and storage of data and how to assist client families in securing their own data. Finally, Dr. Ip also consulted the Behavior Analyst Certification Board's (2014) professional and ethical compliance code guidelines related to boundaries and data management.

THE BEST DECISION POSSIBLE

Dr. Ip took all the information and planned his informed consenting procedures for a separate visit before the beginning of services. He found the Self-Assessment Checklist shown in Exhibit 3.1 helpful to consider as he created his informed consent documentation. This allowed for review of assent with the child (as appropriate) and consent with the parents following a very detailed and in-person visit to establish the basic requirements of the program, discuss the boundaries required, and provide brief training to the various providers on the use of the VPN system and online educational program (which reviewed how the intervention and data tracking/management mobile applications worked in more detail). After this session, Dr. Ip returned with a mobile device, and the team reviewed specifically how to use the device and get connected via VPN. Over the years, Dr. Ip noted that approaching the process in a timely way, step-by-step, worked well to improve the technology knowledge for the team members. Dr. Ip discussed the use of videoconferencing for supervision with his ABA colleagues. There were strong opinions about both using videoconferencing for supervision and training purposes and the limitations videoconferencing presented in the context of ABA therapy (which has been described as a very "hands-on" intervention). Given that videoconferencing would be augmenting a much larger digital therapy program, Dr. Ip determined that the videoconferencing component would pose no particularly increased risk and that, in fact, parents and families were increasingly "online" and preferred this method to the old-fashioned paper-and-pencil tasks.

Case Study 4: Consultation With an Organization With Numerous Employees

RELEVANT EXCERPT FROM THE GUIDELINE

> Psychologists strive to obtain and document informed consent that specifically addresses the unique concerns related to the telepsychology services they provide. When doing so psychologists are cognizant of the applicable laws and regulations, as well as organizational requirements that govern informed consent in this area. . . . Furthermore, psychologists may need to be aware of the manner in which cultural, linguistic, socioeconomic characteristics, and organizational considerations may impact a client's/patient's understanding of, and the special considerations required for, obtaining informed consent. (Joint Task Force, 2013, pp. 795–796)

RELEVANT EXCERPT FROM APA ETHICS CODE: 3.11 PSYCHOLOGICAL SERVICES DELIVERED TO OR THROUGH ORGANIZATIONS

> (a) Psychologists delivering services to or through organizations provide information beforehand to clients and when appropriate those directly affected by the services about (1) the nature and objectives of the services, (2) the intended recipients, (3) which of the individuals are clients, (4) the relationship the psychologist will have with each person and the organization, (5) the probable uses of services provided and information obtained, (6) who will have access to the information, and (7) limits of confidentiality. As soon as feasible, they provide information about the results and conclusions of such services to appropriate persons. (APA, 2017)

Organizational consulting situations often emerge when change that will affect an entire system is required or desired. Given the consequences of such changes on large groups of people, establishing a trusting relationship is paramount for a successful consultation (Freedman & Perry, 2010). There are many avenues to building trust in face-to-face relationships that may not be quite as accessible in telepsychology circumstances, but one strategy that does work in those circumstances and facilitates a trusting relationship is transparent and accessible informed consent.

SETTING: INDUSTRIAL OR ORGANIZATIONAL

Dr. Ann Cheng is an organizational consulting psychologist whose area of specialty is assessing organizational climate and employee satisfaction and morale. She has specific expertise in examining the work–family role interface (Allen, 2013) and the impact of employer family and health care benefits and policies on employee satisfaction and productivity. Dr. Cheng has been working closely with the regional vice president in the local branch of Ace Computing (fictitious name used for purposes of example), a multinational organization, over the past 10 months to identify and develop responses to the work–family role stressors that contribute to employee dissatisfaction. Dr. Cheng held several meetings with the local executives and focus groups of local employees, including supervisors, office workers, production-line component manufacturing workers, and custodial staff. Subsequently, she implemented an intervention that has raised employee satisfaction by a full standard deviation and productivity by almost 20%.

SCENARIO

At the last annual board and shareholders' meeting, the regional vice president reported on Dr. Cheng's intervention and the changes they have monitored in their local setting. The CEO and board members of Ace Computing were very impressed with the changes and have now approached her with the request to provide similar services to all of their branch offices. These include four offices in the United States (in addition to the local branch in Texas with which she has been working), three each in Mexico and Canada, two in Japan, two in the United Kingdom, and one new office in Dubai, United Arab Emirates. Dr. Cheng recognizes that this is an excellent opportunity for her to assess the cross-cultural and international relevance of her work and believes she can deliver the services in a way that is consistent with her own values and the values and culture of Ace Computing, as well as with the "Guidelines for Education and Training at the Doctoral and Postdoctoral Levels in Consulting Psychology/Organizational Consulting Psychology" (APA, 2007). However, she is also concerned that travel to all of the branch offices will be prohibitive. Together, she and the CEO decide that much of the consultation work can occur via telecommunication.

KEY ELEMENTS, CHALLENGES, AND DECISION FACTORS

The client and consultee in this situation are clarified as Ace Computing and its executive board. However, Dr. Cheng will be gathering information at the level of individual employees and units within the organization. Therefore, she will need to clarify how to ensure that everyone involved understands the implications and potential consequences of her work. Given the distance communications strategies to be used, Dr. Cheng will meet directly with only a few individuals in each branch office, but she will be gathering information from all employees. Therefore, she needs to provide written informed consent that clarifies the purpose of the process, how information will be collected, how the telecommunications system that is used to conduct interviews is made secure, how surveys of all employees will be gathered, and how data from both interviews and surveys will be securely stored. She will also need to clarify who has access to and ownership of the data, particularly the extent to which executives and the CEO can access data provided by individual employees. In addition, she will need to clarify whether interviews are recorded and the interviewee is identifiable and whether individual employee surveys, completed via an online data collection server, can be traced back to the individual through IP addresses or other means.

Another essential element in this situation is the variation in regional and national standards regarding informed consent. Dr. Cheng will need to ensure that she clearly understands the ways in which national laws affect privacy, informed consent, and data storage related to all of her initial considerations of informed consent described earlier. In particular, Dr. Cheng will need to research how different countries protect or do not protect confidentiality in online communications. In addition, because she is examining organizational policy implications, she will need to be aware of jurisdictional issues that may influence the ability either to modify policy or to implement the changes she would recommend, in addition to ensuring that her work is culturally informed and relevant across international populations. Finally, Dr. Cheng and the Ace Computing board will need to clarify who will be responsible in the event of a major data breach, such as might occur through an incident of hacking. This also includes careful delineation of what systems are used to collect and store the data and who ultimately controls or owns it.

OPTIONS AVAILABLE TO THE PSYCHOLOGIST

Dr. Cheng consulted with knowledgeable colleagues, reviewed the APA records management guidelines, met with and retained the services of an international IT attorney, and contacted her risk management company representative to identify specific risks and benefits related to the Ace Computing consultation. In addition, Dr. Cheng considered the *Guidelines for the Practice of Telepsychology* (Joint Task Force, 2013) related to the transmission and storage of data and strategies for ensuring that all involved individuals would understand the implications of their involvement through appropriate informed consent.

Subsequently, Dr. Cheng considered the implications of selecting the telecommunications systems she would use to complete the consultation. Ace Computing, of course, had excellent IT capacity and cyber services that would meet all of her needs. Using their system would save substantial costs. However, it could also allow knowledgeable employees access to the data collected from other employees. In addition, storage and maintenance of the data would therefore be overseen by Ace employees; thus, careful controls would have to be established to make use of the Ace Computing systems. Dr. Cheng also considered the potential of contracting with another IT service. In that instance, she would need to ensure that there were no conflicts of interest between the contractor and Ace Computing and would also need to determine that the cybersecurity mechanisms were at least as good as those of Ace Computing. The benefit of an outside contractor would be that Dr. Cheng would have primary access to and control over the information collected.

THE BEST DECISION POSSIBLE

After considering the options available and the legal implications of working with an international organization primarily via telecommunication means, Dr. Cheng agreed to accept this consultation. She was able to gather a knowledgeable team of professionals with expertise in international cybersecurity, workplace law, and language translation. She ultimately decided that working with the existing Ace Computing telecommunications system provided the greatest security for participants and minimized the risk that another company might use the gathered information to its advantage.

However, with the assistance of her attorney, she clarified the boundaries of access Ace managers could have to the collected data and identified a portal to the data that only she and her team could access. Ace Computing ultimately gained control of the deidentified data set so that they could conduct additional follow-up work in the future, and the informed consents specifically noted that all information stored in the final database would have all identifying information (including IP addresses and unique demographic data) removed before Dr. Cheng turned it over to Ace.

Dr. Cheng also worked with her attorney and a team of knowledgeable translators to ensure that all of the informed consent documentation would accurately communicate the rights, commitment, implications, and potential risks of the consultation to all employees in language that was accessible to them. Different versions of informed consent paperwork were prepared for consistency with jurisdictional requirements. In addition, Dr. Cheng assessed some of the policies in place in different countries (including work-based child care, gender equity rules, and worker protections) to ensure that her interview and survey questions were consistent with national laws and cultural norms. Given that there would be limited ability for employees to interact directly with Dr. Cheng, this was identified as an important strategy for decreasing confusion and increasing understanding of the implications of the consultation for individual employees.

Key Points From the Chapter to Remember

This chapter, unlike other chapters in the casebook, presents key points to remember as a self-assessment checklist (see Exhibit 3.1). This format allows psychologists to apply lessons learned and points to remember to their own telepsychology practice for current application as well as planning "thinking forward."

References

Allen, T. D. (2013). The work–family role interface: A synthesis of the research from industrial and organizational psychology. In N. W. Schmitt, S. Highhouse, & I. B. Weiner (Eds.), *Handbook of psychology: Vol. 12. Industrial and organizational psychology* (2nd ed., pp. 698–718). Hoboken, NJ: Wiley.

American Psychological Association. (2007). Guidelines for education and training at the doctoral and postdoctoral levels in consulting psychology/organizational consulting psychology. *American Psychologist, 62,* 980–992. http://dx.doi.org/10.1037/0003-066X.62.9.980

American Psychological Association. (2017). *Ethical principles of psychologists and code of conduct* (2002, Amended June 1, 2010 and January 1, 2017). Retrieved from http://www.apa.org/ethics/code/index.aspx

Behavior Analyst Certification Board. (2014). *Professional and ethical compliance code for behavior analysts.* Retrieved from http://bacb.com/wp-content/uploads/2016/03/160321-compliance-code-english.pdf

Cohen, J. A., Mannarino, A. P., & Deblinger, E. (2006). *Treating trauma and traumatic grief in children and adolescents*. New York, NY: Guilford Press.

Freedman, A. M., & Perry, J. A. (2010). Executive consulting under pressure: A case study. *Consulting Psychology Journal: Practice and Research, 62,* 189–202. http://dx.doi.org/10.1037/a0021247

Health Insurance Portability and Accountability Act, Pub. L. No. 104-191, 110 Stat. 1936 (1996).

Joint Task Force for the Development of Telepsychology Guidelines for Psychologists. (2013). Guidelines for the practice of telepsychology. *American Psychologist, 68,* 791–800. Retrieved from https://www.apa.org/pubs/journals/features/amp-a0035001.pdf

Lovaas, O. I. (1977). *The autistic child: Language development through behavior modification*. Oxford, England: Irvington.

Julie M. Landry Poole and Bruce E. Crow

Confidentiality of Data and Information

4

Psychologists who provide telepsychology services make reasonable effort to protect and maintain the confidentiality of the data and information relating to their clients/patients and inform them of the potentially increased risks to loss of confidentiality inherent in the use of the telecommunication technologies, if any.

—Guideline 4, *Guidelines for the Practice of Telepsychology*

Rationale

The use of telecommunications technologies and the rapid advances in technology present unique challenges for psychologists in protecting the confidentiality of clients/patients. Psychologists who provide telepsychology learn about the potential risks to confidentiality before utilizing such technologies. When necessary, psychologists obtain the appropriate consultation with technology experts to augment their knowledge of telecommunication technologies in order to apply security measures in their practices that will protect and maintain the confidentiality of data and information related to their clients/patients.

The view(s) expressed herein are those of the author(s) and do not reflect the official policy or position of U.S. Army Regional Health Command—Central, the U.S. Army Medical Department, the U.S. Army Office of the Surgeon General, the Department of the Army and Department of Defense, or the U.S. Government.

http://dx.doi.org/10.1037/0000046-005
A Telepsychology Casebook: Using Technology Ethically and Effectively in Your Professional Practice, L. F. Campbell, F. Millán, and J. N. Martin (Editors)

> Some of the potential risks to confidentiality include considerations related to uses of search engines and participation in social networking sites. Other challenges in this area may include protecting confidential data and information from inappropriate and/or inadvertent breaches to established security methods the psychologist has in place, as well as boundary issues that may arise as a result of a psychologist's use of search engines and participation on social networking sites. In addition, any Internet participation by psychologists has the potential of being discovered by their clients/patients and others and thereby potentially compromising a professional relationship. (Joint Task Force for the Development of Telepsychology Guidelines for Psychologists, 2013, p. 798)

As psychologists exercise their responsibility to protect the confidentiality of their patients in traditional in-person therapy, so, too, are they obligated to ensure the same level of protection for their telepsychology patients. Standard 4, Privacy and Confidentiality, of the *Ethical Principles of Psychologists and Code of Conduct* (American Psychological Association [APA], 2017) sets the stage by stating, "Psychologists have a primary obligation and take reasonable precautions to protect confidential information obtained through or stored in any medium." The *Guidelines for the Practice of Telepsychology* (Joint Task Force, 2013) affirm and clarify this responsibility and the implicit obligation of the clinician practicing telepsychology to be aware of the special risks unique to the use of electronic communications. This chapter identifies some of those risks and raises elements to be considered. Although not every risk is enumerated, we hope that the way each one is approached and resolved teaches a framework that can be applied to a multitude of other scenarios.

Case Study 1: Use of E-Mail With Patients

RELEVANT EXCERPT FROM THE GUIDELINE

> Psychologists both understand and inform their clients/patients of the limits of confidentiality and risks to the possible access or disclosure of confidential data and information that may occur during service delivery, including the risks of access to electronic communications (e.g., telephone, e-mail) between the psychologist and client/patient. (Joint Task Force, 2013, p. 798)

SETTING: INDEPENDENT PRACTICE

Dr. Emma Parker belongs to a busy group practice in a large metropolitan area where she treats individual psychotherapy patients. Her patients are generally adults from a relatively diverse population. Although she specializes in eating disorders, she also frequently treats depression and anxiety-related conditions. Dr. Parker and her colleagues began the practice several years ago, but during the past 6 months the practice and its patient base have expanded exponentially.

To successfully navigate the growth of their practice, Dr. Parker and her colleagues recently attended a continuing education course hosted by their state psychological association. The course focused on business strategies and contemporary technology trends among psychologists in private practice. The presenter briefly discussed the benefits of recent technological advances but inadvertently minimized the complexity and unique ethical and legal considerations related to their use.

After the training, Dr. Parker was eager to explore e-mail communication as a means to augment her current interactions with patients. The practice's current consent forms and office procedures included a basic statement indicating that security measures had been taken to ensure protected health information (PHI) was secure during electronic transmission. Despite the brevity and incompleteness of the statement, Dr. Parker reviewed the forms and determined revisions were not required because electronic transmission was specifically addressed. As she began to incorporate e-mail use within her practice, she asked patients if they were comfortable with communicating via e-mail and documented this oral consent in their records.

Dr. Parker found that e-mail communication with her patients was simple, quick, and effective. Realizing how useful it was, she added her e-mail address to her business cards and the practice's website. Her patients also appeared to appreciate the convenience of e-mail messages; several had gradually begun to use e-mail to discuss clinical and therapeutic information. Although Dr. Parker did not plan to use electronic communication for this purpose, she did not give it much thought.

SCENARIO

Emily was a 52-year-old married woman who worked in the finance industry. She had seen Dr. Parker for four sessions of cognitive behavior therapy for generalized anxiety disorder. During their week's session, Emily reported a significant increase in anxiety symptoms, which she attributed to difficulties within her marriage. The day after the session, Dr. Parker received an e-mail from Emily. The subject line read "just one more thing." The long e-mail described Emily's dream the night before and her reaction to the dream, which included the decision to leave her husband. Dr. Parker responded, praising Emily for the breakthrough. She told Emily she looked forward to hearing more at the follow-up appointment the next week.

The following week Emily presented to the session in tears. She told Dr. Parker she left her e-mail open on her home computer by accident, and her husband had read her e-mail to Dr. Parker, as well as Dr. Parker's response. Emily was distraught. She reported that although she felt good about the decision to dissolve the marriage, she had not yet prepared to discuss the decision with her husband. As Emily processed the event in session, she mentioned she had not considered the possibility anyone else would see her personal e-mail messages to Dr. Parker. Dr. Parker realized she had not discussed the inherent privacy risks of e-mail use with Emily or her other patients.

KEY ELEMENTS, CHALLENGES, AND DECISION FACTORS

Although technological advances have proven beneficial within health care settings, the ubiquitous innovations are accompanied by new ethical considerations. The use of e-mail unmistakably provides several advantages, including perhaps the most obvious example of convenience. Psychologists and patients are able to connect at any time from any location. Communication via e-mail additionally allows for rapid correspondence. E-mail communication also may enhance communication and provide a way for clinicians to provide additional support outside of sessions.

Despite the convenience, e-mail use is also accompanied by risks. Deleted e-mails may be easily recovered by Internet service providers. Human error is also a potential privacy threat; e-mails may be inadvertently sent to an incorrect address, exposing the patient's private information to the recipient. Messages may also be accessible by third parties. Finally, e-mail use also allows for a greater potential of boundary violations. Patients may expect a psychologist to be instantly available and responsive.

OPTIONS AVAILABLE TO THE PSYCHOLOGIST

Realizing she had not carefully considered the implications of e-mail communication, Dr. Parker thoughtfully reviewed the *Guidelines for the Practice of Telepsychology* (Joint Task Force, 2013), developed by the APA, the Association of State and Provincial Psychology Boards, and The Trust. She also sought further information from APA Division 46 (Society for Media Psychology and Technology) and reviewed applicable licensing board rules and state laws, as well as the Health Insurance Portability and Accountability Act (HIPAA; 1996) standards of confidentiality.

During her research, Dr. Parker concluded that if she planned to continue using e-mail communication with her patients, she would need to make changes to her current practices to meet the APA guidelines and to ensure she was following all relevant laws and regulations. She created a list of ideas to discuss with her colleagues before implementation. The first item on her list was whether to limit e-mail to administrative content. Dr. Parker recognized benefits and limitations to this approach and therefore determined it would be advantageous to consult with her coworkers before making a final decision.

Dr. Parker also recognized that she should be more deliberate when discussing the general parameters of e-mail use with her patients (e.g., expectations, boundaries). She would need to ensure they were aware that PHI might be included in e-mail exchanges and that it was thus at risk of disclosure. The use of e-mail encryption would also need to be addressed. She considered the need to review with patients their role in maintaining their own privacy and confidentiality. In addition to discussing these topics in person, she planned to include this information within the written office policies provided to patients.

Case Study 2: Facebook Friend Request From a Patient and Supervision

RELEVANT EXCERPT FROM THE GUIDELINE

> Psychologists who use social networking sites for both professional and personal purposes are encouraged to review and educate themselves about the potential risks to privacy and confidentiality and consider utilizing all available privacy settings to reduce these risks. (Joint Task Force, 2013, p. 797)

SETTING: OUTPATIENT PSYCHOLOGY CONSORTIUM INTERNSHIP

Lily was 5 months into her 12-month internship at a rural psychology consortium. The program subscribed to a developmental model of training that focused on personalized training adapted to the trainee's level of functioning and provided a diversified clinical experience. Interns participated in two major placements within integrated primary behavioral care and a traditional outpatient mental health clinic. The structure was designed to allow flexibility for students to shape their clinical rotations on the basis of individual interests within the core framework of the program.

The integrated primary behavioral care placement provided an opportunity to train in the growing area of primary care psychology. Interns served as behavioral health consultants within a primary care setting (e.g., family medicine practice, women's health clinic), assessing and treating patients who presented with behavioral concerns. They also provided feedback to medical providers regarding clinical impressions and recommended treatment. The rotation emphasized the role of a psychologist on a primary care team and the unique ethical issues that arise in primary care settings.

The traditional outpatient mental health rotation provided opportunities for short- and long-term psychotherapy, as well as group, family, and couples therapy. The placement provided an opportunity to work with a wide range of psychiatric conditions in a diverse population. Emphasis was placed on developing and refining skills in clinical interviewing, diagnostic accuracy, treatment planning, interventions, and documentation.

SCENARIO

Mike presented to the outpatient mental health clinic for treatment as a self-referral approximately three months ago due to occupational stressors. He quickly felt comfortable with Lily, who was close to his age and had a similar, extroverted personality. Following only a few sessions, the job-related stress dissipated, and Mike began discussing adverse childhood events he had not previously shared with others.

After their most recent session, Lily received a Facebook friend request from Mike. She was initially surprised by the request but quickly decided to accept. As far as

Lily knew, the consortium did not have any policies that prohibited provider–patient contact on public networks. She had a strong therapeutic alliance with the patient and thought being Facebook friends might enrich that relationship. Additionally, she felt it fit the way she practiced. Although she accepted the request, she made a decision she would not discuss any clinical issues via social media for privacy reasons.

During clinical supervision a few days later, Lily briefly mentioned the friend request while updating her supervisor, Dr. Stark, on her work with Mike. Although she did not intend for it to lead to further discussion, Dr. Stark quickly recognized the topic as an opportunity for professional development. Initially, Lily felt confident about her choice; however, during supervision, she realized it was likely driven, at least in part, by anxiety related to the possible awkward discussion that would result from the rejected request as well as fear of how it would affect the relationship.

KEY ELEMENTS, CHALLENGES, AND DECISION FACTORS

The use of social media was not discussed during Lily's graduate education and training or when she began her internship, and Mike's request was the first time she had experienced a patient invitation to interact on networking sites. The situation also brought to Dr. Stark's attention that the consortium did not have a clear and appropriate written policy on use of social media with patients and that, as a supervisor, he had not addressed this potential situation. Dr. Stark pointed out several issues Lily had not previously considered, including why Mike made the request. Lily assumed Mike wanted a social relationship in addition to their current professional relationship. Before the dialogue with Dr. Stark, Lily did not appreciate that by accepting the friend request, she was accepting a role in a second relationship and one that could compromise confidentiality for her patient. She knew multiple relationships were not unethical per se, but she recognized she would now be faced with the challenge of maintaining effective boundaries because of the blurred line created by the social relationship. She also realized it was possible that the dual relationship might impair her effectiveness as a therapist or even cause harm.

Dr. Stark additionally suggested Lily should consider whether the interactions were relevant to providing care or a way to satisfy a voyeuristic curiosity. He expressed concerns related to patient privacy and confidentiality because social networking platforms are not usually digitally encrypted. He also asked Lily to consider whether people would be able to recognize Mike as her patient, if she would be able to communicate confidentially, and if this was the best venue in which to communicate regarding issues that may be related to Mike's therapeutic work with her.

Lily had not previously thought about disclosure. Mike would learn things about her through Facebook she would not have shared with him otherwise. Mike could identify and contact anyone in Lily's friend list, view an extensive collection of her photos, and read past conversations and anecdotes on her page. Furthermore, Lily might discover things about Mike he had not previously disclosed to her in session. She would need to consider the clinical implications of these disclosures.

Finally, Lily and Dr. Stark thoughtfully discussed the generational difference between them and its effect on them as professionals. Lily and a large proportion of the consortium's patient population grew up communicating in a digital format. She was comfortable using social media sites and did so daily. Conversely, although Dr. Stark had a Facebook page, his daughter had created it, and he was unsure how to use it.

OPTIONS AVAILABLE TO THE PSYCHOLOGIST

Lily and Dr. Stark extended their usual supervision time to discuss further the possible unforeseen problems associated with social media use. Dr. Stark acknowledged that he felt most comfortable limiting Facebook and other networking sites to communication with friends and family, but he realized Lily might not feel the same and knew letting her define what was most comfortable for her as a psychologist was a good lesson. He did, however, suggest Lily should consider how she managed her online presence (e.g., who could find her, what could they find).

Lily planned to look into the privacy controls on the social networking sites she used. Being technologically savvy, she knew even a "private" online presence was public. She also considered having a professional presence separate from her personal page. After much thought and consultation, Lily decided to talk to Mike in his next session about his invitation to determine any therapeutic issues that might be present. She also decided to explain to him that she needed to continue to explore being connected to her patients through social media, and that for now, she was not going to open her personal page to patients. Finally, Lily volunteered to work with Dr. Stark to develop a policy for the consortium on the use of social media and other electronic exchanges with patients.

Case Study 3: Use of Online Search in an Evaluation

RELEVANT EXCERPT FROM THE GUIDELINE

> Psychologists are cognizant of the ethical and practical implications of proactively researching online personal information about their clients/patients. They carefully consider the advisability of discussing such research activities with their clients/patients and how information gained from such search would be utilized and recorded as documenting this information may introduce risks to the boundaries of appropriate conduct for a psychologist. (Joint Task Force, 2013, p. 797)

SETTING: ARMY BEHAVIORAL HEALTH OUTPATIENT CLINIC

Captain (CPT) Jessica Smith was a clinical psychologist in the U.S. Army; she worked in a small behavioral health outpatient clinic within the Department of Behavioral Medicine, which primarily served active duty service members. The clinic providers evaluated and provided treatment for a wide variety of behavioral health conditions, including adjustment disorders, depression, anxiety, and posttraumatic stress disorder. On the basis of the patient population, evaluations were often military specific, including fitness-for-duty evaluations, occupational evaluations, and evaluations for administrative separations.

CPT Smith frequently received consults to perform security clearance evaluations to assess a service member's psychological suitability to receive or retain a security clearance. These evaluations were requested most often after inappropriate conduct had been identified (e.g., criminal behavior, financial irresponsibility). Although evaluations could also be related to the presence of behavioral health conditions, security clearances were most often denied or revoked based on the service member's failure to seek treatment rather than merely the presence of a psychiatric condition.

SCENARIO

Sergeant First Class (SFC) Thompson was referred for a security evaluation after he was arrested for driving under the influence (DUI). The adjudicator noted that although the charges were dismissed, an evaluation was still required. As CPT Smith reviewed the available information, she saw SFC Thompson was also arrested in 1999 and again in 2003 for alcohol-related incidents. In addition, the soldier's medical records contained objective evidence indicative of physical deterioration associated with excessive alcohol use.

CPT Smith contacted SFC Thompson's first line supervisor to obtain collateral information. The supervisor reported the soldier had a history of problematic behavior related to alcohol misuse but indicated disciplinary actions had been lenient due to rank. Despite this historic pattern, the supervisor described the events as past behaviors rather than recent ones; however, he also mentioned he recently saw an Instagram photo of SFC Thompson drinking alcohol at a hail and farewell event. The supervisor suggested CPT Smith look up the picture and provided SFC Thompson's Instagram handle.

KEY ELEMENTS, CHALLENGES, AND DECISION FACTORS

CPT Smith had not previously conducted Internet searches on patients. She felt confident that obtaining material in this manner was legal and did not present an issue with confidentiality because the information was publicly accessible; however, she was uncertain whether an online search was ethical, and if so, under what circumstances. Although she concluded that Googling a therapy patient might affect the therapeutic relationship by blurring boundaries and possibly introducing multiple roles, she felt a search in the context of an evaluation presented a more ambiguous situation.

CPT Smith additionally considered the power differential in the relationship. Although an online search might provide clinically relevant information, SFC Thompson might feel the search was a breach of his privacy and therefore inappropriate. CPT Smith assumed this would affect her ability to establish rapport, and the patient would likely question her professionalism. CPT Smith remained aware of her role in the case and the importance of differentiating a treatment role from an evaluation role.

OPTIONS AVAILABLE TO THE PSYCHOLOGIST

CPT Smith initially considered avoiding the dilemma by simply relying on SFC Thompson's self-report in combination with other available information from collateral sources and medical records. After some additional thought, she concluded that because the supervisor had made her privy to the photo's existence, she would need to address the information in her report and provide a rationale related to her choice about whether to search the Internet for the picture or other relevant information.

Although CPT Smith could conduct the search without the patient's consent (and knowledge), she decided she would feel she had not demonstrated the courtesy and respect the patient deserved and would not meet the aspirational guidelines set forth by the APA. She considered discussing the information the supervisor provided about SFC Thompson but was apprehensive because this might inadvertently affect the supervisor's relationship with the soldier. She also feared the patient might not provide accurate information based on his desire to present a favorable impression of himself.

CPT Smith finally considered requesting SFC Thompson's consent to conduct the online search. If SFC Thompson agreed, she could document the consent and follow up on the information the collateral informant had provided, although she would still need to determine the most appropriate way to use and document any information she discovered.

CPT Smith realized creating and implementing a clear policy about Internet searches and sharing that policy with her patients would reduce the need to make similar decisions in the future. If she chose to begin using information found online to supplement assessments, she would have to consider ways to make these searches a collaborative process to respect the patient.

Case Study 4: Meeting HIPAA and Health Information Technology for Economic and Clinical Health Act Requirements

RELEVANT EXCERPT FROM THE GUIDELINE

> The use of telecommunications technologies and the rapid advances in technology present unique challenges for psychologists in protecting the confidentiality of clients/patients. Psychologists who provide telepsychology learn about the potential risks to confidentiality before utilizing such technologies. When necessary, psychologists obtain the appropriate consultation with technology experts to augment their knowledge of telecommunication technologies in order to apply security measures in their practices that will

> protect and maintain the confidentiality of data and information related to their clients/patients. (Joint Task Force, 2013, p. 798)

SETTING: INDEPENDENT TELEPSYCHOLOGY PRACTICE FROM A HOME OFFICE

Dr. Tom Johnson was a clinical psychologist who was employed by a behavioral health agency within the public sector. He practiced in a suburban area of a large metropolitan city in the northeastern United States where there was a large number of practicing clinical psychologists. He was interested in the prospect of a part-time telepsychology practice from his home as a way to generate additional income with little overhead costs by reaching potential clientele outside of his immediate commuting area. He did not have previous experience with telepsychology but had used videoconferencing at work for business meetings and to visit with family. Although he did not consider himself to be "tech savvy," he was comfortable operating a webcam and believed he could attract clients who would like to receive discreet and confidential psychological services from their home.

SCENARIO

Dr. Johnson wanted to ensure that the telepsychology system and the processes he established would safeguard confidentiality of patient information. He considered obtaining professional consultation for information technology guidance but was concerned about the expense and instead spent time researching other options online.

As Dr. Johnson explored these issues, he concluded that confidentiality was highly related to requirements set forth by HIPAA. He was generally aware of HIPAA requirements to safeguard against the release of PHI but was not familiar with the legal details because he had previously relied on his employer to ensure that information was managed in compliance with HIPAA.

As he conducted his online research, he realized that in his home-based private practice, he would be considered a covered entity within the terms of HIPAA and must therefore comply with requirements to prevent unauthorized disclosures of health information. In his search for a videoconferencing system, he discovered there were considerable references to encryption as a means to ensure the security of videoconference transmissions, therefore protecting confidentiality of the data as it is transmitted; however, he was confused about claims that certain equipment and systems were "HIPAA compliant," which he assumed meant they used appropriate encryption processes.

Because this venture was experimental, Dr. Johnson did not want to make a large monetary investment in a home videoconferencing system. He selected a well-known free service to economize. On the basis of the system's description of encryption technology used for transmissions, Dr. Johnson believed he was selecting a HIPAA-compliant system. Satisfied that he had found an affordable system that transmitted data in an encrypted manner, he prepared to install and configure the system on his home computer.

KEY ELEMENTS, CHALLENGES, AND DECISION FACTORS

Psychologists who meet criteria to be considered a covered entity under the HIPAA Privacy Rule are required to protect individually identifiable health information, which is considered to be PHI. These requirements were expanded under the Health Information Technology for Economic and Clinical Health Act (HITECH; 2009). These requirements apply whether the PHI is held or transmitted in any form or media (Solove, 2013). It is incumbent on psychologists engaged in telepsychology to ensure the videoconferencing system used provides safeguards for PHI in a manner that prevents unauthorized disclosures and maintains confidentiality of the information.

Videoconferencing equipment and systems are not by themselves HIPAA compliant; rather, it is the way they are used that determines whether a psychologist is compliant with HIPAA requirements. The equipment and systems may have elements, such as encryption, that facilitate HIPAA compliance, but the HIPAA Privacy Rule requires a set of actions by covered entities to ensure that health information is protected and remains confidential when PHI is transmitted (APA Practice Organization, 2013). In addition to actions by a psychologist, the actions of a business associate may have an impact on HIPAA and HITECH compliance. If a third party, such as a videoconferencing vendor, transmits PHI on behalf of a covered entity and has access to the PHI, that third party is considered a business associate (U.S. Department of Health & Human Services, n.d.). In these situations, a psychologist who is the covered entity would need a written business associate agreement (BAA) with the videoconferencing vendor that meets the terms of HIPAA and HITECH. Without a BAA, the telepsychologist is at risk for HIPAA noncompliance.

When selecting a videoconferencing system, the telepsychologist must determine whether a BAA is necessary. If the vendor provides encryption and a written BAA, the telepsychologist can have greater confidence that privacy and confidentiality requirements under HIPAA will be met. If encryption and a BAA are not both provided by the vendor, the telepsychologist will need additional verification that a system meets an exception or otherwise meets the terms of HIPAA and HITECH.

OPTIONS AVAILABLE TO THE PSYCHOLOGIST

As Dr. Johnson prepared to set up a telepsychology practice, he realized he was unfamiliar with HIPAA requirements and determined he would need additional information about the provisions of HIPAA and HITECH as they applied to a telepsychology. He likewise discovered that it is difficult to find and access this topic in the professional literature and that much of the readily accessible information was published on the Internet in the form of blogs and informational websites. He found these sites to be variable with regard to citing sources, and at times he found it difficult to judge the merits of various opinions and observations of the authors. With perseverance, he assembled an array of peer-reviewed journal articles and book chapters that addressed these issues. He also discovered some helpful Internet sites that provided reviews of videoconferencing vendors and whether they provided encryption capability that would meet HIPAA requirements. He came to understand that it was important to critically evaluate a vendor's claims to be HIPAA compliant and request that the vendor provide information about how HIPAA compliance is facilitated or achieved.

A fundamental decision Dr. Johnson faced when making plans to establish a telepsychology practice was selecting a videoconferencing system. In the process of researching issues of privacy and confidentiality as they apply to telepsychology, he encountered a common theme that presumes telepsychology sessions transmit PHI and invoke HIPAA rules for privacy and security. As a result, he concluded that he should use a videoconferencing system that had effective encryption methods. He found the technical details about encryption to be confusing, and because he was focused on keeping costs low, he selected a free videoconferencing system that declared its use of encryption would ensure secure data transmissions. Unfortunately, this system did not clearly meet HIPAA Privacy Rule requirements. Additionally, Dr. Johnson did not initially understand the requirements for a BAA, but through his continued research he understood that when a third-party vendor has access to and transmits PHI on behalf of a covered entity, a written BAA must be provided to fulfill HIPAA requirements.

In addition to the encryption and BAA considerations, Dr. Johnson learned about a variety of practices and processes related to privacy and confidentiality. For example, in the Technical Guidelines section of the American Telemedicine Association Practice Guidelines (American Telemedicine Association, 2013), Dr. Johnson discovered a series of recommendations for provider actions to safeguard privacy in the course of practicing telepsychology. These guidelines include recommendations related to the use of mobile devices, videoconferencing software, and storage and transmission of PHI. By reviewing these and similar recommendations from a variety of sources, Dr. Johnson believed he was better prepared to meet HIPAA requirements and to anticipate privacy and confidentiality considerations in the use of telepsychology technology.

Key Points From the Chapter to Remember

- When considering the use of e-mail or other forms of electronic communication with patients, establish written policies addressing not only the specific uses of e-mail and social media that will be acceptable (e.g., scheduling, therapeutic issues) but also how specific risks will be managed and explained to patients to ensure informed consent, such as the accessibility of e-mails to unintended parties, the ability of deleted files to be recovered, the consequences of unencrypted exchanges, the expectation to be instantly available and responsive, and the role of the patient in protecting privacy and confidentiality.
- If you work with an agency, clinic, hospital, or other such entity, be clear about its policies regarding telepsychology, social media, e-mail, and any other form of electronic communication with patients. If there is no written policy, request and document guidance and recommend that such a policy be developed.
- Be very familiar with how to control privacy settings when using electronic communication of any type.

- Supervisors and supervisees need to be proactive in learning about the different levels of digital knowledge and experience each may have and be sensitive to how those differences may influence delivery of services and supervision.
- When conducting an evaluation or providing therapy, psychologists seek information and are informed about current laws, regulations, ethical and professional guidelines and policies, in addition to the therapeutic impact of seeking or receiving information from social media, online searches, or other Internet sources.
- Psychologists who meet criteria to be considered a covered entity under the HIPAA Privacy Rule are required to protect individually identifiable health information, which is considered to be PHI. These requirements are expanded under the Health Information Technology for Economic and Clinical Health (HITECH) Act and apply whether the PHI is held or transmitted in any form or media (Solove, 2013). It is incumbent on psychologists engaged in telepsychology to ensure the videoconferencing system used provides safeguards for PHI in a manner that prevents unauthorized disclosures and maintains confidentiality of the information.
- Videoconferencing equipment and systems are not by themselves HIPAA compliant; rather, it is the way they are used that determines whether a psychologist is compliant with HIPAA requirements. The HIPAA Privacy Rule requires a set of actions by covered entities to ensure that health information is protected and remains confidential when PHI is transmitted (APA Practice Organization, 2013).
- In addition to actions by a psychologist, the actions of a business associate may have an impact on HIPAA and HITECH compliance. If a third party, such as a videoconferencing vendor, transmits PHI on behalf of a covered entity and has access to the PHI, they are considered a business associate (U.S. Department of Health & Human Services, n.d.). In these situations, a psychologist who is the covered entity would need a written BAA with the videoconferencing vendor that meets the terms of HIPAA and HITECH. Without a BAA, the telepsychologist is at risk for HIPAA noncompliance.
- It is important to evaluate critically a vendor's claims of being HIPAA compliant and to request that the vendor provide information about how HIPAA compliance is facilitated or achieved.

References

American Psychological Association. (2017). *Ethical principles of psychologists and code of conduct* (2002, Amended June 1, 2010 and January 1, 2017). Retrieved from http://www.apa.org/ethics/code/index.aspx

American Psychological Association Practice Organization. (2013, September). *HIPAA, What you need to know now. The Privacy Rule: A primer for psychologists.* Retrieved from http://www.apapracticecentral.org/business/hipaa/hippa-privacy-primer.pdf

American Telemedicine Association. (2013, May). *Practice guidelines for video-based online mental health services.* Retrieved from http://hub.americantelemed.org/resources/telemedicine-practice-guidelines

Health Information Technology for Economic and Clinical Health Act, Pub. L. 111-5. (2009).

Health Insurance Portability and Accountability Act, Pub. L. No. 104-191, 110 Stat. 1936 (1996).

Joint Task Force for the Development of Telepsychology Guidelines for Psychologists. (2013). Guidelines for the practice of telepsychology. *American Psychologist, 68,* 791–800. Retrieved from https://www.apa.org/pubs/journals/features/amp-a0035001.pdf

Solove, D. (2013, January 22). *The HIPAA-HITECH regulation, the Cloud, and beyond.* Retrieved from http://www.safegov.org/2013/1/22/the-hipaa-hitech-regulation,-the-cloud,-and-beyond

U.S. Department of Health & Human Services. (n.d.). *Business associates.* Retrieved from http://www.hhs.gov/hipaa/for-professionals/privacy/guidance/business-associates

Ronald S. Palomares and Thomas W. Miller

Security and Transmission of Data and Information

5

Psychologists who provide telepsychology services take reasonable steps to ensure that security measures are in place to protect data and information related to their clients/patients from unintended access or disclosure.
—Guideline 5, *Guidelines for the Practice of Telepsychology*

Rationale

The use of telecommunication technologies in the provision of psychological services presents unique potential threats to the security and transmission of client/patient data and information. These potential threats to the integrity of data and information may include computer viruses, hackers, theft of technology devices, damage to hard drives or portable drives, failure of security systems, flawed software, ease of accessibility to unsecured electronic files, and malfunctioning or outdated technology. Other threats may include policies and practices of technology companies and vendors, such as tailored marketing derived from e-mail communications. Psychologists are encouraged to be mindful of these potential threats and to take reasonable steps to ensure that security measures are in place for protecting and controlling access to client/patient data within an information system. In addition, they are cognizant of relevant

http://dx.doi.org/10.1037/0000046-006
A Telepsychology Casebook: Using Technology Ethically and Effectively in Your Professional Practice, L. F. Campbell, F. Millán, and J. N. Martin (Editors)

> jurisdictional and federal laws and regulations that govern electronic storage and transmission of client/patient data and information, and they develop appropriate policies and procedures to comply with such directives. When developing policies and procedures to ensure the security of client/patient data and information, psychologists may include considering the unique concerns and impacts posed by both intended and unintended use of public and private technology devices, active and inactive therapeutic relationship, and the different safeguards required for different physical environments, different staffs (e.g., professional vs. administrative staff), and different telecommunication technologies. (Joint Task Force for the Development of Telepsychology Guidelines for Psychologists, 2013, p. 797)

In-person practice has conventionally meant maintenance of paper records and, more recently, includes electronic record keeping. The American Psychological Association (APA; 2007) *Record Keeping Guidelines* are detailed and clear on the importance of security, transmission, storage, and disposal of records. Furthermore, the implementation of the Health Insurance Portability and Accountability Act (HIPAA, 1996) Privacy and Security Rules has both assisted health care professionals and challenged them to be alert, vigilant, and informed about the importance of legal and ethical maintenance of client records and the communication to others of client records. Telepsychology introduces additional challenges to the protection and security of records and all client data given that records in this venue are created, maintained, transmitted, and destroyed electronically.

Regardless of their competence in electronic record keeping, psychologists, upon entering into telepsychology, will want to conduct a risk analysis as they develop their record keeping systems and means of protecting data. Access to data is equally important because protection of data and assurance that only authorized individuals have that access are critical to the standard of care for data collection and security. A risk assessment will be valuable in identifying weaknesses and threats to security and in developing means to safeguard transmission of data, such as encryption, firewalls, and robust password systems.

Clients must be partners with psychologists in technology competence and in astute care for their own data and client information. In traditional in-person practice, including agency, inpatient, independent practice, or other settings, psychologists and other authorized staff or facilities were the keepers of data and information regarding services to clients. In telepsychology, the clients also have some, if not all, of the same data on record that are held by the psychologists and other agencies or facilities. Clients do not have a confidentiality obligation for data, but electronic transmission introduces a risk of error, interruption, and unintended disclosure that has not been present in other practice venues. Psychologists have a responsibility to inform clients of risks, be vigilant for a breach in client data, and respond and correct the breach as soon as possible. Increasingly, improved methods to secure, protect, and safely transmit data are available. It is incumbent on psychologists through consultation or additional training to become familiar with and engage in systems that meet the standard of practice.

Case Study 1: HIPAA and Initiating a Telepsychology Practice

SETTING: MULTIDISCIPLINARY HEALTH CLINIC

Dr. Collins, a licensed psychologist, is a partner in a multidisciplinary health clinic. He has been with the practice for more than 20 years but has only recently begun offering telehealth services to clients who live in rural areas. Dr. Collins focuses his work on clients who present primarily with problems that are mood based. In addition, he only provides services to adults. At present, Dr. Collins has only a handful of individuals who are receiving services through telepsychology. In a recent evaluation of those services, he was pleased with the process and level of services he is now able to provide, so he was planning to expand the services to gradually include additional clients from within his practice. However, he first invited his colleague Dr. Victoria, a licensed psychologist and local expert in telepsychology, to meet with him and help him evaluate his telepsychology services. Dr. Victoria had been providing telepsychology services in her own practice setting for more than 5 years, written several research articles for the state psychological association publication and one peer-reviewed journal, and conducted numerous professional development seminars on the use of technology in clinical settings.

SCENARIO

Before the initial offering of telepsychology services, Dr. Collins began his own research and gathered numerous articles and other sources of information for guidance on how to incorporate telepsychology into a clinical practice. He also attended several professional development seminars to learn about the current directions and obtain further guidance on the use of telepsychology in practice settings.

After this fairly extensive gathering of information and careful consideration of how telepsychology could actually enhance the provision of services to his clients, Dr. Collins was excited to begin incorporating telepsychology as an option within his practice's services. He then decided that initially he wanted to keep the scope of services limited to only an audiovisual interactive therapeutic service arrangement with his clients. He ultimately ended up with selecting a subscription-based audiovisual program that used a web-based server for connecting the two parties and did not require either party to download software or purchase additional equipment as long as their computers had a video camera and microphone.

With regard to the selection of clients who would potentially use his telepsychology services, Dr. Collins set a policy of first meeting with the client face to face in his office for a minimum of four sessions. Once he was satisfied that the client was capable of engaging in telepsychology services and had the resources to do so, he then scheduled a separate session to train and practice using the computers and website, as well as go over the additional policies, procedures, and addendums to his privacy and confidentiality policies, before embarking on their telepsychology-based therapy sessions. He also made the decision to offer these services to no more than five clients at any one time to minimize complexity and ensure that he was able to handle the additional demands and evaluate the services without them expanding too fast and becoming difficult to maintain.

After the first year of offering these services, Dr. Collins arranged to have Dr. Victoria, with whom he had worked earlier, review his telepsychology policies and procedures. Drs. Collins and Victoria spent several hours going over the various policies and procedures he had developed, including successes, struggles, and key changes he had incorporated throughout the year. Dr. Victoria congratulated him on his extensive and well-planned process incorporating technology into his clinical practice.

However, before Dr. Victoria would allow Dr. Collins to bask in his perceived moment of glory for having created a successful resource within his practice, she then broke the news that despite all of the careful planning and excellent procedures he had put in place, there was a huge problem with the software he was using for the therapy sessions: It was not compliant with HIPAA, which sets national standards for transmission of electronic health care data. More specifically, it was not compliant with the Security Rule, which focuses on electronic protected health information. In short, Dr. Collins's selection of the web-based services to provide the audiovisual connections created a potential legal issue for him. However, Dr. Victoria reassured him that if he switched to a HIPAA-compliant service provider, all would be well, and he could then truly be pleased with the knowledge that he had developed a successful and secure telepsychology-based service for his clinic.

KEY ELEMENTS, CHALLENGES, AND DECISION FACTORS

When reviewing the work in which Dr. Collins engaged to develop a successful telepsychology service as an addition to his clinic-based services, it should be noted that he did many things correctly. As with any professionals who want to expand their services and knowledge, Dr. Collins first began researching what has been done and evaluated the information he gathered in a manner that would fit his specific practice and needs. He not only read what has been published but also sought professional development activities in which he could hear directly from others who have already been successful in similar processes, as well as interact and have his own questions answered while learning new aspects and creating a process that would be most successful for him.

After gathering information, Dr. Collins started to put the pieces together for the implementation of this new component of his practice. He did not start big, directing a huge portion of his clientele into this new service. Instead, he began slowly by limiting the number of clients using these services to five at any time and, as noted, would constantly evaluate the process not only for his clients but also for himself and the clinic. In sharing this information with Dr. Victoria, Dr. Collins described how he changed various aspects of the service, based on information he learned or ideas that came along to improve it.

Unfortunately for Dr. Collins, somewhere during the process, he failed to consider the various HIPAA requirements that are a part of telepsychology practice despite

Dr. Victoria's earlier consultation. More specifically, he did not understand the requirement to use only HIPAA-compliant software services, ensuring the protection of any electronic protected health information generated through the use of those services. Thus, the surface-level challenge was to ensure that when extending the services being provided by any health care professional, all services were compliant with HIPAA. A deeper level challenge here was understanding that the use of technology created new HIPAA-compliance challenges that needed to be addressed and then appropriately incorporated.

Thus, for Dr. Collins, his decision factors were well thought out and, after Dr. Victoria's review, appeared to be successful. Unfortunately, Dr. Collins was so happy to have found a web-based server that didn't require additional costs, he did not review the HIPAA requirements to ensure compliance across all components of the service. This oversight highlights the importance of going over resources and information and double-checking what is needed for a legal, compliant, ethical, and successful telepsychology practice.

OPTIONS AVAILABLE TO THE PSYCHOLOGIST

The immediate first step Dr. Collins should take is to stop using the non–HIPAA-compliant software services, have his clients see him in his office, and begin researching services that are compliant with federal law. Once he is able to identify a HIPAA-compliant program that meets the specific needs of telepsychology services, Dr. Collins should then be able to resume providing them. However, he should also incorporate a training session with his clients on how to use this new software and ensure they are capable of and comfortable with using it. Additionally, Dr. Collins should contact his malpractice insurance provider or attorney to obtain a consult to discuss any legal obligations he has with his having used a non–HIPAA-compliant service and the potential exposure of his client's electronic health care data.

THE BEST DECISION POSSIBLE

Given the factors in this case, the best decision is to do the following:

- Only use technological services that are HIPAA compliant to ensure protections of clients' health care data.
- Before embarking on the use of technology within one's practice setting, gather information from both published (trusted) resources and other experts through professional development activities and consultation with experienced colleagues.
- Engage clients in face-to-face sessions, including a training session with the hardware and software used in the telepsychology services.
- Invite an expert or experienced colleague who uses telepsychology to evaluate and review policies, procedures, and services.
- Consider consulting with your insurance provider or an attorney to ensure that newly developed policies and services are compliant with local, state, and federal laws.

Case Study 2: Transferring a Telepsychology Training Program to Another Professional

SETTING: UNIVERSITY PRACTICUM AND INTERNSHIP PROGRAM

This year Dr. Singh will be retiring from her position as a psychology professor at Atwater University. She has been on the faculty for more than 35 years, the last 15 of which she served as the psychology practicum and internship director for both the undergraduate and graduate programs. One of her most recent additions to the program was the incorporation of telepsychology in her supervision of students in off-campus placements.

SCENARIO

The newly appointed psychology practicum and internship director is Dr. Juba, who will head up the program at the end of the semester when Dr. Singh retires. Dr. Juba has not previously engaged in any form of telepsychology services. In his first meeting with Dr. Singh to discuss the transition of leadership roles, Dr. Juba explained that he was concerned with the telepsychology services Dr. Singh had instituted and had particular concerns about how to protect confidential information. Dr. Juba was unfamiliar with the equipment and processes in place for these services and was not sure about their purpose. He went on to say that he was uncomfortable being involved in something with which he was unfamiliar and would like to know more about why Dr. Singh had instituted the use of telepsychology services in the field placement processes, as well as their benefits and risks, before moving forward with it.

Surprised by his concerns, Dr. Singh asked to postpone that conversation so she could first prepare and then discuss it with him in more detail during their next transition meeting. Dr. Singh recognized that she needed to provide him with a comprehensive understanding of the use of technology in supervision and to ensure his competence in this skill set so that Dr. Juba would be able to meet the requirements for the security and transmission of the data and information exchanged between him and students and so that he could evaluate properly whether students were guarding against unintended access or disclosure. In her preparations for their conversation, Dr. Singh outlined the decision-making process she initially went through to determine whether she should incorporate telepsychology services into the program and the precautions she took. She listed the positives and negatives for the use of technology, as well as the costs and savings involved, and she described the positive impact she had seen since the inception of the use of telepsychology. Dr. Singh then evaluated the entire implementation of the telepsychology services used in the practicum and internship supervisory process. With this information gathered and reviewed, she then arranged for another meeting with Dr. Juba.

In their meeting, which focused on the use of technology in the practicum and internship programs, Dr. Singh began the conversation by going over the *Guidelines for the Practice of Telepsychology* (Joint Task Force, 2013), pointing out how those guidelines are the foundation of the program she developed. She then discussed the rationale for her use of telepsychology. She explained to Dr. Juba that a vital role the university-based supervisor fulfills is the ongoing communication with and supervision of the students in their field placements. Although each student has a field-based supervisor with whom they work closely at their individual location, the university-based supervisor must also be in continuous communication to ensure that the student's needs for training and support are being met. Before the addition of technology, specifically biweekly audio-video meetings, Dr. Singh found herself often traveling to the various practicum or internship locations for on-site meetings throughout the semester. She was unable to connect with the students as often as she would have liked, especially those who were struggling in their placements for a variety of reasons, and felt the long commutes to the numerous locations had wasted much time. Although Dr. Singh still felt obliged to make one or two physical site visits per placement each semester, she said she was able to be more productive and felt she was actually providing each student with more enhanced supervision than she ever could without the use of technology. She discussed some of the training symposia and conference sessions she had attended to learn more about telepsychology and how other professionals had instituted the use of technology in their practice and training settings. From these training opportunities, Dr. Singh explained how she developed the current program she was using. She also encouraged Dr. Juba to seek out his own training and educational opportunities so that he could learn more about the use of technology and become more comfortable with its use.

While discussing the overall time-savings component the incorporation of technology has given to the internship and practicum program, Dr. Singh also explained to Dr. Juba that additional time needed to be spent up-front to ensure each student was comfortable with and competent in the use of the technology. She described how she spent a portion of her initial orientation meeting with all interns and practicum students each semester going over the proper procedures for using the equipment, as well as covering troubleshooting procedures. By doing this, she was ensuring the students' understood the need to protect the security of client data and information and were compliant with the requirements.

Despite his initial reluctance, Dr. Juba found himself becoming more supportive. When talking about his concerns, he confessed that part of it was his own overall reluctance to use technology, except when he found himself being forced to adapt, across his personal and professional life. He thanked Dr. Singh for her explanation of the rationale for the use of technology, the evident extensive studies in which she engaged before adopting the use of technology, her continued evaluation of the process and outcomes, as well as her enthusiasm for this new component in the internship and practicum program and for helping him understand ways to ensure the security of data and information transmission. He saw the benefits from the addition of technology and ways to protect against risk and now needed to learn more so that he could be more comfortable with it.

With Dr. Juba's acceptance and newly discovered support for the use of technology in the practicum and internship program, Dr. Singh arranged a training session for him to learn about the equipment, procedures, and processes involved. Dr. Singh carefully outlined a plan to walk Dr. Juba through the overall process, discussing the expected uses and overall procedures, and describing ways to ensure compliance with jurisdictional and federal laws and regulations, ethics, and telepsychology guidelines. From her notes and other documents, Dr. Singh then developed a formalized, written manual that explained the various policies, troubleshooting steps, procedures, and processes involved in the telepsychology services to ensure protection of data in transmission and storage, among other important processes included in the psychology practicum and internship programs. Finally, Dr. Singh arranged to meet in person with Dr. Juba to go over the hardware and software used. She gave him a demonstration, and then had him run through a practice scenario using the equipment and software by himself. She also identified potential threats to the integrity of data and information in the form of viruses, theft and damage of devices, malfunctioning hardware, and hackers, among others, and stressed the importance of being aware of current and future threats and developing steps to ensure that security measures were in place for protecting and controlling access to client/patient data within an information system. Finally, she reviewed the policies and procedures she developed to comply with guidelines and directives. Drs. Singh and Juba spent a full afternoon using the equipment and did not conclude the training until Dr. Juba was comfortable enough to use it himself and train others to both use and troubleshoot the equipment and software. At the conclusion of their training session, Dr. Juba was confident that he knew how to engage in basic troubleshooting steps when minor issues arose, as well as whom to call and how to connect with the university's technology department for more advanced help. Later, Dr. Singh followed up again with Dr. Juba to ensure that he still felt comfortable with his new skills, and she provided him with additional resources in the event that he needed assistance in her absence.

KEY ELEMENTS, CHALLENGES, AND DECISION FACTORS

Two key challenges Dr. Singh had to overcome in this scenario were (a) articulating the decision steps she took before incorporating telepsychology supervision services into the practicum and internship program and then (b) encouraging and supporting the continued incorporation of technology within her program. She knew the telepsychology supervision services she incorporated were successful because they were cost-effective and highly valued by the students. Additionally, she knew that she had followed relevant guidelines, research, and other resources to ensure that the program was compliant with relevant laws and requirements. To do that, Dr. Singh needed to review and reconsider her initial rationale and arguments for and against the program enhancement to educate Dr. Juba on the processes that had occurred throughout the start-up and continued use of the virtual supervision services. Dr. Singh needed to find a clear way to explain what and why she had done to an individual who was reluctant to embrace new uses of technology. She knew she needed to give him guidance on how to seek out additional trainings to advance his knowledge, skills, and overall comfort with the use of technology as well as ensure that he understood the telepsychology guidelines and his responsibility not just for ensuring the security of data and transmission but for all of the elements needing attention when using telepsychology.

Similarly, Dr. Juba's first, and largest, challenge was his reluctance to embrace technology, except when forced to do so. Having heard about the success of the telepsychology components within the program, he knew he had to listen and then carefully consider how he would adapt to using it. The final key element—and perhaps the most critical of all—in this scenario is the extensive training and preparation that both Drs. Singh and Juba went through to ensure Dr. Juba could operate the hardware and software to the point where he could train others on the proper use and troubleshooting procedures necessary for basic users. Only then could they both be sure they were safeguarding the security and transmission of data in the process of using technology with students.

OPTIONS AVAILABLE TO THE PSYCHOLOGIST

With the upcoming retirement of Dr. Singh, all decisions around the actions to take were placed directly with Dr. Juba. He knew he was inheriting a successful program, in which the use of technology was considered to be a highlight. Dr. Juba found he needed to gather more information in order to become more comfortable with how the technology was applied and information was protected and to be personally successful with it. He knew he needed to find training opportunities and professional development activities to enhance his knowledge and skills. After an intensive training session with the equipment and software and the guidelines, rules, and regulations, Dr. Juba asked Dr. Singh to supervise his initial attempts with the technology and to help guide his personal growth around his use of technology for the program.

THE BEST DECISION POSSIBLE

Given the factors in this case, the best decision is to do the following:

- Seek guidance and support from others who are using technology in a similar fashion to how you intend to use it.
- Attend professional development activities to enhance and learn new skills around the use of technology.
- Ensure a routine, ongoing process to evaluate telepsychology services, making modifications to improve the program and ensure that data are properly secured.
- When evaluating the use of telepsychology services, also evaluate the various technologies being used, both software and hardware, and update them as necessary.
- When retiring or turning over a program with telepsychology services to another professional, conduct a multifaceted briefing that includes the rationale for and use of technology, the results of all evaluation processes, and assurance that the new individual is competent in the use of all major aspects of the technology and understands the legal and ethical responsibilities of using technology.

Case Study 3: Stolen Laptop

SETTING: PRIVATE PRACTICE

Dr. Davis's private practice is in a downtown office building in a large urban city. For the past 2 years, she has been using an audiovisual, HIPAA-compliant program to conduct therapy sessions with clients who live in rural settings, often 100 or 200 miles away, but all residing in the same state. As Dr. Davis's telepsychology client numbers have grown, she has begun conducting sessions from her home office, where she is able to provide the same level of services to her telepsychology-based clients as she does with her face-to-face clients in her office downtown. Because of these new arrangements, Dr. Davis is now telecommuting from home 2 days a week, scheduling and providing a full range of telepsychology services to clients. The other 3 days a week she is in her office meeting with clients directly or engaging in administrative duties and other typical office duties. Periodically, Dr. Davis will conduct her telepsychology-based sessions with clients from her office, as well as always bringing in these clients for at least one face-to-face session in which they also practice using the computer-based programs before engaging in the distance audiovisual sessions. Because she conducts her audiovisual therapeutic sessions in various settings, Dr. Davis has purchased a lightweight laptop computer that serves as her platform for telepsychology services. She transports it to and from her home and downtown office, where she uses it to conduct therapy, maintain up-to-date information and notes on her clients, e-mail clients, and maintain her schedule. Before she leaves her office each day, Dr. Davis runs a backup program to store the data from her laptop on a hard drive that is kept in the office.

SCENARIO

One evening on her way home from work, Dr. Davis stopped at the dry cleaners. While she was in the store, a thief broke the window on the side of her car and stole her briefcase. Inside the briefcase was her laptop computer with all her files, including notes and appointments for many of her clients. After her initial reaction of shock and feelings of horror, Dr. Davis called the police to report the theft.

After reporting the situation to the police, Dr. Davis then went into "laptop lockdown" mode. That is, when setting up her laptop, she had it programmed with software to allow the capability to remotely lockdown her computer in case it was lost or stolen and thus protect the data it contained from being breached. This program was connected to her cell phone, and once Dr. Davis activated it from her phone, when the laptop was powered up, it would receive the signal sending it immediately into a remotely activated memory erase, followed by a shutdown. (Examples of these types of programs can be found at http://www.druva.com and http://www.absolute.com.)

While making her report to the police about the stolen laptop computer, Dr. Davis was able to retrieve the computer's identification numbers from her office files, such as the computer's make, model, serial number; its machine access code (MAC) number; and two photographs she had taken of her laptop. Because she routinely backed up her computer before leaving the office, Dr. Davis was not worried about losing any data. However, she feared that even though she had taken the precautionary steps to remotely wipe and lockdown the laptop, there was always a chance that her clients' personal information was at risk of being compromised. So Dr. Davis called her malpractice insurance company to obtain guidance on what steps she had to take legally, ethically, and professionally to let the appropriate agencies and individuals know about the potential breach of confidentiality and security loss.

KEY ELEMENTS, CHALLENGES, AND DECISION FACTORS

The critical issue Dr. Davis faced in this situation was the potential loss of client information as a result of a breach of confidentiality and security of her records. However, the decisions Dr. Davis made when she initially began the process allowed her to be more successful in her attempts to limit or prevent the loss of information. She prepared for the potential loss by recording key identification numbers and descriptors of the laptop to provide the police so they could work on the recovery and identification of Dr. Davis as the owner of the laptop.

Dr. Davis also did her research to identify and purchase the software program to lockdown her laptop if it were lost or stolen. Her challenge at this step was to find an appropriate piece of software that she understood how to operate and could do what she wanted—in this case, wipe the memory storage and then shut down the laptop. Dr. Davis began her research on the Internet, reading about various programs and companies that offered the type of software she was looking for. As she narrowed down her options, she also read the reviews and learned more about what the programs did and did not do. Dr. Davis then spoke with several colleagues about the software programs they used, asking for positives and negatives. During this research phase, Dr. Davis attended a conference that had several telepsychology sessions included. She found one that focused on security issues, and she was able to ask the presenter and others in the audience about their opinions, experiences, and recommendations. Upon completion of her data-gathering phase, Dr. Davis had narrowed her search down to two programs that were highly recommended. She then elected to go with the one that a close colleague also used.

Finally, in addition to the software program to lock down the laptop, Dr. Davis had the laptop password protected, so if someone turned on the power, he or she would first have to enter a password. Knowing that simple passwords can often be guessed if the individual knows a few things about the owner, Dr. Davis followed the standard criteria for generating a more secure password. That is, she created a password that was more than eight characters in length, included both uppercase and lowercase letters, numbers, and one or more nonalphabetic characters (e.g., @, #, $, %, ^, &; West Virginia Office of Technology, n.d.).

OPTIONS AVAILABLE TO THE PSYCHOLOGIST

This situation worked out in a positive direction for Dr. Davis because she had been proactive in obtaining security features on the laptop she used to store sensitive and confidential client information. She maintained a set of separate records in her office with descriptive information about the laptop in case she had to report it stolen and would need to identify it if it was ever recovered. More important, Dr. Davis invested in a software program that was able to provide a high level of security to prevent a data breach or unauthorized access to sensitive and confidential information. With guidance from her malpractice insurance provider, Dr. Davis was directed on how to legally and appropriately handle the potential loss with her clients and third-party payers, as well as anyone else she needed to connect with for legal purposes.

THE BEST DECISION POSSIBLE

Given the factors in this case, the best decision is to do the following:

- Research and select a software program that best fits the need to be able to lock down or remotely wipe the memory of a computer in case it is lost or stolen.
- Maintain in a safe location the critical information necessary for identifying your computer to the police in the event that it is lost or stolen.
- Always use passwords that follow standard recommended criteria for passcode protection of your electronic equipment.
- If electronic equipment is stolen, contact your malpractice insurance agency for a professional consult on the recommended actions that should be taken to contact clients, third-party payers, and insurance companies and other legally required steps when there is the loss of patient health information.
- Routinely back up information onto separate secure memory storage, especially from a laptop that is transported from location to location.

Case Study 4: The Importance of Knowing When One Is Using Telepsychology

SETTING: MULTIDISCIPLINARY HEALTH CLINIC

Dr. Palomino is a psychologist working in an outpatient, multidisciplinary health clinic serving a wide range of clients. For the past 10 years, he has been employed with this clinic, engaged in a traditional setting and practice where he only provides direct services to individuals at the clinic. He does not engage, nor does he profess any interest, in expanding the services he provides to include any form of audiovisual technology. Dr. Palomino's practice efforts are predominantly focused on individual, face-to-face therapy sessions, while he periodically leads a few therapeutic groups when circumstances dictate this as an appropriate avenue for services to his clientele.

Although Dr. Palomino does not shy away from using technology in his everyday life, he does not see the utility of trying to incorporate telepsychology into his therapeutic processes at this time. Specifically, he believes that the definition of telepsychology is limited to when one uses telecommunications technology to conduct therapy or meet with clients when they are in different locations. However, within the past 2 years Dr. Palomino has begun to engage in therapeutic follow-up and monitoring with his clients using e-mail and text messages. He has found that periodically being able to connect remotely with his clients has dramatically improved client follow-through with agreed-on therapeutic objectives and ongoing maintenance of skills. Using his phone, Dr. Palomino is able to set up alerts to remind him to connect with clients, send e-mail and text messages when he is away from the office, and keep in touch when emergencies arise. If asked whether this is a form of telepsychology, Dr. Palomino would say it is not, because he is just sending them messages and is not talking with or seeing his clients using technology.

Contrary to Dr. Palomino's perspective, it is important to understand that the generally agreed-on definition of telepsychology services, also referred to as *telepractice, telemedicine*, or *telehealth*, is a broad one that covers the use of any form of telecommunications technology that uses electronic transmission of information over a distance. Examples include the definitions offered by the Centers for Medicare and Medicaid Services (n.d.), the American Telemedicine Association (2014), and the Joint Task Force for the Development of Telepsychology Guidelines for Psychologists (2013).

SCENARIO

One evening while he was riding the local public transportation system home during the crowded rush hour, Dr. Palomino's phone was stolen from his jacket pocket. He was not aware of the theft until he arrived at home and discovered it missing. He was devastated because he had so much personal and work information on his phone. Furthermore, he was angry with himself because for several months he had been thinking that he needed to password protect his phone, but he enjoyed being able to hit the power button and immediately begin working with the various programs, seeing e-mails, responding to text messages, and so on. As he began to realize how devastating this loss was, Dr. Palomino became frantic because he now realized that there was a lot of sensitive information on his phone, including clients' names, contact information, and, more important, e-mails and text messages that were of a therapeutic nature.

Once his anxiety level calmed to a degree that he could refocus and think about what he needed to do next, Dr. Palomino contacted his phone carrier to ask whether they could disable and halt service to the phone. He then called the police to report the theft. Next, Dr. Palomino called his malpractice insurance company for a legal consultation on what steps he needed to take regarding the breach of confidentiality and loss of security for mental health records.

KEY ELEMENTS, CHALLENGES, AND DECISION FACTORS

Because Dr. Palomino did not believe he was engaged in any form of telepsychology services, he had not become properly informed, sought guidance, or gained new knowledge about how best to incorporate telepsychology services into his current practices. Had he reviewed published the professional guidelines on the use of telepsychology (Joint Task Force, 2013) and numerous other resources, both written and in the form of symposia and professional development activities, Dr. Palomino would have realized that he was indeed engaged in a form of telepsychology when he e-mailed and texted his clients in regard to their therapy goals, processes, and his follow-up on their activities. Once he realized that he was engaged in telepractice, Dr. Palomino should have followed the guidelines on how to maintain the security and safety of the information he was creating and transporting on his cell phone.

Another key element in this scenario is the lack of security Dr. Palomino maintained with his cell phone. At a bare minimum, he should have had his cell phone password protected to prevent someone from picking it up and being able to access the sensitive information.

Overall, the perception that using his cell phone for therapeutic interventions was not considered a form of telepsychology and not recognizing the need to protect the information in his cell phone were two key errors Dr. Palomino made. Had he considered that these were indeed a form of telepsychology, he could have begun to question what steps he needed to take to safeguard the confidential, sensitive information he was carrying in his device.

OPTIONS AVAILABLE TO THE PSYCHOLOGIST

Once he realized that using a phone for communications and for storing client-related information was engaging in telepsychology services, Dr. Palomino should have immediately sought guidance on steps to safeguard that information. Researching how to protect the information by reading the available guidance and research, attending professional development events and talking with colleagues and other experts is the first step he should have taken. During this research process, Dr. Palomino should also have searched out resources on general protection of the device he was using to store and transport sensitive information, in this case, his cell phone. For example, the Federal Communications Commission (2015) published a consumer guide to protecting one's smart device. The recommendation includes suggestions to password restrict one's phone and install antitheft software.

After learning about the various requirements and steps to take, Dr. Palomino should have immediately set up his phone with password protection and then installed antitheft software. Contrary to its name, antitheft software does not prevent the actual theft of the device, but most versions allow the individual to locate the device from another web-based device and lock the phone so that even if the thief has the passcode, access to the information in it is not possible. Additionally, many of these software apps also allow the person to remotely remove, or "wipe," the device by deleting contacts, text, and e-mail messages; photos; and user accounts such as Twitter and Instagram. So Dr. Palomino should have taken two key first steps by making his cell phone password protected and installing antitheft software.

Communication encryption software is another type of software that Dr. Palomino should have considered, based on his use of e-mail and texting with his clients. Numerous software companies create applications that encrypt various types of communications (e.g., text, e-mails, phone calls) on cell phones and tablets. By using encryption software, Dr. Palomino could assure his clients that he was taking the appropriate steps to maintain the security and confidentiality of their sensitive and private information.

Finally, Dr. Palomino should have maintained a separate file at home or in the office with the key cell phone identification data that were necessary not only to make the police report but also for his cell phone carrier to be able to ensure his service was terminated and, if possible, remotely wipe the data from his phone. Specifically, Dr. Palomino should have stored the phone's make, model, and serial number. Cell phones will have either an International Mobile Station Equipment Identity (IMEI) or the Mobile Equipment Identifier (MEID). These are unique identifiers for each cell phone and are used by the carriers to determine whether the phone is valid or has been reported stolen. A simple search on the Internet will take one through the process to retrieve these numbers, or if the individual has the original box the phone came in, there is often a panel printed on it with the various numbers and key pieces of information that are used to identify the unique phone. (If the original box is available and it contains the information, one recommendation is to take a picture of the panel with the descriptive information and serial number, print it out, and then store it somewhere secure.)

THE BEST DECISION POSSIBLE

Given the factors in this case, the best decision is to do the following:

- Understand that telepsychology services are broadly defined. There is information and guidance on how to best safeguard, protect, and engage in telepsychology services. Be sure to determine whether you are practicing telepsychology with any of your devices.
- Always have the phone password protected.
- When using a phone to store or access client information, install an antitheft software application to be able to remove the data and lock the device if it is stolen or lost.
- If you use your phone to conduct therapeutic services, including e-mails and text messaging, as well as direct phone calls with the clients, then consider adding a software application that encrypts those communication venues.
- In a safe place, maintain the critical information necessary for identifying your cell phone so you can share that information with the police and your cell phone service carrier in the event that it is ever lost or stolen.

Key Points From the Chapter to Remember

- Perform a risk analysis of your system and method of telepractice at the outset.
- Seek consultation and training to ensure you understand proper security and transmission of data.
- If a breach is suspected or known, be prepared to notify all affected parties and to do all that is possible to control or correct the breach.
- Only use technological services that are HIPAA compliant to ensure protection of your clients' health care data.

- Consult with your insurance provider and with an attorney to ensure that newly developed policies and services are compliant with local, state, and federal laws.
- The evaluation of the use of telepsychology services should include the various technologies being used, both software and hardware, to update them as necessary.
- Routinely back up information onto separate secure memory storage, especially from a laptop that is transported from location to location.
- Research and select a software program that fits your needs best in being able to lock down and/or remotely wipe the memory of the computer in case it is stolen.

References

American Psychological Association. (2007). Record keeping guidelines. *American Psychologist, 62,* 9, 993–1004. http://dx.doi.org/10.1037/0003-066X.62.9.993

American Telemedicine Association. (2014). *Core operational guidelines for telehealth services involving provider–patient interactions.* Washington, DC: Author.

Centers for Medicare and Medicaid Services. (n.d.). *Telemedicine.* Retrieved from https://www.medicaid.gov/medicaid/benefits/telemed/index.html

Federal Communications Commission. (2015). *Protecting your mobile device.* Retrieved from https://www.fcc.gov/consumers/guides/protect-your-mobile-device

Health Insurance Portability and Accountability Act, Pub. L. No. 104-191, 110 Stat. 1936 (1996).

Joint Task Force for the Development of Telepsychology Guidelines for Psychologists. (2013). Guidelines for the practice of telepsychology. *American Psychologist, 68,* 791–800. Retrieved from https://www.apa.org/pubs/journals/features/amp-a0035001.pdf

West Virginia Office of Technology. (n.d.). *Password criteria.* Retrieved from http://www.technology.wv.gov/SiteCollectionDocuments/Security%20Monthly%20Newsletter/2012/Aprilb%202012%20-%20Passwords.pdf

Sara Smucker Barnwell and Margo Adams Larsen

Disposal of Data, Information, and Technologies

6

Psychologists who provide telepsychology services make reasonable efforts to dispose of data and information and the technologies used in a manner that facilitates protection from unauthorized access and accounts for safe and appropriate disposal.

—Guideline 6, *Guidelines for the Practice of Telepsychology*

Rationale

Consistent with [American Psychological Association] APA Record Keeping Guidelines (2007), psychologists are encouraged to create policies and procedures for the secure destruction of data and information and the technologies used to create, store and transmit the data and information. The use of telecommunication technologies in the provision of psychological services poses new challenges for psychologists when they consider the disposal methods to utilize in order to maximally preserve client confidentiality and privacy. Psychologists are therefore urged to consider conducting an analysis of the risks to the information systems within their practices in an effort to ensure full and complete disposal of electronic data and information, plus the technologies that created, stored, and transmitted the data and information. (Joint Task Force for the Development of Telepsychology Guidelines for Psychologists, 2013, p. 798)

http://dx.doi.org/10.1037/0000046-007
A Telepsychology Casebook: Using Technology Ethically and Effectively in Your Professional Practice, L. F. Campbell, F. Millán, and J. N. Martin (Editors)

Psychologists are very familiar with their ethical responsibility to maintain client confidentiality in the creation, access, transfer, storage, and disposal of traditional records and to ensure they are knowledgeable of state and institutional regulations that direct these responsibilities (APA, 2017). Although the APA *Ethical Principles of Psychologists and Code of Conduct* addresses electronic transmission, storage, and disposal "in any medium," they are more general than specific regarding telepsychology, primarily because technology has advanced and provides more opportunities for psychologists and their clients to communicate and work together than were available in 2010.

In their development of Guideline 6 (Disposal of Data and Information and Technologies) of the *Guidelines for the Practice of Telepsychology*, the Joint Task Force (2013), recognizing the differences psychologists face regarding proper disposal of data transmitted and stored in various telecommunication systems versus nonelectronic systems, described how psychologists might apply the guideline in their practices:

> Psychologists strive to securely dispose of software and hardware used in the provision of telepsychology services in a manner that insures that the confidentiality and security of any patient/client information is not compromised. When doing so, psychologists carefully clean all the data and images in the storage media before re-use or disposal consistent with federal, state, provincial, territorial, and other organizational regulations and guidelines. (p. 798)

This chapter provides a more in-depth examination of how psychologists can appropriately apply this guideline in an independent practice setting, a Veterans Affairs hospital setting, a university, and an industrial or organizational setting. The reader is encouraged to note compliance with other telepsychology guidelines throughout the scenario, including knowledge of guidelines and ethical standards, informed consent, confidentiality of data and information, and security and transmission of data and information.

Case Study 1: Cleaning and Disposing of Hardware and Software

SETTING: INDEPENDENT PRACTICE

Dr. Jason Carter was a psychologist in independent practice. He offered assessment and therapy services to adult clients with a diversity of clinical concerns. Dr. Carter's clientele was a relatively mobile population. He served many business executives who traveled frequently for work and college students from a large local university who often returned to their home towns during summers. In addition, Dr. Carter, who spoke several languages, worked with an outreach group that delivered behavioral health services to rural agricultural workers who traveled to the area for seasonal employment.

SCENARIO

An early adopter of telepsychology, Dr. Carter offered videoconferencing and telephone sessions to existing clients who traveled within his licensure jurisdiction. He was knowledgeable regarding regulatory considerations specific to telepsychology, as well as other sources of policy and practical guidance. He resided in a state where the psychology board had adopted guidelines for telepsychology and that required insurance companies to reimburse for telehealth services. Dr. Carter was familiar with state and jurisdictional regulation regarding telepsychology. He was familiar with the *Guidelines for the Practice of Telepsychology* (Joint Task Force, 2013), developed by the American Psychological Association, the Association of State and Provincial Psychology Boards (ASPPB), and The American Insurance Trust (The Trust). He attended several workshops related to telepsychology online and through his state psychological association. He belonged to several online telehealth consultation groups from various professional organizations, from which he could access relevant information.

Dr. Carter was thoughtful in his selection and application of technology products to manage his clinical work. He encrypted his laptop computer's drive in accordance with the recommendations provided by his malpractice carrier (The Trust, 2014) and used only encrypted USB drives to transfer client/patient information. He additionally encrypted and password protected any file with patient information stored on his computer. His electronic medical record provider was a well-established company that offered appointment reminders through secure text, secure e-mail, or interactive voice response technology.

Dr. Carter was diligent in selecting technology products through which he interacted with clients directly. After examining several videoconferencing products, he subscribed to one designed for health care. He conducted telephone sessions from the landline telephone in his office. Dr. Carter used a tablet device with videoconferencing software to conduct sessions with clients and colleagues. Although his videoconferencing program offered a mobile application, he elected not to conduct videoconferencing on his smartphone because he felt that the screen size was too small and he would lose valuable visual data. He did not routinely text with clients, but would occasionally respond to a client's text regarding administrative information using an encrypted text program designed for health care. He communicated only administrative information (e.g., appointment times) with his clients over an encrypted e-mail program designed for health care. He obtained a business associate agreement (as required by the Health Insurance Portability and Accountability Act [HIPAA], 1996) with all technology vendors who could have access to patient information. Overall, Dr. Carter demonstrated an awareness of and compliance with telepsychology guidelines and ethical standards, as well as state and federal regulations. He identified a videoconferencing product that featured encryption and was compliant with HIPAA.

The demand for telepsychology services in Dr. Carter's practice grew. Word of mouth in the local professional community yielded many referrals. Dr. Carter worked closely with the local organization in conjunction with volunteer clinics in rural communities to deliver telepsychology services to clients who engaged in seasonal agricultural work.

In light of the growth in his practice and the demands for telepsychology services, Dr. Carter decided to upgrade and expand several important tools in his practice. He hoped to purchase a new computer and mobile device. He also debated whether to update the e-mail program he accessed through the Internet (e.g., web-based e-mail) and the software he used to conduct videoconferencing. Dr. Carter, who had consistently been a thoughtful telepsychology practitioner, realized that he knew little about best practices related to making these changes.

Dr. Carter was familiar with the APA's (2007) *Record Keeping Guidelines*, including the recommendation that all records, including electronic records, be maintained and disposed of in accordance with HIPAA's Security Rule and other jurisdictional guidelines. In the past, he had destroyed paper records after the amount of time required to maintain them in his jurisdiction. However, he had never before replaced the computer on which he stored client files. Additionally, Dr. Carter had read the *Guidelines for the Practice of Telepsychology* (Joint Task Force, 2013) and understood that he was ethically required to consider client/patient data on the other hardware and software he used to deliver services, including his tablet device, mobile device, and web-based e-mail program and videoconferencing software. He wondered also whether there were other facets of his practice that he would need to address that were as of yet unknown to him. Stated simply, he did know what he did not know.

Could he simply delete his encrypted computer files and dispose of his computer? Dr. Carter's mobile carrier offered discounts to anyone who surrendered their old mobile device. Could he simply surrender his old phone? What were his responsibilities regarding patient information on his mobile device? Could he simply close his encrypted e-mail account or end his contract with his videoconferencing vendor? Dr. Carter realized that this exciting period of growth introduced new challenges. Perhaps more important, he was uncertain where best to pursue the information he needed. Who was best suited to answer his questions?

KEY ELEMENTS, CHALLENGES, AND DECISION FACTORS

Dr. Carter first focused on which facets of his practice would be affected by these changes. He recalled a telepsychology workshop he attended in which the speakers highlighted the value of conducting a self-study that addressed multiple facets of technology use, including the disposal of data. The speakers provided a document for self-guided assessment (see Exhibit 6.1). After reviewing the self-study, Dr. Carter realized that several important aspects of his practice would need to be addressed before updating his office equipment, including

- files with client information stored on his personal computer;
- client contact information stored on his mobile device;
- client information stored in the videoconferencing software on his wireless, mobile computing device that was touchscreen enabled (e.g., tablet);
- the secure text application on his tablet device and smartphone (e.g., Internet-enabled mobile telephone device); and
- his web-based e-mail service.

EXHIBIT 6.1

Components of Self-Study

- Do I store patient information on my personal computer, tablet, or mobile device?
- Do I store patient information on a shared computer, tablet, or mobile device?
- Do I transfer patient information using an external data storage device (e.g., USB drive)?
- Do I store patient information on a cloud-based service?
- Do I maintain client contact information on my mobile device?
- Do I use a software program on my computer (e.g., videoconferencing, e-mail, contact manager) that retains client information (e.g., telephone number, e-mail address, IP address)?
- Do I use a cloud-based service that stores patient information?
- Do I have a business associate agreement with technology product vendors who could access patient information?

Using the criteria in Exhibit 6.1, collegial recommendations, and published standards available through the National Institute of Standards and Technology (NIST), Dr. Carter engaged his self-study.

OPTIONS AVAILABLE TO THE PSYCHOLOGIST

Dr. Carter also sought individualized consultation, reaching out to his online consultation communities. He sent an e-mail detailing his needs to several electronic mailing lists. Community list members offered some guidance and largely encouraged him to pursue more technically sophisticated guidance through the NIST and, perhaps, even an information technology (IT) consultant specializing in health care.

After conducting his self-study and consulting with colleagues, Dr. Carter felt that he needed additional technical guidance to help him address his data disposal needs. He identified the following resources, the first three of which were recommended to him through his online telehealth consultation communities:

- *Guidelines for Media Sanitization* (Kissel, Regenscheid, Scholl, & Stine 2014) and other NIST publications,
- malpractice carrier,
- health care attorney or health care IT consultant, and
- colleague or consultation group.

First, Dr. Carter visited the NIST website to seek specific technical guidance. NIST offered *Guidelines for Media Sanitization* (Kissel et al., 2014), a publication that operationalized some basic terms and approaches related to disposing of data. The guidelines offered Dr. Carter insight into how he might approach data disposal. Dr. Carter was a technologically savvy individual, but he found aspects of the NIST information dense and challenging to operationalize. He reasoned that he would prefer some guidance from someone with experience in the application of NIST principles to health care to ensure that he understood how best to proceed.

Next, Dr. Carter contacted his malpractice carrier to consult with risk management consultants regarding best practices in data disposal. The attorneys provided specific guidance regarding how best to approach deleting client information from his computer (e.g., both deleting files and reformatting his hard drive), his mobile device and tablet (e.g., deleting contacts, removing mobile applications, deleting the call history and/or applying the device's factory reset after he had removed all contacts that he wished to retain), and videoconferencing software (e.g., ensuring that all patient contact information and call history had been deleted from his account, contacting the vendor to further pursue this change). The risk management consultants also referenced NIST standards and helped Dr. Carter conceptualize what information must be addressed before he could dispose of the software and hardware in his office.

Now Dr. Carter possessed an understanding of what information ought to be addressed and how it ought to be addressed. The question that remained was who would be best to perform the tasks. Dr. Carter was somewhat uncomfortable executing the plan. He had never reformatted a computer hard drive or reset a mobile device previously. Online searches yielded videos that could guide Dr. Carter through these steps. Again, he wondered if he could benefit from the guidance of an IT expert with experience in health care. His online consultation community had provided several recommendations, but Dr. Carter worried about the cost this would impose. Still, his time was limited because of his growing practice. Although he hoped to gain instruction to increase his competencies in this aspect of practice, he did not have the time to pursue the information alone. Ultimately, Dr. Carter elected to hire an established information technology consultant who was aware of HIPAA requirements to assist him in the necessary steps of deleting computer files, deleting his computer hard drive, resetting his mobile device, deleting all contacts from his e-mail and videoconferencing programs, and selecting products for his next steps in practice.

Dr. Carter decided that the benefits of an IT consultant outweighed the costs. He contacted the referrals provided to him. The consultant noted that Dr. Carter's considerable work before reaching out would allow them to work efficiently and reduce costs. Although the consultant offered clients a business associate agreement, she noted that she hoped she would have no opportunity to interact with Dr. Carter's client data. Instead, the consultant hoped to provide Dr. Carter with hands-on instruction that would teach Dr. Carter to dispose of client information himself. They met one time for several hours. The consultant visited Dr. Carter at his office. They discussed his needs (e.g., to replace hardware and software) and his desire to learn strategies to manage similar needs in the future. The consultant referenced the APA (2007) *Record Keeping Guidelines* and NIST's (Kissel et al., 2014) *Guidelines for Media Sanitization.* Together they removed all client/patient information from the hardware and software that Dr. Carter used in his practice. The IT consultant noted that the approach she recommended represented an abundance of caution. However, Dr. Carter was pleased to have a straightforward path to managing the disposal of client/patient information moving forward and preferred to adopt a conservative approach.

THE BEST DECISION POSSIBLE

Exhibit 6.2 summarizes Dr. Carter's data removal plan. After disposing of the data together, Dr. Carter and the IT consultant discussed next steps for his practice. The IT consultant reinforced Dr. Carter's responsible practices of selecting telecommunications products for his practice (e.g., new videoconferencing software, e-mail, text programs) that were designed specifically for health care and that offered a business associate agreement. The consultant encouraged Dr. Carter to consider a more streamlined approach (e.g., a single vendor that offered several of these products) to simplify future data disposal efforts. Dr. Carter ultimately elected to use encrypted e-mail and text programs integrated into his electronic medical record. After reviewing the pros and cons of other products, he selected a videoconferencing program with expanded functionality (e.g., superior privacy protections) and a reduced cost.

Documenting the changes in his hardware and software, Dr. Carter noted the steps that he took to arrive at his approach to data disposal. He recorded relevant information on the methods and procedures he used to dispose of the sensitive information. He recorded information on all of the hardware that he recycled or replaced (e.g., model, serial number, where he originally purchased the equipment). He authored a brief policy regarding how he would take steps to dispose of sensitive information in the future. He provided brief information to new clients and posted a copy of the

EXHIBIT 6.2

Dr. Carter's Data Removal Plan

- Hardware:
  - Delete all files from laptop computer.
  - Reformat computer hard drive and USB drives.
  - Complete "factory reset" or "hard reset" for mobile device and tablet.
  - Ensure that no patient information remains on encrypted external storage devices (e.g., USB flash drives) by deleting files and reformatting the drive.
  - Recycle hardware with local technology recycling company or with vendor offering rebate.
- Software:
  - Delete all contacts and call history from text, e-mail, and videoconferencing programs.
  - Uninstall software and mobile applications from all hardware.
  - Log in to any web-based interfaces (e.g., e-mail program, web management for secure text account) to delete any stored information (e.g., stored patient information, call logs of prior clinical contacts).
  - Contact the vendors for web-based services to inquire how to ensure that all deleted information was permanently deleted from any future access.
- Future Steps:
  - Select software and mobile applications designed for health care.
  - Obtain a business associate agreement from all vendors.
  - Consider authoring a policy regarding data disposal to be shared with clients during informed consent.
  - Ensure that informed consent document includes a review of risks and benefits regarding technology use, as well as some basic information regarding record maintenance and disposal.

policy on his website. He stored the detailed information in his own records, alongside other documents such as informed consent procedures, releases of information procedures, and other documents in his practice. He updated his own documentation (e.g., HIPAA privacy policy) with information regarding his new procedures.

Although Dr. Carter was an exceptionally knowledgeable telepsychology practitioner, his struggle to conceptualize data disposal offers insight into a fundamental challenge of technology use in health care. Psychologists possess extensive training in the science, practice, and ethics of psychology, but little experience in IT. Despite this, technology's increasingly prominent role in psychology requires psychologists to stretch beyond their training and expand their competencies. Dr. Carter's decision to seek guidance from an IT expert while bolstering his own competencies represents an ethical practice that is fundamental to psychology: seeking consultation in an emerging area of practice. By acknowledging the limitations of his knowledge base and recognizing an opportunity for growth, Dr. Carter advanced his telepsychology practice, offered improved access to care, and rendered himself better able to manage his practice and consult with his colleagues facing similar challenges.

Case Study 2: Disposal of Cookies and Malware

RELEVANT EXCERPT FROM THE GUIDELINE APPLICATION

> Psychologists also strive to be aware of malware, cookies, etc., and dispose routinely of them on an ongoing basis when telecommunication technologies are used. (Joint Task Force, 2013, p. 798)

SETTING: INDUSTRIAL AND ORGANIZATIONAL

Dr. Jack Murphy was a fairly recent graduate of an industrial and organizational (I/O) psychology program, with several major conglomerate companies for clients since he had apprenticed with a well-established consulting psychologist for supervised practical training before obtaining licensure as a psychologist. Dr. Murphy was eager to get his career underway and recognized the value in spending money to make money. He had invested in excellent and coordinated gear for his office and ensured via an expert IT consultation that he was aware of, developed policies for, and implemented the most ethical and technologically savvy I/O practice within a several-state area.

SCENARIO

As a consulting I/O psychologist, Dr. Murphy was interested in applying innovative technology to enhance his busy practice. His training model had involved telecommunications for both scheduling and interviewing many client contacts but he was now interested in hosting web-based consultation forums, trainings (both interactive live and store and forward formats), and even conducting contact interviews and assessments via a web portal and online assessment services. He was often hired by international companies to assess productivity and personnel efficiencies throughout the company that could span several thousand individuals in various divisions around the country (and sometimes the globe). Data collection costs could be reduced greatly by using online strategies that could clump data sets and minimize personal contact with the individuals being assessed. This would also decrease his travel and consulting expenses, making services more streamlined and fiscally efficient for his clients. The challenges that Dr. Murphy faced in considering these potential services were significant, however. Dr. Murphy wondered what would happen if a virus got into the e-mail system he used to send out invites to the surveys? How could he ensure that cookies were not left on the evaluation devices that employees would be using, and what types of systems and methods would be the most secure for protecting against hacking or infiltration by external parties? Developing methods for technology-based evaluation and assessment that meet the needs of the client along with the *Guidelines for the Practice of Telepsychology* (Joint Task Force, 2013), particularly related to malware, cookies, and unfortunate instantaneous technology events, was critical for Dr. Murphy's practice. He knew all too well the woes of another telepsychologist whose e-mail had been hacked by a virus and sent some untoward solicitations to both colleagues and clients and another whose technologically sophisticated borderline patient hacked into his electronic records system and set malware in place to permanently delete the server.

OPTIONS AVAILABLE TO THE PSYCHOLOGIST

Dr. Murphy decided to seek consultation from an IT expert and search for innovative products that might meet his needs. He generated the following list of discussion items to address with his consultant:

- How could firewalls protect his server from hackers and/or decrease the functionality of his interactive consulting software?
- Could online portals for data collection and retention systems solve his storage needs?
- Would passwords be enough to protect his system and consulting clients' needs?
- How could he ensure he was not leaving cookies on his devices, and, furthermore, how could he assist his many survey respondents to do the same?
- Was there a mechanism to erase and remove e-mails once they were viewed?
- Were there efficient e-mail methods that could maintain confidentiality and guard against security risks?
- Was there a method that he could use that would ensure the technology both he and his clients (and thousands of survey respondents) could use such as single-use technologies (i.e., providing tablets for the sole purpose of data collection)?
- Were there legal aspects that he needed to consider? Dr. Murphy was concerned that he may be engaging in interjurisdictional practice because his clients were worldwide. Were there special federal guidelines or requirements for data transmittal?

- What would be the licensure implications for obtaining information from employees in other countries or states? Had he considered the types of services that might be allowed without licensure from the location where the services were provided?
- How would all of these security measures be best addressed in the informed consent process? Was this even necessary, and what level of detail was acceptable?

THE BEST DECISION POSSIBLE

Dr. Murphy managed to complete several of his important to-do items to further the development of his office. He recognized that he would not require much overhead in office space, which could be set aside for computer and server IT consultation. He also realized that not all jurisdictions license the practice of I/O work: All jurisdictions license clinical, counseling, and school specialties in the practice of psychology, but less than half license I/O and consulting psychologists. Dr. Murphy recognized that awareness and compliance with the regulatory rules regarding licensure would be important both for the jurisdiction from which he would be consulting and the jurisdiction of the organizational client. Dr. Murphy sought legal consultation to establish best practices related to his understanding of and comfort with the distinct, respective regulatory definitions of title and scope of practice that might conflict with the proposed work. He also confirmed with his malpractice carrier that he indeed had purchased the most robust policy for his unique practice setting.

Case Study 3: Developing Data Disposal Policies

RELEVANT EXCERPT FROM THE GUIDELINE APPLICATION

> Psychologists are encouraged to develop policies and procedures for the destruction of data and information related to clients/patients. . . . Psychologists are encouraged to document the methods and procedures used when disposing of the data and information and the technologies used to create, store, or transmit the data and information, as well as any other technology utilized in the disposal of data and hardware. (Joint Task Force, 2013, p. 798)

SETTING: VETERANS AFFAIRS HOSPITAL

The U.S. Department of Veterans Affairs (VA) supports the use of telepsychology through policy creation, postdoctoral training programs in telepsychology, and the implementation of telemental health services throughout the nation's largest health care system. A typical VA telemental health program connects mental health clinicians (psychologists, psychiatrists, social workers, among others) to veterans in VA medical centers, community-based outpatient clinics, and veteran residences via live videoconferencing.

Historically, VA telepsychology clinicians used large, costly (e.g., \$3,000–\$10,000) desktop videoconferencing units to deliver videoconferencing care to clients. However, in recent years, clinicians increasingly used a simpler solution that consisted of an inexpensive (e.g., \$50–\$100) web camera with integrated microphone attached to an Internet-enabled computer (Smucker Barnwell, Juretic, Hoerster, Felker, & Van de Plasch, 2012). Software applications (e.g., Cisco Jabber, FaceTime, Vidyo) that were "patched and operated in accordance with Federal and Department security policies and guidelines in order to mitigate known and future security vulnerabilities" (U.S. Department of Veterans Affairs, 2014) provided the necessary security and connection for videoconferencing and were relatively inexpensive.

SCENARIO

The transition from larger, costly desktop videoconferencing units to inexpensive software-based solutions for clinicians was an important step in the dissemination of telepsychology services throughout the VA. Less costly equipment made telepsychology a more viable option for VA medical centers with smaller equipment budgets and fewer IT staff resources to maintain the complex hardware. With many VA systems receiving recommendations from leadership to expand telemental health programming, a simpler technical solution for the clinician was welcome. Some VA facilities were required to train most mental health staff in the provision of telemental health services over a several-month period. Without the ability to transition to smaller, less costly technology options, rapid, large-scale expansion of services would have been delayed significantly.

The transition away from the larger desktop videoconferencing units also introduced a new concern for many telemental health programs: what to do with the old hardware. In most instances, the hardware would be placed in a VA community-based outpatient clinic, where it would provide telepsychology clinical care for clients who are seen there. Those pieces of hardware that were outdated would be decommissioned and recycled.

Dr. Ellen Blanche was a psychologist who was navigating this process in her local VA. As team leader for her VA telemental heath program, she developed policies for her team in conjunction with her VA's facility leadership, the Office of Telehealth Services, and her regional Veterans Integrated Service Network (VISN) telehealth leadership. As a psychologist, Dr. Blanche's application of telepsychology was guided by the *Guidelines for the Practice of Telepsychology* (Joint Task Force, 2013), best practice publications from the American Telemedicine Association (ATA), and consultation from the robust telemental health consultation community in the VA nationwide. Dr. Blanche worked with her VA's local leadership to author policies for her staff related to information security, privacy, and confidentiality when using technology. She advocated for integrated information regarding technology use into facility informed consent documentation. She ensured that all staff verbally apprised clients of the risks and benefits of the technology products that they used. She also encouraged clinicians to apprise clients of their own roles in securing their protected health information (e.g., password protecting electronic devices they used to communicate with her, ensuring privacy in a room where they had a videoconferencing or telephone session, others). Dr. Blanche and her team of psychologists were thoughtful and thorough regarding the creation of telehealth policies.

Dr. Blanche was pleased when she learned that her team would be transitioning from the traditional desktop videoconferencing hardware to software programs. She understood that this would mean a lower operating budget for the program, the opportunity to recruit more psychologists to deliver telehealth care to veterans, and an overall simpler technology infrastructure. She also realized that, despite her thorough approach to policy development, she was uncertain of what to do, if anything, with the old equipment.

OPTIONS AVAILABLE TO THE PSYCHOLOGIST

Dr. Blanche understood from reading the APA *Guidelines for the Practice of Telepsychology* (Joint Task Force, 2013) that the old hardware could have protected health information on it. She felt ethically compelled to ensure the proper disposal of this information. However, she knew little regarding the maintenance of this equipment. Like many large-scale hospital systems, the VA possesses competent, thorough IT staff. As the team leader for her VA's telemental health program, Dr. Blanche was well acquainted with her IT staff at the VA. Her IT department worked closely with the national Office of Telehealth Services and was familiar with the demands of HIPAA (1996), the Health Information Technology for Economic and Clinical Health Act (HITECH; 2009), and other regulations governing protected health information. Was it appropriate for her to convey her concerns regarding the patient data potentially stored on her equipment to the IT staff? As a competent telepsychologist, Dr. Blanche was still not a technologist and did not possess the training to digest and critique IT policies per se. Although she recognized that she needed a positive working relationship with her IT department and did not wish to be perceived as distrusting IT staff, she was uncomfortable *not* asking any questions. Was there a role for the mental health professionals in disposing of the data? What should be her team's policy regarding this important matter? Dr. Blanche felt clear that she was required to advocate for ethical data disposal, but she wished to manage the issue diplomatically.

The IT department at Dr. Blanche's VA was collaborative, competent, and well-versed in the needs of telehealth. However, Dr. Blanche recalled the guidance that

> psychologists are encouraged to develop policies and procedures for the destruction of data and information related to clients/patients. . . . Psychologists are encouraged to document the methods and procedures used when disposing of the data and information and the technologies used to create, store, or transmit the data and information, as well as any other technology utilized in the disposal of data and hardware. (Joint Task Force, 2013, p. 798)

EXHIBIT 6.3

National Institute of Standards and Technology Recommendations for Media Sanitization

- After sanitization, a paper or electronic certificate of media disposition should be completed for each piece of electronic media that has been sanitized.
- For a large number of devices with data of very low confidentiality, an organization may choose not to complete the certificate.
- The certificate should record at least the following details: product manufacturer, model and serial number; organizational identifier (if applicable); media type (i.e., what is it) and source (i.e., user or computer the media came from); sanitization description; method used to remove data (i.e., overwrite, cryptographic erase, etc.); sanitization tool used; verification method (i.e., full, quick sampling, etc.); postsanitization destination (if known); and data backup (if applicable).

Note. Adapted from "Guidelines for Media Sanitization, NIST Special Publication 800-88, Revision 1," by R. Kissel, A. Regenscheid, M. Scholl, and K. Stine, 2014 (http://nvlpubs.nist.gov/nistpubs/SpecialPublications/NIST.SP.800-88r1.pdf). In the public domain.

She realized that her efforts to generate policies for other aspects of telepsychology practice for her team had neglected the issue of data disposal.

Dr. Blanche decided that whatever the role of her clinicians, even if it was one of noninvolvement, her team ought to have a clearer understanding of IT data disposal practices and a policy for their own data disposal efforts. To pursue the information necessary to generate this policy, Dr. Blanche set a meeting with the head of her facility's IT department. To further educate herself on the technical requirements for data disposal, Dr. Blanche spoke with her IT staff contact, who suggested that she familiarize herself with the NIST (Kissel et al., 2014) *Guidelines for Media Sanitization*. She reviewed some of the basics of NIST media sanitization (see Exhibit 6.3) with her team.

Dr. Blanche met with her IT department lead. She was not surprised to learn that the IT department had already developed a detailed data disposal plan that complied with NIST standards. As a psychologist, however, Dr. Blanche sought to determine how she could develop a data disposal policy and documentation process appropriate for her team as well as the expanding number of telepsychologists in the larger hospital system. This meeting was critical in providing the information necessary to inform policy creation. She expressed her concerns, and listened. Following is an excerpt from the meeting:

Dr. Blanche: Thank you so much for meeting with me. My team and I are delighted to be receiving new equipment. As you know, I am hoping to discuss how the information stored in the old equipment will be managed. I know that our IT department has policies that manage the disposal of protected health information. The upgrade in equipment and scheduled removal of the old videoconferencing units really highlighted for me that I do not understand these policies well. So please, bear with me as I try to understand how my team can be good partners in the established data disposal process and follow our professional guidelines regarding good practice.

IT: Thanks, Dr. Blanche, for calling this meeting. It's a great opportunity for us to teach the staff we support regarding their equipment and how best to maintain it. We will be moving the old videoconferencing hardware to new locations within the health care system. Our practices require us to perform a reset of the videoconferencing units, clearing all information and restoring it to the state in which it existed when we first installed it. Sensitive information can be stored in several places on your videoconferencing units. Perhaps the most obvious is the Contacts list and the call history. Our policies prohibit clinicians from storing any patient information in the Contacts portion of the hardware, and we recommend that clinicians intermittently purge call logs. And we double-check.

Dr. Blanche: That's a great point. I know that my team knows never to store information in the Contacts section, but I wonder if we are purging call logs.

IT: The videoconferencing unit call logs display the patient's videoconferencing account "address," which typically includes a portion of the patient's name. This is why we recommend that clinicians clear the call logs to ensure no one could tell when and to whom calls were placed. Again, we will reset the entire device when we dispose of data using a special program that erases it. A good analogy would be mobile devices: The mobile phones and tablets that telemental health clinicians use to call patients and, sometimes, deliver care in remote locations. We intermittently update these devices for those staff approved to have them. When we collect the old device from clinicians, we purge all contacts and call log information.

Dr. Blanche: I didn't even think about the mobile devices!

IT: If you are developing a policy to help your staff think through data disposal, I would recommend that you include all hardware that is used to communicate with patients—videoconferencing units, mobile phones, and tablets.

Dr. Blanche: That's great input. So once you take these devices away, how do you keep track of what happens to them? How do you make sure the data are destroyed?

IT: Each of your devices possesses a bar code. That bar code is scanned whenever it is "checked out" or "checked in" by a clinician. Important steps of our protocols ensure that the IT staff member who checks it in clears all the information possessed on that device. We use a special program to delete data and reformat the device to its factory settings. Then we plug the device in and manually check to make sure that nothing remains. Our practices conform to NIST media sanitization guidelines, and we maintain a digital certification of the reformatting.

Dr. Blanche: That is very helpful. How can my clinicians help?

IT: They can be diligent not to store inappropriate information, such as patient names or patient IP addresses, on the device, and to purge the call logs regularly. And of course, they can always follow basic security protocols to ensure that sensitive patient data are never placed at unnecessary risk: password protect the device, secure the devices when not in use, and limit use of the devices to professional activities.

KEY ELEMENTS, CHALLENGES, AND DECISION FACTORS

Following the meeting with facility telehealth stakeholders, Dr. Blanche felt reassured that the data were being disposed of properly. She also felt empowered to create a policy that addressed ethical demands and documentation needs. Together with her IT department and facility telehealth coordinator, Dr. Blanche drafted a policy that reminded psychologists never to store patient information on their devices used to deliver clinical care (e.g., videoconferencing hardware, tablets, mobile devices) and to purge call logs at the end of each use. She reminded psychologists to secure hardware when not in use and to limit use to professional activities. She also developed a documentation checklist that psychologists could use for their own record keeping when devices were replaced. Exhibit 6.4 shows an example of the completed documentation.

EXHIBIT 6.4

Example of Documentation

Clinician Name: Dr. Ellen Blanche

Date equipment installed: 10/12/2009 **Date removed:** 5/11/2013

Equipment Type, Brand, and Model: Desktop videoconferencing. Tandberg, MXP 1700

Serial Number Provided through VA IT: 1200MQ2

Name of VA IT Staff Member Who Removed Equipment: Adam Smith

Reason for Equipment Removal: Upgrade to Cisco Jabber software

All Contact Information Deleted: 5/10/11 **All Call Logs Deleted:** 5/10/11

Method Used: Call logs and contact information deleted manually. VA IT will reset device in accordance with Office of Telehealth Services and will document this deletion in accordance with National Institute of Standards and Technology Guidelines.

It is notable that this documentation was not technically detailed. Instead, it reflected an accountability and thoughtfulness regarding the disposal of equipment that was consistent with the *Guidelines for the Practice of Telepsychology* (Joint Task Force, 2013). This documentation was not standardized through the VA, and it acted in addition to the IT sound practices. Still, this effort ensured that Dr. Blanche, a psychologist, strived to attain a high ethical standard of accountability for information disposal and required psychologists on her staff to do the same. Dr. Blanche's efforts also helped to provide leadership to the growing numbers of mental health professionals who would be using videoconferencing at her hospital for the first time.

THE BEST DECISION POSSIBLE

Dr. Blanche's story parallels the experience of many psychologists in large health care systems as well as independent practice. Many psychologists may elect or even be required to have technological aspects of their practice managed by technology experts (e.g., IT departments, technology companies, consultants for independent practitioners). This allocation of responsibility represents an advantageous division of labor among specialists, but it does not relieve the psychologist of her duty to understand the technology that she uses and how it affects her patients/clients. Dr. Blanche negotiated the demands of maintaining a positive working relationship with her technologist colleagues while simultaneously ensuring that her workplace's policies promoted ethical data disposal. In the end, she authored a policy that was simple, straightforward, and complementary to the practices of the technologists with whom she worked. In this way, Dr. Blanche and her team meaningfully participated in competent data disposal and provided additional ethical accountability to a small process in a large system.

Case Study 4: Storage Technologies

RELEVANT EXCERPT FROM THE GUIDELINE APPLICATION

> Psychologists are aware of and understand the unique storage implications related to telecommunications technologies inherent in available systems. (Joint Task Force, 2013, p. 798)

SETTING: UNIVERSITY COUNSELING CLINIC

Dr. Saritha Rata is the director of the university counseling clinic (UCC) that has recently embarked on a partnership with rural nurse practitioners to provide telepsychology services to remote areas within the state. Doctoral-level counseling psychology students, supervised by Dr. Rata, provide services at the UCC. Dr. Rata has been licensed as a psychologist in the state of the university for 12 years. The remote communities of disparate needs include First Nations populations, oil workers, and children. At times, graduate psychology students provide services in the rural communities in person and receive telesupervision from a licensed psychologist via HIPAA-compliant state-based care network videoconferencing. At other times, graduate psychology students provide telepsychology services from within the university clinic setting to patients located in remote communities (e.g., outpatient physical medicine office or a school counselor's office via HIPAA-compliant state-based care network videoconferencing). This is a unique and mutually beneficial opportunity for patients in underserved areas with high needs, community clinicians, and students. The community mental health perspective that provides a foundation for the student's clinical learning serves them well as they rotate through this practicum position.

Before establishing the telepractice service model, Dr. Rata and the licensed psychologist supervisors prepared ahead by consulting with colleagues in established telepractice training centers to obtain guidance regarding appropriate student training curriculums for this medium of care. The faculty supervisors decided that establishing a highly conservative model of informed consent and description of practices, as well as seeking their own supervision for telepractice services, would ultimately provide the best level of training and be consistent with best care practices. The faculty and students experimented with using the state-based videoconferencing before commencing with their patient-based services. Faculty members were aware that a certification in e-practice was anticipated for licensed providers in the future, and they structured their graduate curriculum to include the requirements to prepare students for the future practice standard.

A key component on which Dr. Rata focused was to carefully review all aspects of the jurisdictional legal requirements for telepractice (often found in the licensure board statutes or regulations), the described enforcement of these requirements (generally located in the licensure board rules), and any policy documents or white papers their jurisdictional board had established. Dr. Rata was surprised to find that within her jurisdiction, regulations for telepractice to patients outside the jurisdiction (more to follow in Guideline 8) were actually found within licensure statutes for professions and occupations. She determined, however, that to minimize complications, the clinic would only provide services within the jurisdiction in which the university was located and in which the supervisors were licensed. Further, Dr. Rata reviewed HIPAA (1996), the Children's Online Privacy Protection Act (1998), and HITECH (2009) regulations and spent time with the university legal counsel as well as her risk management legal consultant to ensure that the services planned were provided within these federal guidelines, as well as the Family Educational Rights and Privacy Act (1974), given the training setting and university-based clinic.

Dr. Rata was familiar with the *Guidelines for the Practice of Telepsychology* (Joint Task Force, 2013), jointly developed by APA, ASPPB, and The Trust. She was also an active member of the Association of Psychology Training Clinics and was a member of relevant professional organizations focusing on the use of telecommunications technology and psychology. She obtained specific content for discussion with her faculty colleagues, as well as posting on electronic mailing lists regarding collaboration and sharing of resources and lessons learned from other clinics and colleagues around the nation.

SCENARIO

In developing the UCC remote project, Dr. Rata had many questions about the technology used, electronic medical records, management of student records, university computing policies, Title IX sexual violence reporting requirements, whether business associate's agreements were required for the state network for telecare, and general practical considerations of how to manage note taking for distant patients, distant supervisees, word documentation and encryption, online word processing products available through the university, cloud storage on campus, student cloud storage, HIPAA offsite vendors versus university-approved vendors, as well as interjurisdictional issues in data storage. Beyond this, availability of records for patient access, providing reports to patients and security issues, what to do with recorded telepractice sessions (retention, storage, disposal), who has access to what and how, and the additional complicating layer of testing materials (i.e., copyright status) were all suggestions her training clinic colleagues indicated would be important for her to consider.

KEY ELEMENTS, CHALLENGES, AND DECISION FACTORS

There were several elements for Dr. Rata to consider with her colleagues. The first was the protection of the public to which the supervised students would be providing services. The patients would be referred by a nurse practitioner in their local area, and services would be available through this nurse practitioner's clinic setting. As such, there was potential for a secure receiving site of services, with immediate access to medical care or emergency services. The second element Dr. Rata contemplated was the experience and richness potential of the training opportunity that students could have through such a practicum setting. However, guidelines for the requirements of supervision within her jurisdiction as well as program accreditation requirements would need to be considered. If students were providing services in the remote area, although the nurse practitioner would be available for medical assistance, a licensed supervisor would need to be available to provide telesupervision if imminent concerns arose (or to view the session live). Finally, students would need to be provided a curriculum to support the nuances and challenges related to remote care within a rural setting. Fortunately, the program already had a community outreach curriculum in place. Beyond the jurisdictional, ethical, and legal considerations, Dr. Rata finally considered the demands that a telepractice clinic would place on her colleagues, such as increased on-site supervision and increased clinical caseloads with both students and faculty learning and requiring supervision or consultation. She ensured that before implementation, her colleagues were comfortable with the level of care and procedures for services that would be developed and that the acceptance of referrals began at a slow pace to ensure comfort with the process and the developed procedures.

The most significant challenge that Dr. Rata faced with this process was the amount of time required to thoughtfully consider all these elements, time involved in consulting with knowledgeable colleagues in telepractice, meeting with appropriate consultants (i.e., attorneys, IT specialists, university and medical setting personnel involved in telepractice) while maintaining her current workload of teaching and supervision. In addition, she knew that mental health services were significantly lacking in the rural communities and that local providers were struggling to meet the mental health needs of their patients. Dr. Rata worked expeditiously to plan and led her colleagues through this process. She included students and the nurse practitioner community provider in all aspects of the development and worked at planning for challenges to minimize potential risks or problems she knew were inherent in telepractice and telesupervision work (e.g., dropped connections, poor video quality, problematic video or audio feeds). She set in motion several consultations at the outset of the development process such that planning and IT, legal, and community consultation could simultaneously occur to reduce the timeline for implementation. Also included in the implementation was continued consultation at various stages to evaluate the operational services and problem solve concerns or deficits.

OPTIONS AVAILABLE TO THE PSYCHOLOGIST

Dr. Rata could simply have jumped in and engaged with the community nurse practitioner to test the waters and see how a single patient service would go and develop the practicum along the way. She could also have limited the services to only telesupervision, resulting in significant travel and time costs for the graduate student. She could have limited the services to only consultation with the nurse practitioner on case conceptualization and brief counseling. Services could have been limited to one specific need (i.e., anxiety management). Yet none of these options seemed to capture the full potential of the service for anyone involved, including patients, rural referral source, students, and licensed faculty.

THE BEST DECISION POSSIBLE

Dr. Rata and her colleagues carefully weighed the costs and benefits of these aspects of providing care and determined that the unique setting could offer patients increased access to care, focusing the nurse practitioner on the more demanding cases (e.g., personality disorders), and made general practice cases available to students who might not typically have the opportunity to work with these rural-based individuals and families. With a moderate investment of time in consultation, Dr. Rata and her team were able to create a beneficial experience for patients, reduce the demand on community providers, provide a meaningful experience for their graduate students, and limit increased demands for faculty supervisors.

Key Points From the Chapter to Remember

- Engage in thoughtful questioning, review, and consultation with knowledgeable others to determine what you don't know, what you need to know, and what resources you need to access and obtain (e.g., Joint Task Force, 2013,

Guidelines for the Practice of Telepsychology; Kissel et al., 2014, NIST *Guidelines for Media Sanitization*) and then develop a plan of action before engaging in the disposal of data and devices used in telepsychology.

- Carefully review all aspects of jurisdictional legal requirements, including title and scope of practice and possible exemptions for telepractice and telesupervision (often found in the licensure board statutes or regulations) for all involved jurisdictions, the described enforcement of these requirements (generally located in the licensure board rules), and any policy documents or white papers your jurisdictional board has established regarding provision of telepsychology services, protection of privacy, and disposal of information and records.
- Have a clear understanding of the IT data disposal practices of any setting in which you work or consult.
- Remember that you are accountable for proper information disposal. You are not relieved of your duty to understand the technology you use and how it affects your patients/clients even if you work in or for an agency, business, hospital, or other setting.
- Before disposing of hardware, be sure to remove all client/patient information from hardware and software due to transfer or storage of such information. This includes, at a minimum, deleting contacts, removing mobile applications, deleting the call history, and/or applying a device's factory reset; with videoconferencing software, ensure that all patient contact information and call history have been deleted from your account and contact the vendor to further pursue this change.
- Make efforts not to store inappropriate information (e.g., patient names, patient IP addresses) on devices, and purge call logs regularly.
- Follow basic security protocols to ensure that sensitive patient data are never placed at unnecessary risk: password protect the device, secure the devices when not in use, and limit use of devices to professional activities.
- Inform clients/patients on the importance of and how they can safeguard and protect their privacy on devices they may use.
- Seek frequent consultation from knowledgeable legal, computer and server IT, and malpractice experts.
- Document steps taken to ensure proper disposal of information and technologies.
- Continue to be well-informed of changes and developments in legal requirements and technological developments.

References

The American Insurance Trust. (2014, September). *Choosing encryption software.* Retrieved from https://www.trustinsurance.com/resources/articles/choosing-encryption-software

American Psychological Association. (2007). Record keeping guidelines. *American Psychologist, 62*, 9, 993–1004. http://dx.doi.org/10.1037/0003-066X.62.9.993

American Psychological Association. (2017). *Ethical principles of psychologists and code of conduct* (2002, Amended June 1, 2010 and January 1, 2017). Retrieved from http://www.apa.org/ethics/code/index.aspx

Children's Online Privacy Protection Act, 15 U.S.C. §§ 6501–6506, Pub. L. 105–277, 112 Stat. 2681–728. (1998).

Family Educational Rights and Privacy Act of 1974, 20 U.S.C. §1232g. (1974).

Health Information Technology for Economic and Clinical Health Act, Pub. L. 111-5. (2009).

Health Insurance Portability and Accountability Act, Pub. L. No. 104-191, 110 Stat. 1936. (1996).

Joint Task Force for the Development of Telepsychology Guidelines for Psychologists. (2013). Guidelines for the practice of telepsychology. *American Psychologist, 68,* 791–800. Retrieved from https://www.apa.org/pubs/journals/features/amp-a0035001.pdf

Kissel, R., Regenscheid, A., Scholl, M., & Stine, K. (2014, December). *Guidelines for media sanitization* (NIST Special Publication 800-88, Revision 1). Gaithersburg, MD: National Institute of Standards and Technology. Retrieved from http://nvlpubs.nist.gov/nistpubs/SpecialPublications/NIST.SP.800-88r1.pdf

Smucker Barnwell, S. V., Juretic, M. A., Hoerster, K. D., Felker, B. L., & Van de Plasch, R. (2012). VA Puget Sound telemental health service to rural veterans. *Psychological Services, 9,* 209–211. http://dx.doi.org/10.1037/a0025999

U.S. Department of Veterans Affairs. (2014, November 30). *FaceTime*. Retrieved from http://www.va.gov/TRM/ToolPage.asp?tid=7953

Bruce E. Crow and Julie M. Landry Poole

7 Testing and Assessment

Psychologists are encouraged to consider the unique issues that may arise with test instruments and assessment approaches designed for in-person implementation when providing telepsychology services.
—Guideline 7, *Guidelines for the Practice of Telepsychology*

Rationale

Psychological testing and other assessment procedures are an area of professional practice in which psychologists have been trained, and they are uniquely qualified to conduct such tests. While some symptom screening instruments are already frequently being administered online, most psychological test instruments and other assessment procedures currently in use were designed and developed originally for in-person administration. Psychologists are thus encouraged to be knowledgeable about, and account for, the unique impacts of such tests, their suitability for diverse populations, and the limitations on test administration and on test and other data interpretations when these psychological tests and other assessment procedures are considered for and conducted via telepsychology. Psychologists also strive to maintain

The view(s) expressed herein are those of the author(s) and do not reflect the official policy or position of U.S. Army Regional Health Command—Central, the U.S. Army Medical Department, the U.S. Army Office of the Surgeon General, the Department of the Army and Department of Defense, or the U.S. government.

http://dx.doi.org/10.1037/0000046-008
A Telepsychology Casebook: Using Technology Ethically and Effectively in Your Professional Practice, L. F. Campbell, F. Millán, and J. N. Martin (Editors)

> the integrity of the application of the testing and assessment process and procedures when using telecommunication technologies. In addition, they are cognizant of the accommodations for diverse populations that may be required for test administration via telepsychology. These guidelines are consistent with the standards articulated in the most recent edition of Standards for Educational and Psychological Testing (American Educational Research Association, American Psychological Association, and the Council on Measurement in Education, 1999). (Joint Task Force for the Development of Telepsychology Guidelines for Psychologists, 2013, p. 798)

Psychometric and clinical assessment has long been an area of strength for psychologists and a skill set that distinguishes them from other mental health professionals. Their responsibility for ethical conduct with assessments extends to development, training, administration, scoring, interpretation, explanation and release of data, and maintenance of security and integrity of many different instruments while also considering the standardization, reliability, validity, and limitations of such instruments. Psychologists are keenly aware of the detrimental effects that improper care of the assessment process can cause to the public. The responsibility is no less demanding when consideration is given to conducting assessments via telepsychology. In fact, because there is limited research and psychometric data on such use, psychologists are called to a high standard of protecting and ensuring proper care in conducting assessments using telepsychology. In this chapter, we propose several situations that require the psychologist to question actively what additional precautions and preparation are needed when using telepsychology.

Assessment and Testing Via Videoconferencing

Current guidelines for, and ethical considerations of, testing in a videoconferencing modality feature the application of face-to-face protocols for standardization of testing conditions and environmental controls to videoconferencing. As telepsychology advances, assessment, including aspects of administration, may be conducted online, and protocols developed specifically for telepsychology services will be used. The field is beginning to produce scholarly works that investigate the effectiveness of telepsychology services primarily in the areas of forensics, neuropsychology, and general assessment. Representations of the research lines include the following.

FORENSIC PSYCHOLOGY

Forensic assessment videoconferencing is gaining popularity (Adjorlolo & Chan, 2015), signaling the need for competence specific to the forensic setting as well as technical competence in this area of practice. The use of social media, Internet search engines, and other means of networking raises questions regarding their use in conducting forensic evaluation and users' privacy (Pirelli, Otto, & Estoup, 2016).

TELENEUROPSYCHOLOGICAL ASSESSMENT

Studies investigate the reliability of an online battery of tests compared with face-to-face testing. These tests were used in suspected dementia cases and included the Mini-Mental State Exam (MMSE), Hopkins Verbal Learning Test—Revised, Digit Span, the Boston Naming Test, Letter and Category Fluency, and Clock Drawing. Highly similar results were found between the videoconferencing and face-to-face conditions (Cullum, Hynan, Grosch, Parikh, & Weiner, 2014). Another study investigated the use of videoconferencing testing compared with in-person evaluation for cognitive impairment. Importantly, further study is needed to determine modifications for specific testing online and separate normative data (Cullum & Grosch, 2013).

Similarly, another investigation made use of the Repeatable Battery for the Assessment of Neuropsychological Status (RBANS; test for cognitive impairment) and found the videoconferencing to be effective compared with face-to-face testing. RBANS scores were reliably correlated, thus supporting remote administration (Galusha-Glasscock, Horton, Weiner, & Cullum, 2016).

GENERAL TELEPSYCHOLOGY ASSESSMENT

Two additional studies conducted with a sample of rural American Indians and a VA sample support the reliability and feasibility of videoconferencing administration compared with face-to-face conditions. In one study, comparable results were achieved with alternative forms of the MMSE, Clock Drawing, Digit Span, Oral Trails, Hopkins Verbal Learning, Letter and Category Fluency, and the Boston Naming Test administered in face-to-face and videoconferencing conditions (Wadsworth et al., 2016). In doing matched testing on global cognition, attention, and visuospatial function, videoconferencing conditions were found to be comparable to face-to-face conditions among outpatient VA geropsychology patients (Grosch, Weiner, Hynan, Shore, & Cullum, 2015).

In addition to specialty population research, several studies were conducted that advance application in general telepsychology assessment. These studies provide an overview of the integration of telecommunication modalities (Parakh, Ghosh, & Mehta, 2014); highlight data regarding limitations of telepractice, cultural, ethical, and safety considerations (Luxton, Pruitt, & Osenbach, 2014); and give attention to benefits of videoconferencing, practical concerns, and recommendations for integrity of assessments (Luxton, Pruitt, & Jenkins-Guarnieri, 2015).

Case Study 1: Assessment of Suicidality

RELEVANT EXCERPT FROM THE GUIDELINE

> When a psychological test or other assessment procedure is conducted via telepsychology, psychologists are encouraged to ensure that the integrity of the psychometric properties of the test or assessment procedure (e.g., reliability

> and validity) and the conditions of administration indicated in the test manual are preserved when adapted for use with such technologies. (Joint Task Force, 2013, p. 798)

SETTING: ARMY TELE-BEHAVIORAL HEALTH HUB

The behavioral health care system within the Department of the Army includes several tele-behavioral health (TBH) hubs. Like traditional outpatient behavioral health care clinics, these hubs provide services that are unavailable at military installations because of local provider shortages, access to care issues, the need for specialty care unavailable at the installation, and other issues. Using secure videoconferencing, the clinic staff provide a wide range of psychological services to active duty service members and their family members throughout the continental United States.

Dr. Cooper is a civilian clinical psychologist who has been employed by the Department of the Army for the past 6 years. Currently, she works full time in a TBH clinic where she provides services primarily to active duty service members. Dr. Cooper sees both individual psychotherapy patients and assessment patients and specializes in the treatment of insomnia.

SCENARIO

Lieutenant (LT) Grey is a single 23-year-old African American active duty army officer. He presented to his local behavioral health clinic as a walk-in due to a recent increase in depressive symptoms. He was triaged by a licensed clinical social worker and scheduled for follow up 1 week later with a local psychiatrist. The psychiatrist diagnosed LT Grey with major depressive disorder, single episode, severe, and began treatment with an antidepressant. LT Grey was also referred to a local psychologist within the same clinic for psychotherapy, but he was subsequently scheduled in the TBH clinic at his request because of the long wait time to see a traditional face-to-face provider.

One month after initially seeking treatment, he is scheduled for an initial therapy intake evaluation with TBH psychologist Dr. Cooper. Before the evaluation, Dr. Cooper reviews the available medical records and sees that the most recent encounter written by the psychiatrist describes suicidal ideation and a specific plan. The notes also indicate that the patient suffers from clinical depression, has extremely poor self-esteem, recently broke up with his girlfriend, acknowledges that he often acts impulsively (i.e., drinking and driving), and has a poor relationship with his mother.

After a personal introduction and verification of patient identity, Dr. Cooper begins to introduce the limits of confidentiality. Before she is able to finish, LT Grey interrupts to say he "refuses" to be hospitalized because he feels it is unacceptable for an army officer to be treated in an inpatient psychiatric ward. Dr. Cooper empathically listens to his concerns and asks questions to gather additional information. LT Grey explains he recently began a new position within an armored brigade combat team, and he already feels out of place among the other brigade staff officers because of differences in his education and training. He is worried his peers and superior officers will lose respect for him if he needs to be hospitalized for behavioral health reasons. He also acknowledges feeling embarrassed about his suicidal thoughts and depressive symptoms. LT Grey reports that the depression and thoughts of self-harm have improved since initiating psychotropic medication 2 weeks ago, and he insists to Dr. Cooper that he will only get better with the addition of the talk therapy.

Dr. Cooper validates LT Grey's emotions and normalizes the fears and concerns he expressed. She explains that inpatient psychiatric hospitalization is not necessarily required when a patient experiences suicidal feelings and thoughts. She clarifies that further assessment is needed in order to make the most appropriate treatment decision.

KEY ELEMENTS, CHALLENGES, AND DECISION FACTORS

During an initial telepsychology encounter, the psychologist must determine whether the patient is appropriate for outpatient care and for assessment or treatment (or both) administered via telepsychology. These determinations are based on similar criteria (e.g., imminent risk to self or others), but occasionally patients who are suitable for outpatient treatment are not ideal candidates for telepsychology. Exclusion decisions may be based on the severity of symptoms, poor treatment compliance, and/or complex management. Additionally, the psychologist must assess for any diversity-related issues (e.g., language, cognitive impairments) that would necessitate accommodations if telepsychology assessment and/or treatment were conducted (see Guideline 2: Standards of Care in the Delivery of Telepsychology Services; Joint Task Force, 2013, pp. 794–795).

A review of the available literature related to suicide assessment via telepsychology could provide additional aid in the psychologist's decision making. The use of remote management for behavioral health emergencies (i.e., suicide) can be traced back to 1953 when the Samaritans Service offered crisis counseling via telephone for United Kingdom and Ireland residents (Godleski, Nieves, Darkins, & Lehmann, 2008). In 1963, the first suicide prevention telephone service in the United States, "Call Bruce," originated in San Francisco (San Francisco Suicide Prevention, 2007). A national suicide prevention hotline was eventually established by the U.S. Substance Abuse and Mental Health Services Administration with a specific military component added in 2007. As the evidence base establishing the comparability of remote and face-to-face treatment has developed, providers are increasingly engaging in remote suicide risk assessment (Godleski et al., 2008).

On the basis of the growing focus on evidence-based treatment, the psychologist would also likely want to determine whether there is an evidence-based, suicide-specific assessment or treatment available for use with telepsychology patients. The Joint Task Force for the Development of Telepsychology (2013) guidelines encourage psychologists to consider whether the assessment tool may be used in such a way that the integrity of the application of the assessment process is maintained. The psychologist should be aware of and knowledgeable about the accommodations required for suicide assessment via telepsychology. Additionally, the task force recommends that patient treatment notes in the medical record specify the assessment was conducted via telepsychology and describe any accommodations or modifications made to the assessment.

Another important consideration related to telepsychology suicide assessment is the requirement for the psychologist to rely on the remote location's administrative staff. The staff will be responsible for ensuring that the patient completes any necessary paperwork and for protecting the security of the assessment process during completion of the required forms (e.g., observing to ensure the patient is not using a cell phone or discussing with others). The administrative staff must additionally return the completed materials to the psychologist on time and in a manner that protects the patient's confidentiality and protected health information. Depending on the training and skills of the staff, this may require additional considerations on the part of the psychologist (see Guideline 1: Competence of the Psychologist; Guideline 2: Standards of Care in the Delivery of Telepsychology Services; Joint Task Force, 2013, pp. 793–794).

OPTIONS AVAILABLE TO THE PSYCHOLOGIST

Dr. Cooper concludes that she has two options. Given the information gathered from the medical records and the initial discussion with LT Grey, she may decide that further assessment via telepsychology is inappropriate and alert the remote location's TBH clinic staff that the patient requires traditional face-to-face assessment and disposition due to the current clinical presentation. Or she may consider conducting further assessment herself.

If Dr. Cooper refers the patient for face-to-face assessment, the traditional provider may be able to detect subtle nuances that could be indistinguishable via telepsychology. The provider would be more familiar with local resources and available treatment options at the military installation or surrounding. Additionally, the on-post provider may have a working relationship with the treating psychiatrist.

Referral to another clinician would also mean that the patient would need to see yet another provider. If LT Grey is referred, he will have been evaluated by four providers since initially seeking treatment just 1 month ago. Considering the embarrassment he currently feels, the lack of continuity of care may prevent him from continuing treatment and may exacerbate the dissatisfaction he felt with behavioral health services when trying to schedule a therapy appointment. It is also likely he will be rescheduled with Dr. Cooper at a later time if he is seen by the in-person provider and deemed appropriate for outpatient care. This may lead to difficulty developing rapport and an effective therapeutic alliance between Dr. Cooper and the patient.

Conversely, Dr. Cooper may decide to conduct the assessment herself. The patient has already shared his concerns and fears with her. If she is able to continue the telepsychology assessment, she will demonstrate respect for his privacy, which will likely be paramount in building a successful relationship with the patient due to his fear of the potential career impact stigma might cause. Additionally, she may be able to respect the patient's wishes and prevent hospitalization if successful treatment interventions are implemented via telepsychology. Also, the patient is already in the room with Dr. Cooper. As discussed earlier, referring him to a local clinician for triage would involve another provider and could imply to the patient that the providers do not care about him.

Dr. Cooper feels most comfortable assessing and treating suicidality through the application of collaborative assessment and management of suicidality (CAMS). Although the CAMS approach is empirically validated for the assessment and treatment of suicidality, administration via telepsychology has not been studied; therefore, Dr. Cooper has another decision to make. She may choose not to administer the CAMS if she feels the technique cannot be used in such a way that the integrity of the assessment process is maintained. However, she may decide she is comfortable making the necessary accommodations to assess the patient using CAMS via telepsychology. These accommodations may include different seating arrangements (i.e., face to face via TBH rather than side by side), two sets of forms rather than one shared between the patient and provider, or seeking assistance through the administrative staff to forward the patient's form with the patient and vice versa.

On the basis of the presenting problem, Dr. Cooper is interested in obtaining additional information about her patient's diagnosis and psychological status and assessing for treatment planning. In the army, TBH is delivered by the provider at one military treatment facility (MTF) and received by the patient at another MTF. Dr. Cooper has experience with administering the Minnesota Multiphasic Personality Inventory—2 (MMPI–2) to patients in her office but not through TBH. She requests the patient site MTF administer the assessment and forward her the results. She prepares the patient by explaining the rationale for the assessment as well as the procedures and conditions. Dr. Cooper coordinates with the support staff at the remote location to send her the computer-generated scoring report by secured e-mail.

In addition to the MMPI–2, Dr. Cooper also considers including conventional projective measures. In the past she has found the Thematic Apperception Test to be beneficial for gaining insight into issues to incorporate in the treatment. Dr. Cooper searches for guidelines or precedence in virtual administration of the Thematic Apperception Test or other projective testing, but the search does not produce any related publications. In an attempt to replicate conventional administration, she arranges to have the behavioral health technician at the remote site join the patient in the treatment room and hand cards to him as Dr. Cooper provides instructions and records the narrative given by the patient.

Dr. Cooper has used psychological testing and assessment to assist with determining diagnosis, treatment planning, and conduct a comprehensive assessment of suicidality. She found that by making relatively minor adaptations to conventional assessment procedures, she was able to capitalize on the benefits of structured psychological assessment in support of her telepsychology patient care.

Case Study 2: Referral in Lieu of Telepsychology

RELEVANT EXCERPT FROM THE GUIDELINE

> Psychologists are thus encouraged to be knowledgeable about, and account for, the unique impacts of such tests, their suitability for diverse populations, and the limitations on test administration and on test and other data interpretations when these psychological tests and other assessment procedures are considered for and conducted via telepsychology. (Joint Task Force, 2013, p. 798)

SETTING: UNIVERSITY COUNSELING CENTER

John recently began the clinical psychology internship program at a large university counseling center. In this setting, both individual and group therapy are provided, as well as psychological assessment and various types of evaluations. There is a strong sense of collaboration and support, and interns are considered junior colleagues rather than subordinate trainees. Both telepsychology (campus clinic to campus clinic) and traditional face-to-face services are provided by the counseling center.

SCENARIO

John is assigned a telepsychology evaluation with a first-year medical student who presents to the clinic with concerns related to concentration and attention complaints. The patient denies a history of similar problems or a diagnosis of attention-deficit/hyperactivity disorder. After a thorough clinical interview and review of available medical records, John posits that the patient's difficulties are likely due to a recently sustained head injury. The counseling center's organizational policies require psychological assessment in any case where academic accommodations or medication may be clinically indicated. John also knows that neuropsychological testing would be beneficial in assessing for cognitive impairment as well as type and localization of any damage subsequent to the concussion.

John discusses the case with his supervisor during their next meeting. Rather than give him instructions as to how to proceed, his supervisor encourages him to consider the referral question, the evaluation requirements subsequent to the center's policies, and the available resources. John also spends time looking up research related to psychological assessment via telepsychology.

KEY ELEMENTS, CHALLENGES, AND DECISION FACTORS

John finds several journal articles on the use of assessment measures administered via videoconferencing. Kobak's (2004) study was designed to determine whether the mode of administration affected the psychometric properties of the Hamilton Depression Rating Scale. The results demonstrate psychometric equivalence of remote and face-to-face administration. A similar study examined face-to-face versus remote administration of the Montgomery–Åsberg Depression Rating Scale. The researchers found comparability of face-to-face administration and remote administration, including both telephone and videoconference (Kobak, Williams, Jeglic, Salvucci, & Sharp, 2008). A more recent study compared videoconference and face-to-face assessments for veterans evaluated using the Clinician-Administered PTSD Scale (CAPS) for Posttraumatic Stress Disorder. The results of the study show significant correlations between administration of the CAPS via videoconferencing and face to face (Porcari et al., 2009). Litwack et al. (2014) also found strong correlations between face-to-face assessment and telepsychology assessment of the CAPS.

Research on the assessment and treatment of traumatic brain injury via telepsychology is scarce; however, there is growing evidence showing neuropsychological assessment via videoconferencing demonstrates good agreement with traditional in-person assessment (Hildebrand, Chow, Williams, Nelson, & Wass, 2004; Jacobsen, Sprenger, Andersson, & Krogstad, 2003; Kirkwood, Peck, & Bennie, 2000; Loh et al., 2004; Vestal, Smith-Olinde, Hicks, Hutton, & Hart, 2006). Overall, studies suggest assessment conducted through verbal instructions and responses may be more reliable than others, although other tasks may be amenable to modification for TBH purposes (Cullum & Grosch, 2013).

Despite the supportive evidence base, John must consider whether testing via telepsychology is feasible given the available resources. The counseling center routinely uses psychological assessment tools via online administration; however, on the basis of the presenting problem, John determines that these instruments are inappropriate for this particular evaluation. He concludes that a full neuropsychological test battery is needed.

OPTIONS AVAILABLE TO THE PSYCHOLOGIST

John initially decides to administer the Halstead–Reitan Battery via telepsychology. He presents this idea to his supervisor, who praises his recognition of suspected brain damage but says the center does not have all of the necessary tests. She reminds him that administration via telepsychology would necessitate training a technician at the remote location in the use of the assessment measures due to measures that require stimulus manipulation.

John considers using a more limited battery based on the center's assessment library but decides full assessment is the best option for the patient. His supervisor suggests referral to a local neuropsychologist who occasionally performs assessments for university students. Despite the supervisor's suggestion, John has several concerns about making a referral for testing. The patient would need additional appointments—testing, testing feedback, final determinations related to academic accommodations, among others. Because of the multiple appointments, the evaluation will take several weeks to complete.

Further consultation with his supervisor and the other interns alleviates some of these concerns. John realizes it is in the patient's best interests to receive a full neuropsychological battery administered in person according to the accepted norms rather than a limited assessment administered via telepsychology. The in-person administration conducted by a neuropsychologist would ensure standardized administration of the assessment.

Case Study 3: Army Electronic Assessment Battery

RELEVANT EXCERPTS FROM THE GUIDELINE

> Psychologists are encouraged to be cognizant of the specific issues that may arise with diverse populations when providing telepsychology and make appropriate arrangements to address those concerns. (Joint Task Force, 2013, p. 798)
>
> When administering psychological tests and other assessment procedures when providing telepsychology services, psychologists are encouraged to consider the quality of those technologies that are being used and the hardware requirements that are needed in order to conduct the specific psychological test or assessment approach. (Joint Task Force, 2013, p. 798)

SETTING: REGIONAL TBH HUBS

The U.S. Army utilizes regional TBH hubs to provide remote telepsychology services to military hospitals across the United States. Several military-unique psychological evaluations are required by various army regulations before certain types of administrative separations and for determining suitability for specific advanced military training or special duty assignments. These evaluations are often conducted through telepsychology whereby soldiers report to their local behavioral health clinic and complete their evaluation in a room configured to receive TBH.

Procedures are performed in accordance with the Army Tele-Behavioral Health Operations Manual (U.S. Army Medical Command, 2012). Army policies require soldiers to complete a battery of computerized preappointment questionnaires before a clinic-based or TBH encounter. The standardized assessments are administered via the army's Behavioral Health Data Portal (BHDP), which was developed by the army as a psychological assessment tool that uses a standardized battery of questionnaires for initial and follow-up assessments and assesses domains such as general psychological distress, depression, anxiety, posttraumatic stress, substance and alcohol abuse, relationship problems, and suicidal and homicidal ideation. The BHDP enables the psychologist to obtain baseline measurements and to measure changes over time during the course of treatment. The BHDP is an example of electronic psychological assessment that can be used in a telepsychology setting. The BHDP is designed so that a psychologist can access patient information from any location along with the patient's electronic medical record. Because all surveys and questionnaires are electronically and immediately scored, the psychologist has rapid access to results as soon as the patient completes their responses.

SCENARIO

Major (MAJ) Smith is an active duty army clinical psychologist who provides telepsychology services at one of the army's TBH hubs. Staff Sergeant (SSG) Clark has been referred for a suitability assessment in consideration of selection for special duty as an Army recruiter. Recruiters are typically midlevel or senior noncommissioned officers, many of whom would benefit from psychological counseling after multiple combat deployments and exposures to psychological trauma. Recruiters are often assigned to locations distant from military health care facilities and work independently for long hours. Standards of conduct for recruiters are high because they are readily visible as public representatives of the army. Preassignment evaluations are required to determine whether there are behavioral health conditions that would interfere with a soldier's ability to perform recruiter duties.

SSG Clark has been on active duty since 2002, having enlisted to serve in the military to fight against anti-U.S. terrorists. His first combat deployment was in 2003 during the ground invasion in Iraq, and he served two subsequent combat tours, one in Iraq and one in Afghanistan. His military occupational specialty is infantryman, and he has served a total of 3.5 years in combat with many intense combat exposures. He has never requested or been referred for behavioral health treatment, although he wondered if he should have been.

SSG Clark has been scheduled by his local army behavioral health clinic for an appointment to see MAJ Smith, and in accordance with army policies, SSG Clark is asked for consent to receive this behavioral health service via TBH before scheduling. SSG Clark has given consent, citing his familiarity and comfort with talking to his family over the Internet during his multiple deployments. When SSG Clark arrives at his home station clinic on the day of his appointment, he is seated at a computer kiosk behind a privacy screen and completes the questionnaires on the BHDP. He notifies the reception desk staff when he's done, and he is logged off the session. He is soon greeted by a behavioral health assistant in the waiting room, who escorts him to the TBH room and orients him to the TBH equipment.

The questionnaires completed by SSG Clark before this initial assessment included a standard intake battery. The results were electronically transmitted to MAJ Smith in real time as each questionnaire was completed, and he reviewed the results before beginning the TBH session with SSG Clark. MAJ Smith also reviewed SSG Clark's electronic medical record at the TBH Hub location to review SSG Clark's medical and behavioral health history as documented by his local health care providers as well as those at previous assignment locations. MAJ Smith is notified by clerical staff at SSG Clark's location that he is in the TBH room and ready to be seen. MAJ Smith opens the TBH session at his location and is greeted by the assistant, who introduces SSG Clark to MAJ Smith before leaving the room. Major Smith ensures that SSG Clark understands the purpose of the evaluation and limits of confidentiality because the results of the evaluation will be provided to his chain of command.

MAJ Smith observes that SSG Clark appears to fully comprehend his questions and maintains good eye contact with the video monitor in the TBH room. His speech is clearly audible, he is a native U.S. citizen, educated entirely in U.S. public schools, and English was his only language in his home of origin.

MAJ Smith notes that the questionnaires that measure general psychological distress, depression, sleep disturbance, and PTSD have positive indications of probable psychiatric disorder. In addition, SSG Clark acknowledges a lifetime history of suicide ideation, occurring during a recent period of intense relationship problems, although he denies any current plan or intent. In SSG Clark's medical record, MAJ Smith discerns that with the exception of occasional brief symptomatic treatment of insomnia, he has denied any behavioral health concerns during several primary care visits for various routine and minor medical issues. During his clinical interview with SSG Clark, MAJ Smith inquires about specific responses from the screening questionnaires and carefully expands his interview around these potential symptoms to elicit a more comprehensive and salient behavioral history.

Upon completion of the evaluation, MAJ Smith discusses the significance of SSG Clark's clinical history and assessment results. He informs him that although he has not previously disclosed behavioral health concerns to health care providers, he is clearly experiencing symptoms of probable psychiatric disorder and may be at increased risk for suicide thoughts. He discusses the expected benefit of more formal psychological evaluation and behavioral health treatment and offers to provide a referral to the behavioral health clinic at SSG Clark's home station. SSG Clark agrees and indicates that he feels relief knowing there may be help for the symptoms he reported. MAJ Smith also discusses the fact that he will be informing SSG Clark's chain of command that until further evaluation and a course of treatment, he will need to be deferred from further consideration for recruiter duty. SSG Clark acknowledges this requirement and admits he was secretly worried that if required to serve as a recruiter, he would fail and think more seriously about suicide. MAJ Smith prepares a memorandum for SSG Clark's commander and sends it electronically to the clerical staff at SSG Clark's location to be delivered to his unit.

KEY ELEMENTS, CHALLENGES, AND DECISION FACTORS

MAJ Smith periodically refers to the *Guidelines for the Practice of Telepsychology* and is familiar with the testing and assessment recommendations that psychologists are encouraged to be cognizant of specific issues that may arise with diverse populations when providing telepsychology and to make appropriate arrangements to address those concerns. He is aware of caveats when obtaining informed consent to use TBH for this assessment situation because the evaluation is required by the Army and soldiers may feel obligated to consent to TBH despite any reservations they may have. He is mindful that there may be barriers to establishing rapport for some soldiers in a TBH encounter that may influence his ability to achieve an accurate assessment. He closely monitors whether SSG Clark's nonverbal communication appears degraded by the field of view and picture quality of the monitor and whether this inhibits SSG Clark's willingness to disclose important clinical information. Likewise, MAJ Smith is also attentive to the possibility that because his military rank is higher than his patient's, SSG Clark may be motivated to appear unaffected by behavioral health symptoms.

Although the BHDP was developed by the army and is a routinely administered assessment procedure for all outpatient behavioral health encounters, MAJ Smith is aware that the Joint Task Force for the Development of Telepsychology Guidelines for

Psychologists (2013) advises that he consider the quality of the technologies being used to support psychological assessment via telepsychology. He understands this to mean that he is expected to understand the effects of the BHDP technology on the administration process for the questionnaires that compose the assessment battery. Although MAJ Smith is aware that the kiosk where the BHDP is administered is stocked with high-quality computer and monitor equipment, he confirms with SSG Clark that questions on the BHDP were readily understood and there were no concerns or problems with completing the questionnaires.

MAJ Smith has also studied the BHDP Users Guide to ensure he understands the manner in which the questionnaires are presented and the methodology used to score them. He notes that the manual does not completely describe the basis for various cut-off scores, and he finds that he needs to refer to additional documents and publications to confirm that interpretation guidelines by test authors or publishers are correctly reflected in the automated scoring programs.

OPTIONS AVAILABLE TO THE PSYCHOLOGIST

Army policies require that behavioral health patients give specific consent for evaluation or treatment via TBH and always retain the option for clinic-based encounters. In many cases, there is a shorter wait time for a TBH provider or greater access to a provider with a specialty skill, especially given that many military installations are in relatively remote areas of the United States. Because the patient gives this consent before scheduling the TBH appointment and before meeting the telepsychologist, MAJ Smith ensures that SSG Clark fully understands that he has a choice between TBH and a clinic-based appointment. MAJ Smith is prepared to help SSG Clark reschedule with a clinic-based provider at his home station location if he chooses. Likewise, as the TBH session proceeds, MAJ Smith is prepared to suspend the evaluation if he determines that the TBH medium compromises his ability to complete an accurate and appropriate assessment. He pays close attention to whether the manner of presentation of the BHDP or the quality of the technology precludes accurate interpretation of the assessment results. He is aware that even if his patient is completely amenable to and comfortable with TBH, the technology used in the TBH application of psychological assessment measures may alter administering, scoring, and recording of the assessment in a way that impedes his clinical decisions.

During this evaluation, MAJ Smith determines that SSG Clark seems quite comfortable with the TBH medium and is comfortable discussing symptoms that have bothered him for a period of time but for which he did not think help was available. He determines that he was well oriented to the BHDP kiosk and reported that it was easy for him to navigate through the different assessment modules. He is confident that the BHDP assessment technology provides an accurate recording of SSG Clark's responses and that his responses were a good representation of his clinical status on the psychological domains assessed.

In the course of the assessment, MAJ Smith must determine whether this one-time evaluation has detected a need for further assessment or referral to treatment.

If a referral is needed, MAJ Smith will need to know how to contact appropriate staff at SSG Clark's location. Similarly, if during the evaluation session MAJ Smith determines his patient presents with acute distress and needs urgent or emergency management, he will need to invoke patient safety procedures.

MAJ Smith determines that additional assessment is indicated but that SSG Clark is not in acute distress or in need of an urgent referral, nor does MAJ Smith need to contact his commander because there are no current concerns about risk of harm to self or others.

Case Study 4: Child Psychological Assessment

RELEVANT EXCERPT FROM THE GUIDELINE

> In addition, psychologists may consider the use of a trained assistant (e.g., proctor) to be on premise at the remote location in an effort to help verify the identity of the client/patient, provide needed on-site support to administer certain tests or subtests, and protect the security of the psychological testing and/or assessment. (Joint Task Force, 2013, p. 798)

SETTING: RURAL PRIMARY CARE CLINIC

Dr. Myers is a fellowship-trained and board-certified child psychologist in a midwestern U.S. metropolitan city that is home to the state's largest public university. A part of her practice is to provide telepsychology services to clients in rural areas of her state, and she frequently receives referrals to evaluate children with disruptive behaviors at school. Her referrals often come from pediatricians and family medicine physicians in primary clinics in small and medium-sized towns. Gaining access to psychological services can be difficult for families who live a considerable distance from a specialty practice psychologist, such as a child psychologist. There is an increasing use and acceptance of telepsychology as a solution to increase access to behavioral services for families in rural and remote areas that would otherwise face travel time and cost barriers (Nelson, Barnard, & Cain, 2006; Nelson & Bui, 2010).

SCENARIO

Dr. Myers receives a referral requesting psychological evaluation for Katy, a 9-year-old fourth-grade student who attends public elementary school in her small rural town with a population of 2,000. Katy has received medical care from a family medicine physician at a nearby health clinic since her birth. She has enjoyed good health, and with the exception of routine childhood illnesses, physicals, and immunizations, she has not needed other medical care. But Katy's parents have been concerned by increasing problems with her behavior. During the past year, she has become increasingly "touchy," and it seems to her parents that minor stressors readily escalate to tantrums and argumentative behavior. At the midpoint of the school year, her teachers begin sending home notes to notify her parents that Katy has not been turning in homework, seems to have trouble paying attention in class, and is having trouble learning new material. She has become "pushy" on the playground, and other children complain that she is "too rude." The school recently requested a parent conference and suggested that Katy be evaluated for possible learning disability, attention-deficit problems, or emotional and behavioral problems. In accordance with the school's protocol, the school psychologist conducts intellectual and academic achievement testing to address the academic problems noted by the teacher and to determine whether Katy met criteria for learning disability services; she also conducts classroom observations and mood disorder screening to identify symptoms that may be interfering with school functioning.

The school administrators inform Katy's parents that they do not provide or make referrals for psychological testing to diagnose psychiatric disorder, but if her parents are concerned about that possibility, they can obtain an evaluation from a child psychologist of their choosing. Katy's parents are indeed concerned that she may need treatment for a psychological condition that was causing the problem behaviors. Katy's school counselor does not have specific suggestions for obtaining the evaluation but is aware that there are child psychologists in the university town, some 100 miles away. The counselor suggests that Katy's parents might be able to get a referral from Katy's doctor "to see someone." Katy's parents make an appointment with their family physician and explain the situation, asking for help in locating a child psychologist. Katy's doctor tells the parents that he does not know a child psychologist to whom he can refer them for an in-person evaluation, but he informs them that their primary care clinic recently began offering telepsychology at their location. Katy's parents are interested and quite relieved they will not need to drive 200 miles round trip for an evaluation that is unfamiliar to them. Katy's family doctor makes the arrangements, and they are scheduled for an appointment with Dr. Myers the next week, right after school gets out for the day.

Dr. Myers has provided the clinic with an information sheet that is given to parents of the children who are scheduled with her. The information sheet provides an introduction and photo of Dr. Myers, a statement of professional credentials, a description of services, and a series of frequently asked questions that detail what to expect when meeting with a telepsychologist. Katy's parents know that during the first appointment, Dr. Myers will meet with the parents and Katy together, as well as privately with the parents and privately with Katy. When Katy and her family come to the first appointment they are greeted by a pediatric licensed practical nurse (LPN), who explains that she works as an assistant to Dr. Myers and will be their point of contact at the local clinic. Katy's family is shown the room where they will meet Dr. Myers, and the nurse explains how the equipment works and that she will assist with adjusting audio and video settings at the start of the encounter with Dr. Myers.

Dr. Myers meets with the family for two sessions to complete an intake and gather relevant clinical history. After the end of the first session, Dr. Myers asks Katy's parents to complete several checklists of her behaviors and requests that Katy's primary and secondary teacher complete a teacher-specific version. In between the first and second sessions, Dr. Myers reads the results of the testing by the school psychologist as well as the classroom behavioral observation summary, then reviews Katy's school and medical records. At the second session, Dr. Myers provides more details about the assessment she has planned that she believes will answer the concerns raised by Katy's teachers and her parents. The LPN assistant has ensured that documents sent to and from Dr. Myers have been securely transmitted electronically and that paper copies of questionnaires and checklists are scanned in a readable fashion.

At the third session, Dr. Myers administers a computerized Continuous Performance Test (CPT) to assess attention-related problems, with proctoring by the LPN assistant. The proctor ensures that Katy understands the task and stands by in case she has any trouble completing the CPT. Katy takes the test on a computer that is set up within view of the telepsychology camera, and while she works with the CPT, the proctor notes behavioral observations. In addition, Dr. Myers also observes Katy's behavior during testing and maintains a quiet presence. The psychologist asks Katy to draw a paper-and-pencil picture of her family; after she finishes, the assistant scans the picture to Dr. Myers, who asks Katy to talk about each family member. Dr. Myers also instructs the proctor to guide Katy through age-appropriate paper-and-pencil self-report measures of depression and anxiety.

After Dr. Myers has collected and reviewed all testing and questionnaire data, behavioral observations, school and medical records, and clinical interview information, she prepares her report in which she fully acknowledges that the assessment was conducted via telepsychology with the assistance of a proctor. She further notes potential limitations on her assessment findings that emanate from modifications in the testing procedures or from the testing environment. For this evaluation, she has determined that the total assessment and all available data support a diagnosis of attention-deficit/hyperactivity disorder, predominantly inattentive presentation, and that the assessment data are not consistent with other psychiatric diagnoses.

KEY ELEMENTS, CHALLENGES, AND DECISION FACTORS

The guidelines emphasize that it is important for psychologists to consider that a proctor or assistant may be a benefit or even a necessity to ensure that psychological tests are appropriately administered and that the integrity of the assessment condition is maintained.

When Dr. Myers set up her telepsychology practice with children, she recognized that she would need to make some adaptations to the manner of her practice. She is aware that building rapport with her patients is often essential to eliciting their optimal performance or willingness to provide frank and candid disclosure of personal information. In her clinic-based practice, she conducts her own psychological testing and is therefore able to directly discern whether her patient understands testing instructional sets and seems motivated and engaged in the task at hand. She is also able to make direct observations of behaviors exhibited during testing that supplement the test scores and provide meaningful clinical context.

In her telepsychology practice, she relies on an assistant at the remote or patient site location to achieve these same parameters. Dr. Myers accepts that it is her responsibility to train her assistant and supervise her ability to meet all standards for correctly administering psychological testing. She is also aware the assistant must ensure an appropriate environment of assessment conditions is maintained that is comfortable and supportive for the patient and free from distractions.

OPTIONS AVAILABLE TO THE PSYCHOLOGIST

When Dr. Myers received the referral for Katy, she recognized her behaviors as ones that are often addressed through a comprehensive assessment to rule out neurodevelopmental learning problems, attention-deficit problems, or psychiatric disorder. For each patient, Dr. Myers makes an initial assessment whether the child is comfortable with the telepsychology testing environment and whether there are likely to be confounds that would preclude an appropriate remote assessment. She knew that previous assessments through telepsychology for similar referrals were successful, although some adaptations were necessary to administer the tests at a distance. The primary adaptation for Dr. Myers is the use of a trained assistant to serve as a proctor for testing and at times directly administer the tests. As Dr. Myers considered the specific potential tests, she did so based on her initial assessment of congruence among the test, the patient, and the testing conditions. One essential role for Dr. Myers's assistant is to facilitate rapport to optimize clinical validity of the assessment outcome. Dr. Myers prefers to meet a child and his or her parents for one or more initial sessions and to observe the interaction of the child with the patient site assistant, as well the child's manner of responding to the testing environment. If the child appears too uncomfortable, anxious, or otherwise affected by the testing setting, Dr. Myers is prepared to recommend to the parents that a clinic-based setting may be a better option. Likewise during the assessment, Dr. Myers arranges to observe the child taking the tests and his or her interactions with the proctor. She is prepared to suspend the testing if she believes that the telepsychology conditions are having a negative impact on the child's performance. Finally, Dr. Myers solicits feedback from her patients and their parents about the telepsychology testing experience and uses this information to improve her telepsychology practice.

Key Points From the Chapter to Remember

- Psychologists make sure that the psychometrics of tests and the conditions under which the manual prescribes administration are maintained when adapted for technology.
- The testing environment must either be modified or maintained to meet criteria of test protocols.
- Psychologists should be aware of distractions or any other stimuli in the remote environment that could affect performance or the test environment protocols.

- Psychologists must be cognizant of factors that could arise regarding diverse populations (e.g., language, culture, impairments) and correct or accommodate those factors.
- Psychologists must be deliberate in choosing or using technologies that are used and the hardware needed to conduct the test or assessment.
- Psychologists must be prepared to account for and explain differences in results obtained from face-to-face versus remote administration of tests.
- Psychologists must be aware of and able to explain any modification or accommodations made for telepsychology service.
- Psychologists must be alert to and use norms that are developed for telecommunication technologies.
- Psychologists must be aware of potential limitations of testing conducted through telecommunications technologies and ready to explain the effects of the limitations.

References

Adjorlolo, S., & Chan, H. C. (2015). Forensic assessment via videoconferencing: Issues and practice considerations. *Journal of Forensic Psychology Practice, 15,* 185–204. http://dx.doi.org/10.1080/15228932.2015.1015363

Cullum, C. M., & Grosch, M. (2013). Special considerations in conducting neuropsychology assessment over videoteleconferencing. In K. Myers & C. L. Turvey (Eds.), *Telemental health: Clinical, technical, and administrative foundations for evidence-based practice* (pp. 275–293). Waltham, MA: Elsevier.

Cullum, C. M., Hynan, L. S., Grosch, M., Parikh, M., & Weiner, M. F. (2014). Teleneuropsychology: Evidence for video teleconference-based neuropsychological assessment. *Journal of the International Neuropsychological Society, 20,* 1028–1033. http://dx.doi.org/10.1017/S1355617714000873

Galusha-Glasscock, J. M., Horton, D. K., Weiner, M. F., & Munro Cullum, C. (2016). Video teleconference administration of the Repeatable Battery for the Assessment of Neuropsychological Status. *Archives of Clinical Neuropsychology, 31,* 8–11. http://dx.doi.org/10.1093/arclin/acv058

Godleski, L., Nieves, J. E., Darkins, A., & Lehmann, L. (2008). VA telemental health: Suicide assessment. *Behavioral Sciences & the Law, 26,* 271–286. http://dx.doi.org/10.1002/bsl.811

Grosch, M. C., Weiner, M. F., Hynan, L. S., Shore, J., & Cullum, C. M. (2015). Video teleconference-based neurocognitive screening in geropsychiatry. *Psychiatry Research, 225,* 734–735. http://dx.doi.org/10.1016/j.psychres.2014.12.040

Hildebrand, R., Chow, H., Williams, C., Nelson, M., & Wass, P. (2004). Feasibility of neuropsychological testing of older adults via videoconference: Implications for assessing the capacity for independent living. *Journal of Telemedicine and Telecare, 10,* 130–134. http://dx.doi.org/10.1258/135763304323070751

Jacobsen, S. E., Sprenger, T., Andersson, S., & Krogstad, J. M. (2003). Neuropsychological assessment and telemedicine: A preliminary study examining the reliability of neuropsychology services performed via telecommunication. *Journal of the International Neuropsychological Society, 9,* 472–478. http://dx.doi.org/10.1017/S1355617703930128

Joint Task Force for the Development of Telepsychology Guidelines for Psychologists. (2013). Guidelines for the practice of telepsychology. *American Psychologist, 68,* 791–800. Retrieved from https://www.apa.org/pubs/journals/features/amp-a0035001.pdf

Kirkwood, K. T., Peck, D. F., & Bennie, L. (2000). The consistency of neuropsychological assessments performed via telecommunication and face to face. *Journal of Telemedicine and Telecare, 6,* 147–151. http://dx.doi.org/10.1258/1357633001935239

Kobak, K. A. (2004). A comparison of face-to-face and videoconference administration of the Hamilton Depression Rating Scale. *Journal of Telemedicine and Telecare, 10,* 231–235. http://dx.doi.org/10.1258/1357633041424368

Kobak, K. A., Williams, J. B., Jeglic, E., Salvucci, D., & Sharp, I. R. (2008). Face-to-face versus remote administration of the Montgomery–Åsberg Depression Rating Scale using videoconference and telephone. *Depression and Anxiety, 25,* 913–919. http://dx.doi.org/10.1002/da.20392

Litwack, S., Jackson, C., Chen, M., Sloan, D., Hatgis, C., Litz, B., & Marx, B. (2014). Validation of the use of video teleconferencing technology in the assessment of PTSD. *Psychological Services, 11,* 209–294.

Loh, P. K., Ramesh, P., Maher, S., Saligari, J., Flicker, L., & Goldswain, P. (2004). Can patients with dementia be assessed at a distance? The use of telehealth and standardised assessments. *Internal Medicine Journal, 34,* 239–242. http://dx.doi.org/10.1111/j.1444-0903.2004.00531.x

Luxton, D. D., Pruitt, L. D., & Jenkins-Guarnieri, M. A. (2015). Clinical assessment in clinical videoconferencing. In P. W. Tuerk & P. Shore (Eds.), *Clinical videoconferencing in telehealth* (pp. 203–220). New York, NY: Springer International.

Luxton, D. D., Pruitt, L. D., & Osenbach, J. E. (2014). Best practices for remote psychological assessment via telehealth technologies. *Professional Psychology: Research and Practice, 45,* 27–35. http://dx.doi.org/10.1037/a0034547

Nelson, E.-L., Barnard, M., & Cain, S. (2006). Feasibility of telemedicine intervention for childhood depression. *Counselling & Psychotherapy Research, 6,* 191–195. http://dx.doi.org/10.1080/14733140600862303

Nelson, E.-L., & Bui, T. (2010). Rural telepsychology services for children and adolescents. *Journal of Clinical Psychology, 66,* 490–501.

Parakh, M., Ghosh, D., & Mehta, V. S. (2014). Web based assessment: New avenues in psychological testing. *Indian Journal of Health and Wellbeing, 5,* 504–506.

Pirelli, G., Otto, R. K., & Estoup, A. (2016). Using Internet and social media data as collateral sources of information in forensic evaluations. *Professional Psychology: Research and Practice, 47,* 12–17. http://dx.doi.org/10.1037/pro0000061

Porcari, C. E., Amdur, R. L., Koch, E. I., Richard, D. C., Favorite, T., Martis, B., & Liberzon, I. (2009). Assessment of post-traumatic stress disorder in veterans by videoconferencing and by face-to-face methods. *Journal of Telemedicine and Telecare, 15,* 89–94. http://dx.doi.org/10.1258/jtt.2008.080612

San Francisco Suicide Prevention. (2007). Retrieved from http://www.sfsuicide.org/about-sfsp/history

U.S. Army Medical Command. (2012). *Tele-behavioral health operations manual.* Fort Sam Houston, TX: Author.

Vestal, L., Smith-Olinde, L., Hicks, G., Hutton, T., & Hart, J., Jr. (2006). Efficacy of language assessment in Alzheimer's disease: Comparing in-person examination and telemedicine. *Clinical Interventions in Aging, 1,* 467–471.

Wadsworth, H. E., Galusha-Glasscock, J. M., Womack, K. B., Quiceno, M., Weiner, M. F., Hynan, L. S., . . . Cullum, C. M. (2016). Remote neuropsychological assessment in rural American Indians with and without cognitive impairment. *Archives of Clinical Neuropsychology, 31,* 420–425. http://dx.doi.org/10.1093/arclin/acw030

Stephen T. DeMers, Eric A. Harris, and Deborah C. Baker

8 Interjurisdictional Practice

Psychologists are encouraged to be familiar with and comply with all relevant laws and regulations when providing telepsychology services to clients/patients across jurisdictional and international borders.

—Guideline 8, *Guidelines for the Practice of Telepsychology*

Rationale

With the rapid advances in telecommunication technologies, the intentional or unintentional provision of psychological services across jurisdictional and international borders is becoming more of a reality for psychologists. Such service provision may range from the psychologists or clients/patients being temporarily out of state (including split residence across states) to psychologists offering their

---

Editors' Note: Despite the challenges outlined in this chapter, interjurisdictional telepsychology practice, both its facilitation and regulation to ensure competent ethical practice, is a high priority for all constituencies involved. The federal government is promoting telepractice across many fields. At the time of this printing, the Association of State and Provincial Psychology Boards had developed and is promoting an interstate compact for interjurisdictional telepsychology practice and temporary in-person practice. The American Psychological Association, The Trust, and other professional associations are providing guidance, programing, and services, including malpractice coverage. There are private companies sprouting up to address the infrastructure challenges and the training needs and provide technical support and consultation. This broad commitment to establishing structures will allow for effective, ethical, and legal telepsychology practice to be more readily available for patients and more easily provided by psychologists in the future.

http://dx.doi.org/10.1037/0000046-009
A Telepsychology Casebook: Using Technology Ethically and Effectively in Your Professional Practice, L. F. Campbell, F. Millán, and J. N. Martin (Editors)

> services across jurisdictional borders as a practice modality to take advantage of new telecommunication technologies. Psychological service delivery systems within such institutions as the U.S. Department of Defense and the Department of Veterans Affairs have already established internal policies and procedures for providing services within their systems that cross jurisdictional and international borders. However, the laws and regulations that govern service delivery by psychologists outside of those systems vary by state, province, territory, and country (APA Practice Organization, 2010). Psychologists should make reasonable efforts to be familiar with and, as appropriate, to address the laws and regulations that govern telepsychology service delivery within the jurisdictions in which they are situated and the jurisdictions where their clients/patients are located. (Joint Task Force for the Development of Telepsychology Guidelines for Psychologists, 2013, p. 799)

The *Guidelines for the Practice of Telepsychology* (Joint Task Force, 2013) conclude with a focus on special considerations created when one engages in telepsychology practice across state or provincial territorial boundaries. Regulation of all professional services, including those provided by psychologists, is governed by state and provincial laws, not federal regulations or statutes. This guideline recognizes that the power of and opportunities presented by new digital technologies make the routine provision of interjurisdictional telepsychology practically inevitable. It also recognizes that psychologists and other mental health professionals are likely already providing such services. Additionally, this guideline acknowledges that "the laws and regulations that govern service delivery by psychologists outside of those (federal) systems vary by state, province, territory, and country" (APA, 2010, as cited in Joint Task Force, 2013, p. 799), so it is incumbent on the psychologist to be "aware of the relevant laws and regulations impacting telepractice both where the psychologist is located and where the patient or client is located (if different from where the psychologist is)" (Joint Task Force, 2013, p. 799).

It is important to note that concerns about other jurisdictions' requirements mentioned in this guideline pertain mostly to providing services to clients in different jurisdictions than those in which a psychologist is licensed, and they likely may not apply if a psychologist is using telehealth technology to provide services to a client who is in the same state where the psychologist is located and licensed to practice psychology. To be sure, however, even within the same jurisdiction, the application of regulations, being familiar with rules and regulations approved by the state, as well as changes, and familiarity with the interjurisdictional status of telepsychology practice in one's state are critically important. The psychologist's state licensure laws and other relevant state policies govern that interaction, and the same risk management strategies apply. Current licensing laws, intended to protect consumers within that state, were developed at a time when psychological interventions were provided in person where the psychologist and client are in the same state and, often, the same room. Some states and provinces have adopted special provisions for the delivery of psychological services using telecommunications technology. Psychologists providing such services within their home state or any state where they hold a license to practice should make sure they are familiar with and comply with any relevant state statute or rule that has been promulgated by their own state board of examiners involving boundaries, informed consent, confidentiality, and other factors that carry across modalities.

However, many states, provinces, and territories have not updated or amended their laws or rules to address telepsychology practice. The typical psychology licensing act in force today did not anticipate the remote provision of services through a variety of technological modalities. Attempts to apply current laws to the provision of digital interjurisdictional transactions, including the provision of medical and psychological services, have been unsuccessful in producing agreement among commentators and different governmental agencies as to what is or is not permitted. This lack of consensus makes clear guidance about provision of professional services in which a client is located in a different jurisdiction than the psychologist difficult. For this reason, Guideline 8 (Joint Task Force, 2013, p. 799) does not offer specific direction for lawfully engaging in telepractice across jurisdictional lines.

Questions to Consider for Interjurisdictional Practice of Telepsychology

The lack of uniformity among states' laws and the lack of a clear legal mechanism for facilitating interjurisdictional practice prompt a number of key questions that must be addressed to practice telepsychology across jurisdictional boundaries in compliance with current laws and rules. These questions are listed and discussed next.

WHERE DOES THE TRANSACTION ACTUALLY TAKE PLACE?

This question is at the root of the legal controversy over which set of laws govern interjurisdictional transactions. Where does the therapy legally occur when a psychologist provides services from where he or she is licensed to a client who is located in another state where the psychologist is not licensed? Because we do not yet have laws and regulations governing transactions in cyberspace, a decision has to be made as to which jurisdiction's laws and policies govern—the state where the psychologist is located and licensed or the state where the client is located and receives services? This is an important distinction because it affects actions a psychologist must take in certain circumstances. For example, State A may require a psychologist to break confidentiality if a client threatens self-harm or harm to an identifiable third party, whereas State B provides no exceptions to confidentiality to address potential violence by the client. The requirements for record keeping and a client's access to records may differ from one jurisdiction to another. If insurance benefits are involved, one state may require coverage for telehealth services, whereas another state may not have such a mandate. At the time of this writing, 29 states plus the District of Columbia have enacted insurance mandates prohibiting insurance companies from refusing to cover health care services provided via telehealth if those same services would be covered if provided in person (Baker, 2015). Absent specific federal or multijurisdictional guidance, appropriate professional delivery of services is not entirely clear-cut.

IS THE PSYCHOLOGIST REQUIRED TO BE LICENSED WHERE THE CLIENT IS?

A number of jurisdictions take the position that the client's state or province has regulatory jurisdiction and that health care providers must therefore be licensed where the client is at the time services are rendered regardless of whether the services are provided in person or via telehealth technology. For example, California has a telehealth statute that specifically requires that health care providers who deliver health care services to clients in California via telehealth must be licensed in California (Telehealth Advancement Act, 2011). Similarly, Georgia requires providers who offer health services to Georgia residents via telehealth be duly licensed (Georgia Telemedicine Act, 2015). In fact, the Georgia State Board of Examiners of Psychologists "will report out-of-state psychologists to their respective licensing boards for practicing psychology via these means in the state of Georgia without a Georgia license" (Georgia Comp. R. & Regs., 2004). Mississippi defines the practice of psychology to include any of the enumerated services or interventions that are provided to individuals, families, groups, systems, organizations, and the public whether via face to face, telephone, Internet, or telehealth (Miss. Code Ann., 2015). This view that providers are considered to be practicing in the state where the client is located and therefore subject to that state's licensure requirements has been affirmed at the federal level as well. However, federal opinion on the issue is also divided. A federal agency has opined that "In the absence of specific agreements . . . states may not discipline healthcare professionals not licensed in their state if patient harm occurs as the result of the provision of health care services by an out of state practitioner" (Wakefield, 2010). State boards of examiners are authorized by their state to discipline psychologists licensed in their state and, with few exceptions, do not have the authority to discipline psychologists who are licensed in other jurisdictions. As a result, licensing boards typically refer complaints to the jurisdiction in which the psychologist is licensed.

Although some licensure exceptions may exist, such as the temporary practice provision found in most states' psychology practice acts, those exceptions are not intended to facilitate long-term practice into another state without a license. States differ as to who may be exempt from psychology licensure requirements. For example, one state may exempt those who teach psychology or who engage in research and provide services to organizations or institutions, whereas a neighboring state may not recognize all of those exemption categories. Certain state laws or procedures, such as the process for contacting emergency services when a client is in crisis or even initiating involuntary commitment proceedings, may authorize only certain providers licensed in the state where the client is. Significantly, this means that providers licensed and practicing in another state may have neither the legal authority nor the qualified immunity to report suspected abuse or hospitalize a client who is in a different state.

WHY IS THE PSYCHOLOGY LICENSING BOARD IN THE CLIENT'S STATE CONCERNED ABOUT A LICENSED PSYCHOLOGIST IN ANOTHER STATE?

It is important to keep in mind that the role of the licensing board is to protect the health, safety, and welfare of the state's residents and to make sure that its laws and regulations are enforced. The state establishes procedures for licensing health care providers and regulating their practice within the state as well as providing a forum wherein concerns about a licensee can be submitted to the licensing board. The board can evaluate the merits of the complaint and, if necessary, investigate and even discipline the provider. Whether communicating with a client by telephone, videoconferencing, or e-mail, the licensing board's objective is to ensure that qualified individuals are providing services to clients within the state in a safe, appropriate, and ethical manner. So it is important for the licensing board to know who is providing services or engaging in licensable activities in the state.

Where opinions likely differ, however, is on the kind of authority the licensing board has over an out-of-state psychologist. This is where the state's authority under the Tenth Amendment of the Constitution to regulate activities within its borders may conflict with the Constitution's Commerce Clause, which reserves Congress's right to regulate interstate commerce. As discussed earlier, the rationale for state licensing boards' oversight of licensed health care activities is based on the consumer protection mandate. Depending on the individual state's laws and regulations, the penalty for practicing without a license may vary from an administrative remedy (e.g., a cease and desist order, an injunction) to a civil fine or even a criminal offense (in most cases, a misdemeanor but in at least one state, a felony).

For those who engage in unauthorized practice within the state, the state's authority to impose a penalty is clear. It is not clear whether or how a state's jurisdictional authority extends to someone outside of its jurisdictional boundaries, however. Without jurisdiction, the state cannot impose penalties of any kind. Given the lack of consensus about which jurisdiction has regulatory authority over health care services provided via technology in cyberspace, what follows looks at how the courts have interpreted who has jurisdiction when providers and patients are in different states.

Minimum Contacts Analysis for State's Jurisdiction Over Out-of-State Practitioners

State jurisdiction over citizens of other states has been the subject of case law around the country. The courts' determination is based on the application of the "minimum contacts" rule to the specific facts and circumstances of an individual case. Under the minimum contacts rule, a state "cannot assert personal jurisdiction over an out-of-state resident in a civil proceeding unless he has purposefully availed himself of the privileges and benefits of conducting activities within the forum" (*International Shoe Co. v. Washington*, 1945).

No bright line test has emerged to define exactly what facts constitute sufficient contacts by the provider aimed at the forum state (i.e., the state in which a lawsuit is filed). So the courts have ruled both ways, finding in some cases that the out-of-state practitioner is subject to the state's jurisdiction and deciding under other circumstances that jurisdiction is lacking.

Generally, the courts have not exercised jurisdiction in cases where the patient travels to another state where the provider resides or is located for diagnosis and treatment. However, in those cases where the doctor–patient relationship crossed state lines, the courts tended to focus on the kinds of contacts or activities and the frequency that the provider had with the forum state in determining whether it had jurisdiction in the underlying malpractice case.

In most cases, the courts have held that the mere fact that a patient received treatment in the state where the practitioner is located and returns to his or her own state where the effects of such treatment might be felt is insufficient to confer jurisdiction. In those cases, the courts determined that any contacts the provider might have had within the forum state were routine, follow-up actions, not the acts constituting diagnosis and treatment giving rise to the malpractice claims. Activities deemed by the courts as insufficient for jurisdiction include sending a refill prescription to a pharmacy in the patient's state for medication that plaintiff had been prescribed previously (*Wright v. Yackley*, 1972), follow-up calls checking on the patient's status (*Prince v. Urban*, 1996), and sending letters confirming diagnoses and treatment recommendations made outside the forum state (*Bradley v. Mayo Foundation*, 1999).

Conversely, it appears that the courts have been inclined to find jurisdiction in those cases where the patient successfully alleged an ongoing provider–client relationship across state lines. Examples of the facts indicating an ongoing relationship include mailing prescription medications to the patient in the forum state (*Bullion v. Gillespie*, 1990) and providing subsequent advice about treatment and medication via telephone calls to the patient in the forum state (*Walsh v. Chez*, 2006). For example, in *Jones v. Williams* (2009), the California court ruled that weekly telephone therapy provided by a therapist licensed in New Mexico to a patient in California, as well as the therapist's traveling to California at that patient's request to provide in-person therapy, was sufficient for the provider to be subject to California's jurisdiction.

But the most notable case is *Hageseth v. Superior Court of San Mateo County* (2007) in which a Colorado psychiatrist was charged with practicing medicine in California without a license, a felony, for prescribing psychotropic medications to a California resident through an online pharmacy. California decided to extradite Hageseth to California to stand trial. The psychiatrist tried to argue that California had no jurisdictional authority to prosecute him as he was never in California nor had he acted through any agent in California. However, the California appellate court ruled that although he wrote the prescription in Colorado, he knew or should have known that the online prescription would be filled and mailed to the individual in California, thereby resulting in unlicensed practice of medicine being "consummated" in California and thus meeting the minimum contacts test. On that basis, the appellate court ruled that California had jurisdiction.

It is hard to draw clear conclusions about how to rationalize the different court interpretations of the minimum contacts rule and apply them to actual cases that psychologists encounter. Most case law that explicates telepractice is taken from the medical profession; extrapolation to psychology does not yet have a rich history of case law. The clearest guidance comes from the court's interpretation in *Prince v. Urban* (1996). In this case, a patient traveled from California to a center of medical excellence in Illinois to get treatment for headaches. When she returned to California, she communicated regularly with the doctors in Illinois to get follow-up care and advice. When she did not get better, she tried to bring suit in California claiming that the telephone conversations with the doctors constituted practice in California, giving the California courts jurisdiction. The court said no, enunciating the following three principles that determined whether the minimum contacts test would be met and would give the patient's location state jurisdiction:

1. Was the doctor–patient relationship created because of a systematic and continuing effort by the doctor to provide services in the client's state or was the location incidental?
2. Were the doctors' services grounded in any relationship that they had with the state (i.e., did they have offices in the state, were they seeking reimbursement for the services from the state)?
3. Did the state's interest in providing good medical care for its citizens outweigh the potential and severity of any reasonably anticipated harm?

The court's language in analyzing the third principle above is important and instructive:

> In the case of personal services, focus must be on the place where the services are rendered, since this is the place of the receiver's (here the patient's) need. The need is personal, and the services rendered are in response to the dimensions of that personal need. They are directed to no place but to the needy person himself/herself. . . . [The] "dominant interest" of a state regarding patients/clients is "not that they should be free of injury by out-of-state doctors, but rather that they should be able to secure adequate medical services to meet their needs wherever they may go." (*Prince v. Urban*, as cited in *Wright v. Yackley*, 1972)

The following four principles offer a preliminary basis for risk management guidance to psychologists contemplating providing telepsychology to patients:

1. The relationship between the psychologist and the patient comes from the patient's initiative and not as the result of the psychologist's attempt to advertise services interjurisdictionally or the psychologist's participation in a commercial enterprise that provides interjurisdictional services.
2. There is a clear rationale that providing services using telepsychology would be at least equal, if not superior, to those services which the client could receive through an in-person referral to a provider in the client's jurisdiction.

3. The psychologist takes reasonable steps to ensure the competence of his or her work and to protect clients and others from harm. This means psychologists at a minimum are conversant and compliant with all of the telepsychology guidelines developed by the Joint Task Force (2013).
4. The psychologist has conducted a conservative assessment of the client's diagnosis, history, and risk level and determined that these factors do not contraindicate providing services via technology.

If these conditions are met, then one may have a persuasive argument that the state's interest in providing good medical care to its citizens outweighs the potential and severity of any reasonably anticipated harm posed by an out-of-state clinician providing services. It would also be unlikely that the state would seek to take action in such a case given the difficulty and uncertainty of action. Further, allowing these services does not leave consumers dissatisfied or feeling harmed without recourse. They can always file a complaint with the licensing board of the state in which the psychologist is licensed and providing services. Although this could create logistical issues that would make it hard for the psychologist's licensing board to investigate and adjudicate, it would not be impossible.

Regulators might agree with the described risk management strategy but would very likely view interstate telepsychology practice as a high-risk venture. There is currently no legal mechanism that would permit a psychologist to engage in telepractice in another state where he or she is not licensed (other than the temporary practice statutes mentioned earlier). So unless a psychologist has multiple licenses or is exempt from licensure, regulators would contend that the psychologist engaging in interstate telepractice is not lawfully practicing psychology in those other states and is thus risking some disciplinary consequence.

Admittedly, pursuing or prosecuting psychologists engaging in unlawful interjurisdictional telepractice may be quite difficult. States have limited resources they can devote to disciplinary proceedings against psychologists. Pursuing out-of-state psychologists who provide services to clients in their states involves a number of legal and procedural difficulties that would require considerable financial expense, time, and energy. To proceed criminally against a psychologist, a state would have to extradite the offending psychologist. The question of whether a state could impose civil fines is also debatable. Some believe the state may be limited to issuing a cease and desist order or other injunctive relief. A cease and desist order is commonly issued for the in-person practice of psychology by other mental health professionals and can be issued to psychologists practicing in the jurisdiction without a license. This is a common and easily employed strategy. However, the consequences of a cease and desist order, a fine, or certainly any criminal complaint against a psychologist for practicing without a license could be significant. Although it may be difficult to imagine that a state would use its scarce resources to prosecute a psychologist who complies with the preceding guidelines and carefully considers ethical and lawful professional practice standards or guidelines, the circumstances of the individual client as well as the potential risks of such practice given current uncertainties should give any prudent psychologist reason to proceed with great caution.

Given the short length of time that interstate telepsychology has been practiced, there are limited actuarial data about the disciplinary risks involved. There are some data to suggest that many psychologists are providing telepsychology services across state lines. There are cases in which state licensing boards issued cease and desist orders, but few, if any, reported disciplinary sanctions against an out-of-state licensed psychologist for providing telepsychology services to a client within that state's licensing board jurisdiction.

Nevertheless, it is important to note that these issues are unresolved at the time of this writing and certainly not unique to telehealth or telepsychology. Witness the fact that it is still not clear whether consumers of Amazon and other large online retailers have to pay state sales taxes. The issues related to interjurisdictional practice will take time and effort to resolve before a practitioner can safely understand the new "rules of the road" when it comes to interjurisdictional telepsychology. The increasing demand for telehealth services has, however, cast a sharper focus on these issues, resulting in some stakeholders calling for either a national or federal solution to the current interjurisdictional barriers or other possible state-based solutions to facilitate interstate telepractice to help clarify these unresolved issues.

Federal Initiatives to Address Interstate Practice

The growing demand for telehealth services has prompted increasing calls at the federal level either to institute policies or to remove obstacles to better facilitate telehealth practice around the country. One idea is to institute a national health care provider licensure system analogous to driver's licenses. The provider would obtain licensure in the state of his or her residence. That license would be recognized by other states if the provider is practicing in another state. Should the provider change his or her residence, then the expectation is that he or she would then move licensure to the new state. However, there is much resistance from state regulators and other stakeholders to this idea because of concerns about federalism, decreased ability to oversee appropriate credentialing of providers, and a lack of means for disciplining bad actors.

Other proposals call for lifting existing practice restrictions. For example, in 2011, Congress passed the Servicemembers' Telemedicine and E-Health Portability (STEP) Act that allows health care providers credentialed in the U.S. Defense Department (DoD) to treat military personnel at any location regardless of where the provider or patient is located, so long as the provider is practicing within the scope of his or her authorized duties. Specifically, the STEP Act expanded the DoD state licensure exemption to allow credentialed providers to work across state borders without having to obtain a new state license, expanded the definition of exempt health care professional to include qualified DoD civilian contractors, and removed the service location requirement to allow for care regardless of where the health care professional or patient is located. The DoD, however, has jurisdiction over its employees apart from location and can determine the location of any employee, thereby making the DoD an entity that commands authority that jurisdictions do not have. Further, the DoD has state-of-the-art technology that allows services to be rendered by a military psychologist in Austin, Texas, to a deployed military person in a foreign country.

A similar proposal for the Department of Veterans Affairs (VA) has been pursued in Congress. The Veterans E-Health & Telemedicine Support (VETS; 2015a, 2015b) Act would allow a licensed health care professional credentialed through the VA to provide telehealth services anywhere in the United States including the District of Columbia, or a U.S. commonwealth, territory, or possession, regardless of whether the provider or patient is located at a federal government facility. The current version of the VETS Act (HR 2516; 2015a) and its companion bill (S 2170; 2015b) were introduced in 2015.

Likewise, federal legislators have been lobbied to ease restrictions under Medicare for telehealth services. One example is the TELEmedicine for MEDicare (TELE-MED) Act (2015a, 2015b). This bill seeks to amend the Social Security Act to allow a Medicare provider to provide telehealth services to a Medicare beneficiary who is in a different state from the one in which the provider is licensed or authorized to provide health care services. This proposal would vest authority in the state where the provider is licensed to regulate the delivery of health care services, instead of the state where the patient or beneficiary is. Like the VETS Act, the TELE-MED Act has been introduced over the past few congressional sessions. The current bills (S1778 and HR 3081; 2015a, 2015b) were introduced during the summer of 2015.

Another legislative example is the Medicare Telehealth Parity Act (2015), which seeks to expand incrementally the coverage of telehealth services under the Medicare program. Specifically, this proposal seeks to extend the definition of "originating site" (location where the patient receives services via telehealth) to include any federally qualified health center, any rural health clinic, and the patient's home (for outpatient mental and behavioral services, hospice care, home dialysis, or home health services). It would add respiratory therapy, physical therapy, occupational therapy, audiology, and speech pathology to the lists of covered telehealth services and approved telehealth providers. It would also increase the geographic areas where Medicare beneficiaries would be eligible to receive telehealth services because Medicare currently limits coverage to mainly rural areas. The current proposal (HR 2948) was introduced in July 2015.

Those are a few examples of the growing number of legislative proposals introduced in Congress to facilitate telepractice. Although many have not progressed very far through the legislative process, these concepts are gaining traction among legislators as calls for solutions from the health care and patient communities, as well as the technology industry, continue to build.

Multistate Licensure Compacts

Concurrent with increasing legislative activity at the federal level, some regulatory bodies are considering the multistate compact as a mechanism to facilitate interjurisdictional telepsychology practice (IJTP). The Nursing Licensure Compact grants registered and licensed practical and vocational nurses licensed in any of the current 25 compact states the ability to practice, physically or electronically, in both their home state and other compact states (National Council of State Boards of Nursing, 2000). If a nurse moves to another jurisdiction, the nurse would either need to declare a new primary residence if in another compact state or obtain licensure by endorsement if in a noncompact state. There is a separate compact for advanced practice nurses.

The Federation of State Medical Boards (2013) recently developed the Interstate Compact to Expedite Medical Licensure and Facilitate Multi-State Practice. This compact would allow for qualified physicians seeking licensure in multiple states to pursue expedited licensing in all compact states. Its focus is license portability and uniform licensing requirements. Therefore, the medical compact still requires physicians to obtain medical licenses in each state where the physician practices. The compact would not grant a multistate licensure similar to the Nursing Licensure Compact. In 2015, 11 states enacted enabling legislation establishing the compact.

In 2015, the Association of State and Provincial Psychology Boards (ASPPB) announced the development of a similar compact proposal, the Psychology Interjurisdictional Compact (PSYPACT), which would authorize licensed psychologists in PSYPACT states to engage in "telepsychology and temporary in-person, face-to-face practice of psychology across state lines." Like the Nursing Licensure Compact and the medical compact, participating state licensing boards would agree to share information about licensure verification, complaints, and investigations. The Medical Board Compact requires licensure in each compact state; however, the PSYPACT for psychologists would be similar to the Nursing COMPACT in which psychologists would only be required to be licensed in their home jurisdiction. However, the authority to revoke a psychologist's license would rest with the licensing board in the jurisdiction where the psychologist is licensed. Starting with the 2016 state legislative season in the United States, ASPPB's plan was to introduce PSYPACT legislation in several states open to such initiatives. PSYPACT, like other compacts, is written such that at least seven states must pass the compact legislation before PSYPACT can become operational.

Until a mechanism like PSYPACT takes effect and is operational in all 50 states and U.S. territories, the challenges of practicing psychology across state lines without multiple licenses remain. In this chapter, the authors present three case studies that highlight the complexities of telepsychology practice when practicing across state lines within the regulatory environment at the time this was written. The risk management and regulatory perspectives for each case study are described and contrasted. Readers can evaluate their own situations and gauge the potential risks and benefits. Not surprisingly, all sides will not necessarily agree on an approach, underscoring why practitioners should give careful consideration to how to proceed if they are thinking about engaging in telepsychology across state lines. It should be noted that specific states identified in any of the case examples are used strictly for illustrative purposes, demonstrating the thought process for considering whether to engage in telepsychology across jurisdictional lines.

Case Study 1: IJTP for Continuity of Care

Dr. Innovative has been licensed in Rhode Island for 15 years. During that time, she has specialized in working with adolescents and young adults. She has experience working for college counseling centers in the past, although she is now exclusively in private practice. She had been seeing a now 18-year-old client for 3 years. Her client will be going to college in Colorado in the fall and wants to continue treatment with Dr. Innovative via phone or videoconferencing. The parents are strongly supportive of this.

The client comes from an upper-middle-class family and experiences considerable stress and tension precipitated by high academic performance expectations both internally and externally. She works hard and often has problems completing work because of anxiety that her work is not good enough. Her parents are divorced and still in some conflict with one another, which has caused considerable discomfort for the client on occasion. There is a great deal of pressure on the client from parents who greatly value intellectual performance and professional success. The client reports feeling that pressure acutely and has periods of intense anxiety. The client has a diagnosis of generalized anxiety disorder rendered by a previous therapist with which Dr. Innovative concurs.

The client also uses the treatment to deal with normal developmental issues faced in late adolescence and her concerns about going to college. She had a couple of failed treatment episodes during the period of conflict between the parents and before Dr. Innovative took over the client's care. Dr. Innovative and the client have a very strong alliance, and the client feels Dr. Innovative has helped her greatly. She says that she would not start with someone else while away at college because she says it would be too much trouble to get to know someone new, and she is doubtful it would work anyway. The parents are willing to pay out-of-pocket. The client will see Dr. Innovative in person when she returns home during breaks, including Thanksgiving, Christmas, spring break, and over the summer.

The client has a psychiatrist who has prescribed a minimal dosage of a benzodiazepine for anxiety. Her psychiatrist is willing to monitor her medications and to see her on vacations but will only do this if Dr. Innovative continues on the case because he feels it isn't responsible to prescribe when he doesn't know the therapist.

Dr. Innovative considers herself to be a novice in using technology. She has some knowledge of how to operate safely online, but she has never used videoconferencing technology except to Skype with her relatives, children, and friends. Dr. Innovative is willing to consider taking on the challenge but seeks advice about what she would have to do to minimize risk.

RISK MANAGEMENT PERSPECTIVE

The first step is to consider the clinical presentation involved by comparing the proposed telepsychology treatment to making a referral to a competent colleague in Colorado for in-person therapy or referring to the university counseling center. The university counseling center has its limitations because its aim is to provide short-term counseling services, which is not what this client wants nor would it be the optimal treatment.

There are certainly a number of competent private practitioners in the vicinity of the college, but one would have to be found, and it would be hard to determine in advance whether the relationship would work out as well as the current relationship between the client and Dr. Innovative. Further, a new psychiatrist would have to be recruited. Finally, the new psychologist would not be available during vacations and both the client and her parents would want Dr. Innovative to be available during these times.

All of these issues lead to the conclusion that most likely, continuing the existing, already beneficial therapy relationship presents the best chance for success. Of course, Dr. Innovative should consider whether the client's dependence on her is developmentally problematic and whether it is a good time for the client to separate. If Dr. Innovative determines that her continuation would be the most productive option, then there are a number of other issues she should consider:

1. Dr. Innovative would have to carefully examine the telepsychology guidelines developed jointly by APA, ASPPB, and The Trust (Joint Task Force, 2013). Because she has little experience in providing services remotely but has considerable experience with providing psychotherapy services both to this client and others with similar issues, she might have some doubts about her competence. To increase her confidence, she might seek out consultation from a colleague who has actual experience in the area, read some of the many articles that are available online about providing remote services, and seek assistance from her ongoing consultation group of seasoned therapists. Dr. Innovative has a learning curve ahead of her in achieving technical competence, clinical competence online as different from in-person, informed consent adaptation, and other significant competency factors.
2. Dr. Innovative should then check to see what kind of temporary practice is permitted in Colorado by a psychologist licensed in another state. Colorado allows for 20 days of practice in a calendar year so long as the psychologist discloses to those he or she is serving that he or she is not licensed in Colorado. That means that Dr. Innovative could legally provide 20 sessions to her client, which would allow her to provide a telepsychology session every other week during the academic year. Dr. Innovative and her client could even choose to conduct extended 2-hour sessions if it were determined to be clinically appropriate.

   Additionally, Dr. Innovative should check to see whether Colorado has a policy about telepractice, and after she discovers that it does have such a policy, she should become familiar with it to ensure compliance. Colorado adopted a telepractice policy applicable to all mental health providers (Department of Regulatory Agencies, 2015) that outlines the issues the mental health provider must identify and address before providing therapy electronically. Not only does this policy recommend that the "initial therapeutic contact be in person and adequate to provide a conclusive diagnosis and therapeutic treatment plan" but the clinician needs to comply with the licensing laws and provide periodic face-to-face visits. Additionally, the policy states that a provider of telepractice needs to identify and address several other criteria both with regard to his or her practice and to challenges that may exist and which are specific to providing psychotherapy electronically. Complying with such a policy is important to risk management.

3. Dr. Innovative ought to do some research about what kind of communication platform would be optimal and meet Health Insurance Portability and Accountability Act (HIPAA; 1996) requirements. A number of online sites provide comprehensive reviews that she could access to research the question. She could also seek the advice of more experienced colleagues through either her state association or divisional electronic mailing lists. Before Dr. Innovative agrees to this arrangement, she might propose that she and the client conduct a couple of videoconferencing sessions to see whether they each feel comfortable with the differences from in-person sessions.
4. Despite the fact that the client is technically an adult, Dr. Innovative could insist on access to the client's parents during the time she is away at school as a condition of her undertaking this kind of treatment. If there are problems at school, Dr. Innovative wants to be sure that she and the parents can operate as a team to support the client.
5. Further, it is recommended that Dr. Innovative seek the client's agreement to check in with the college counseling center to inform them that she is in treatment with Dr. Innovative and provide them with authorization to communicate with Dr. Innovative in the unlikely event that a crisis might arise. In the event of a crisis, the university would be in a much better position to take immediate action.
6. Dr. Innovative might also negotiate some ground rules about the client's behavior during the sessions aimed at creating an environment conducive to therapy. For example, she could require that the client shut down all electronic communication devices, video, music, or other potential distractions during their telepractice sessions. If the client has a roommate, there will need to be negotiation to ensure that the client has the necessary privacy. Dr. Innovative and the client should also have a backup plan should the technology fail or be interrupted as will almost certainly happen from time to time (see Standards of Care, *Guidelines for the Practice of Telepsychology*, Joint Task Force, 2013).
7. Dr. Innovative could clarify with both the client and her parents that since she does not have a great deal of experience providing this mode of treatment that she reserves the right to stop the treatment with time to terminate appropriately if she feels that it is not working (see Standards of Care and Competence, *Guidelines for the Practice of Telepsychology*, Joint Task Force, 2013).

What is the risk to Dr. Innovative? Although unlikely, the client could prove to be unready for college and develop severe anxiety or depression and become suicidal. She could find herself involved with drugs, irresponsible or abusive romantic partners, or even be the victim of sexual assault. Parental disputes could develop about whether

Dr. Innovative is doing a good job. All of these issues could lead to the client's being or feeling harmed. In any and all of these situations, although it may be unlikely, a complaint could be filed with the Colorado psychology licensing board, where the college is located.

If a complaint were filed in Colorado, Colorado would have no jurisdiction over Dr. Innovative and would be limited to either forwarding the complaint to Rhode Island or issuing a cease and desist order. A cease and desist order could be challenged in federal court, although it is unlikely that Dr. Innovative would have the resources to do so, nor would it be advisable to expend the energy involved in such action. However, from a risk management perspective, a cease and desist order does not constitute discipline, although it would have to be listed on applications and could have some consequence for Dr. Innovative. If she chooses to provide telepsychology to her client, Dr. Innovative's risk management strategy would be to provide short-term, limited telepsychology services to her existing patient under the temporary practice provision so long as she follows the requirements and identifies the issues outlined in Colorado's psychology licensing board policy on telemental health. In this case, Dr. Innovative would notify the counseling center and the licensing board of her temporary practice, therefore protecting against a complaint about her right to practice. She could still be subject, of course, to a complaint regarding her specific work with the client just as she is when she sees clients in her office face to face.

At this point, there is little actuarial data that a board has ever processed a complaint or attempted to discipline someone for providing telepsychology services to a client who receives the services in a state different from the one in which the psychologist is located and licensed. There is an increased interest from psychologists who are deciding to engage in this kind of interjurisdictional practice because they feel that it is in the best interests of their clients to continue their investment in helping them with their issues.

The risk for Dr. Innovative, based on the case law and data, is very low. Dr. Innovative is almost certain to have cases in her caseload that present higher risk than this one would present. In the end, when advising psychologists who seek guidance on this issue, risk management consultants go over the case carefully, help the psychologist figure out the pros and cons, including the risk, and leave the choice of whether to continue to the psychologist's personal and professional discretion.

REGULATORY PERSPECTIVE

Colorado, like several other states, has rules related to the provision of psychological services that specifically require the provider to be licensed or certified in Colorado unless the provider meets one of the exemptions. One of those exemptions is practicing under the temporary practice provision that allows a psychologist to practice for 20 days in Colorado without being licensed in Colorado as long as the psychologist is licensed in his or her own state. Providing telepsychology under the temporary practice provision also requires compliance with Colorado's regulations. If Dr. Innovative does not follow the requirements of the temporary practice provision and the telepractice policy, the Colorado board may issue a cease and desist order to Dr. Innovative or report her to the Rhode Island psychology board, with significant consequences for the clinician. For example, even if no sanction is ever assessed, Dr. Innovative would have to disclose in applications for liability insurance or licenses in subsequent states that she had been the subject of a disciplinary complaint or restriction on her license. Consequently, the importance of fully understanding the rules and regulations for temporary practice and telepsychology practice cannot be overestimated. Therefore, in review, it is recommended that Dr. Innovative do the following:

1. Carefully review and consider Colorado's rules or regulations related to the provision of telepsychology services whether within the state or outside the state. Checking with the Colorado State Board of Psychologist Examiners would be the best way to get this information even though there are a number of other ways to research this question.
2. Review Colorado's provision for temporary practice and structure her sessions with her client to be compliant with that. If Dr. Innovative concludes the treatment her client needs cannot be provided within the temporary practice provision requirements and the telepractice policy, she should advise the client and her parents that regardless of the prior relationship, the client would be best served through referral to another licensed provider in Colorado.
3. Consult with colleagues who have expertise and experience in the area of telepractice and her professional malpractice carrier to help her consider all factors before proceeding with providing telepsychology to her client in a different state.

One other avenue for Dr. Innovative is whether a multistate compact has been adopted by the legislatures in Colorado and Rhode Island. If so, then Dr. Innovative could practice in Colorado as long as she is licensed in one of the compact states. Dr. Innovative would still need to consider, however, the telepractice policy as well as all the other concerns about patient privacy, security, and emergency care outlined in the risk management section.

Case Study 2: Industrial–Organizational Setting

Dr. Business is a licensed industrial–organizational (I/O) psychologist with 20 years of experience and a highly regarded professional reputation as a management consultant. Dr. Business is approached by a large U.S. corporation about running a personnel management and evaluation effort for the company's national workforce spread across five states as an independent contractor, not as an employee. Although Dr. Business is licensed in three states, he only has a license in one of the five states where the company has facilities and wants him to evaluate employees. That state is where the company has its main corporate offices. The company tells Dr. Business that they want him to design and implement an online assessment system that will use employee self-ratings plus ratings from peers and supervisors to evaluate employee performance and recommend advancement, retention, or termination based on his findings.

The company stresses to Dr. Business that he is not making the final decision in these cases but that his input will have a major influence on the company's final decision. The company further states that they are looking for someone with his skills and abilities who can deliver these assessments using online tools and possibly interviewing, but there is no money to support travel to provide face-to-face service.

Dr. Business considers the possible risks to him from assessing individuals and recommending advancement, retention, or termination for employees located in a state where he is not licensed. However, he accepts the contract by reasoning that, first, he is not the ultimate decision maker for these employees and, second, that he is licensed where the company's headquarters is located. Dr. Business feels that the company, not the employee, is his client, and therefore he can legally perform these services by using informed consent to make the employees aware of the purpose of his assessments.

RISK MANAGEMENT PERSPECTIVE

The first thing that Dr. Business would have to consider is whether I/O psychology is part of the practice of psychology or is otherwise exempt in the states where he was not licensed. That is, many jurisdictions do not require licensure for consulting or I/O psychologists because they are not health service providers. Dr. Business would need to be aware of licensure status for his specialty before beginning services. Assuming the states in which he needs to work are not exempt, he would be at some risk.

Unlike in Case Study 1 (IJTP for Continuity of Care), there is no question that the company's physical presence in the five states would meet the "minimum contacts" test and, therefore, gives the licensing boards jurisdiction. On the other hand, because all of the professional activities take place where the psychologist is licensed, it might be hard to argue that he is actually practicing across state lines. If the psychologist exclusively used empirical instruments to assess the candidates, it would probably be safer. The actual interviews with someone in a different state would make the process riskier.

In this case, full informed consent is crucial, which requires that Dr. Business also have a clear written contractual understanding with the company as to what the company plans to do with the information and that it will be adequately protected. Dr. Business would be wise to follow the APA (2017) Ethics Code Standard 3.11, which enumerates the requirements for informed consent when working with an organization rather than an individual client.

The company could protect itself from some of its liability exposure by having contracts with employees that either include compulsory arbitration agreements or clauses specifying that the contract would be subject to the laws of the state where the company's home office is located.

But none of this would prevent a disgruntled employee from filing a complaint against Dr. Business with the licensing board in the place where the employee is a resident, and if Dr. Business is not licensed in the same state, this licensing board could take jurisdiction. It could assess fines that the company could agree to pay if this happened, or the licensing board could charge the psychologist with practicing psychology without a license, a criminal offense.

A better solution might be to have the psychologist hire licensed individuals to administer the tests, but it is critical for Dr. Business to determine what each state allows in its licensing laws. If licensed individuals credentialed to practice in the state provide such services, they could also conduct the employee interviews, which could then be forwarded to Dr. Business, who could then do the analysis and advise the company. That would not seem to violate any licensing laws. However, the company might be reluctant to spend the money for these additional professionals.

If a multistate compact were in force, if consulting and I/O psychologists were not required to be licensed in a given state, or if the state allows temporary practice, this case would have a better solution. In the meantime, psychologists have a significant responsibility to follow ethical guidelines and state laws.

REGULATORY PERSPECTIVE

This scenario presents a challenging set of issues. Assuming the company is operating with the best intentions to recruit and retain the most qualified and talented employees possible and that Dr. Business is both competent and willing to develop a valid and reliable assessment system based on the latest employee selection research and best practices, several major obstacles to accepting this arrangement still remain:

1. Is the telepsychology approach of remote evaluations being sought by this company the most valid and appropriate way to provide these employees with assessments? Should an employee feel harmed by the results of such an assessment and decide to take legal action against the company and perhaps the psychologist, can the services provided be justified through a strong evidentiary basis for taking such an approach? This use of telepractice may be efficient and cost-effective for the company and lucrative for the psychologist, but is it valid and defensible for the individuals being assessed?
2. Despite the company's protestations, who is the client? The psychologist and the company may agree that the company is the client here. Then, however, the employees will need to be provided with clear informed consent about the nature and purpose of the evaluations and the confidentiality (or lack of confidentiality), as well as the additional factors noted in the APA (2017) Ethics Code Standard 3.11 afforded in this professional interaction with Dr. Business.
3. Finally, given the high stakes nature of the assessments being planned and conducted by Dr. Business and the fact that livelihoods and careers may be negatively affected, one can anticipate that some employees may challenge the adequacy of their results. Let's say an employee objects to the company assessment and ends up being terminated. If the employee feels harmed by the input from the assessment conducted by Dr. Business, where does he or she receive recourse? If the employee was working in Texas and also evaluated there, but the company is headquartered in California and Dr. Business

is licensed in California but not Texas, which state licensing board has jurisdiction over the professional behavior of Dr. Business? In which state was the professional service of Dr. Business provided? Or was it provided in cyberspace and thus beyond the jurisdiction of either Texas or California? For these reasons, Dr. Business should decline to accept this consulting arrangement unless he is willing to obtain a license in every jurisdiction where an employee will be evaluated.

Case Study 3: IJTP Therapy Practice

Dr. Digital is an early-career psychologist who is interested in leveraging technology and social media to expand his practice. Dr. Digital sees a number of adolescents and young adults within his practice, so he is comfortable using technology to communicate with some of his established clients for limited purposes. He would like to expand his use to grow his practice. He has received solicitations from several online therapy companies interested in adding licensed mental health therapists to their panels. One of the companies, TalkTherapy (a fictitious company used as example), not only offers videoconferencing but also therapy via text messaging and online public forums.

In looking at TalkTherapy, Dr. Digital believes that as part of the application process, he needs to submit information demonstrating that he is actively licensed in good standing in his particular mental health care discipline. The time commitment for working with TalkTherapy appears to be flexible. Its website claims that subscribers may chat with a licensed therapist wherever they may be and at any time.

But what is not clear to Dr. Digital from reviewing the company's website is how the company assigns or connects one of its therapists to a subscriber, whether the company confirms and documents that a subscriber is matched to a therapist appropriately licensed in the jurisdiction where the subscriber is located, or how a session is scheduled once a subscriber logs on to the site. In addition, Dr. Digital is not sure whether he is expected to confirm the identity of individuals with whom he may be connected through the website or whether the company is responsible for that.

The company does state that its therapists are licensed, pass background checks, and are vetted by the company's advisory board. It also claims that it tries to match subscribers to therapists who have special expertise, if applicable, to each individual's needs. But Dr. Digital is not sure how to document his virtual interactions (both videoconferencing and text messaging) with users through this platform. He is not sure whether he is expected to maintain information beyond what the APA (2007) *Record Keeping Guidelines* recommend or whether he is expected to provide a diagnosis or offer psychotherapy based on issues that may arise during his interactions with subscribers.

Furthermore, in his existing private practice, Dr. Digital does accept some forms of insurance and bills the insurance company directly on behalf of the clients he sees in person. Therefore, he is a "covered entity" under HIPAA and is subject to HIPAA's Privacy Rule and Security Rule requirements. He is unclear as to whether he needs to be concerned about whether his involvement with a company like TalkTherapy ought to comply with HIPAA. Although the company states that it is HIPAA compliant, there is no mention of offering a business associate agreement to the therapists who sign up as providers, nor is there mention of whether it is also Health Information Technology for Economic and Clinical Health Act (HITECH; 2009)–compliant.

In addition, some of the types of clients Dr. Digital works with may be considered high-risk—for example, high school students who have been bullied by their peers and young adults who have either been abused as children or are currently in abusive relationships. He wonders whether he should note that as an area of expertise should he decide to join the TalkTherapy network. Because he is not certain that he will know where the subscriber may be located at the time of a videoconferencing or text messaging conversation, he is not sure whether this platform would be appropriate for dealing with those kinds of cases.

RISK MANAGEMENT PERSPECTIVE

There is no question that Dr. Digital would be considered to be an agent of TalkTherapy, a national business that expressly intends to offer services in his and other states. This would clearly meet the "minimum contacts" test and would allow any state where a client resides to assert legal jurisdiction. The fact that this is a national company would also make it more likely that a state licensing board would consider taking action because the company and its business model present a greater threat to consumers than a solo practitioner who is providing services to a client where there is a reasonable justification for providing services other than a commercial motivation. So Dr. Digital would have to be certain that the only clients he is referred actually reside in the state where he is licensed. He should also be aware that if there is a problem and a complaint is filed, he is likely to be evaluated not only on the work that he actually did with the client but on the model that the company is using.

Even if Dr. Digital could establish that the only clients who would be referred to him actually reside within his state, there are a number of questions about the way the program operates that raise clinical issues that could create serious risk management concerns. Dr. Digital does not know how TalkTherapy screens potential clients for appropriateness. Are they interviewed by mental health professionals? Is there any attempt to screen out those who may be inappropriate for teletherapy? If not, Dr. Digital would need to have the ability to conduct an evaluation to determine whether the referred clients would be appropriate for his practice and decide not to provide services to those whom he deems inappropriate.

How is informed consent provided to potential clients? Would Dr. Digital be able to provide clients with the appropriate HIPAA notice forms, or would he have to trust TalkTherapy to provide them and secure the appropriate client signatures? What if clients had questions about confidentiality and limits to confidentiality? Who would answer them? What about parental consent, if the clients are minors? He would need to assess whether he would have any direct access to the clients referred to him or whether all communication would have to go through TalkTherapy. Would a client have to pay in advance to reach Dr. Digital? If so, what would happen if his client had an urgent clinical need and payment was a problem?

Would Dr. Digital be able to establish appropriate ground rules to make sure that remote therapy would meet appropriate professional standards? Would he be able to make a contract with clients to ensure that they were in places that provided adequate privacy and minimized distractions? This would be particularly important with individuals who are accustomed to lives of multitasking and other electronic distractions and could easily leave their cell phones on during treatment.

It is possible that TalkTherapy would have satisfactory answers to all of these questions, but the more that Dr. Digital would have to delegate important legal and ethical responsibilities to TalkTherapy, the more vulnerable he would be if TalkTherapy does not perform them appropriately. If there were a complaint, Dr. Digital would be held responsible for the acts that TalkTherapy performed.

REGULATORY PERSPECTIVE

Dr. Digital seems to have identified a number of troubling and possibly risky aspects of joining the TalkTherapy platform. First, and perhaps foremost for purposes of this chapter, Dr. Digital has not been able to obtain assurance that he will only receive referrals from subscribers residing and receiving services in the state where he holds a license to practice psychology. Although the flexibility of TalkTherapy sounds attractive, it also suggests the very real possibility that therapists are linked with subscribers without regard to the state of residence of either therapist or subscriber. Unless Dr. Digital can obtain such assurance, he is risking a complaint and potential sanction from a state licensing board where he provides services without holding a license. This could come in the form of a cease and desist letter or a charge of practicing without a license.

Even if TalkTherapy assures Dr. Digital that he will only be sent subscribers residing in his state of licensure, he will still need to consider whether his state allows the delivery of psychological services using telecommunications technology and under what circumstances and with what patient safeguards. If his state has passed guidelines for use of technology in the practice of psychology, then Dr. Digital will need to make sure his work with TalkTherapy complies with those guidelines. If his state has not passed telepsychology guidelines, then he has an even larger burden to consider whether this practice modality can be defended as reasonable, competent, and ethical should any complaint arise.

Finally, Dr. Digital's concerns about adequate record keeping, compliance with HIPAA and HITECH requirements, and provisions for emergency situations given the potentially high-risk population must also be satisfied before joining this online therapy service.

Key Points From the Chapter to Remember

- The psychologist must evaluate whether he or she is really interested in providing these kinds of services. There is a certain amount of work in becoming competent to provide the services, including becoming familiar with the Telepsychology Guidelines developed by the APA, ASPPB, and The Trust Joint Task Force (Joint Task Force, 2013) and achieving the technological competence necessary to provide remote services. Also, providing services across state lines involves some disciplinary risk.
- It is important to consider the clinical rationale for providing mental health services remotely via telecommunications technologies. Is the client a good candidate for these services? Is he or she motivated? How serious are his or her symptoms, and how much do they interfere with the client's functioning? Does the client have the capacity to pay for the services out-of-pocket?
- The psychologist ought to carefully consider whether he or she is attempting to market his or her practice online or across state lines. Is the client requesting telepsychology due to work demands, illness, or other reasons?
- The client's location is an important factor to take into account. The psychologist must confirm where the client will be when the telepsychology services would be provided. Is the patient in state or in another jurisdiction? In addition, the psychologist ought to determine whether the client's presence in another jurisdiction is a temporary or time-limited situation. Is the client permanently located in or transferring to another location? Are there equal or better options that do not involve interjurisdictional practice? Can a local emergency contact be arranged?
- It is incumbent on the psychologist to ascertain whether the state or jurisdiction where the client is or will be located has specific policies about telepsychology that would affect the mental health professional wanting to provide telehealth services. If the client is receiving services through federal benefits (e.g., DoD, VA), what are the relevant federal agency policies for providing telehealth services?
- The psychologist should carefully review and consider a state's rules or regulations regarding what kind of temporary practice is permitted in the state by a psychologist licensed in another state and whether it would accept telepractice within the temporary practice framework. Checking with the state's board of psychologist examiners would be the best way to get this information, even though there are a number of other ways to research this question.
- The psychologist is strongly encouraged to consult with his or her professional liability carrier, colleagues, and professional association to make a risk management decision about providing telepsychology services across state lines.

There is clearly no easy answer for when and how a psychologist may provide services via telecommunications technologies to a client who is in a state where the psychologist is not licensed, but, as always, psychologists benefit from consulting with others; keeping the welfare of the client foremost; researching and keeping current regarding regulations, laws, guidelines, and ethics codes; and using a risk management strategy that encourages looking at all options in concert with potential consequences.

References

American Psychological Association. (2007). Record keeping guidelines. *American Psychologist, 62,* 993–1004. http://dx.doi.org/10.1037/0003-066X.62.9.993

American Psychological Association. (2017). *Ethical principles of psychologists and code of conduct* (2002, Amended June 1, 2010 and January 1, 2017). Retrieved from http://www.apa.org/ethics/code/index.aspx

American Psychological Association Practice Organization. (2010). Telehealth: Legal basics for psychologists. *Good Practice, 41,* 2–7.

Association of State and Provincial Psychology Boards. (2015). *Psychology interjurisdictional compact (PSYPACT).* Retrieved from http://www.asppb.net/?page=PSYPACT

Baker, D. (2015, August). Federal and state telehealth policies and regulations. In L. F. Campbell (Chair), *Developing a road map for telepsychological practice: APA guidelines and regulatory developments.* Symposium conducted at the annual convention of the American Psychological Association, Toronto, Ontario, Canada.

Bradley v. Mayo Foundation, No. 97-204, 1999 U.S. Dist. LEXIS 17505 (E.D. Ky. Aug. 10, 1999).

Bullion v. Gillespie, 895 F.2d 213 (5th Cir. 1990).

Department of Regulatory Agencies, Division of Professions and Occupations. (2015). *Colorado State Board of Psychologist Examiners policies: §30-1 Teletherapy policy—Guidance regarding psychotherapy through electronic means within the state of Colorado.* Retrieved from https://drive.google.com/file/d/0B-K5DhxXxJZbT3I3aWJITVl1YnM/view?pref=2&pli=1

Federation of State Medical Boards. (2013). *Interstate medical licensure compact.* Retrieved from http://www.licenseportability.org

Georgia Comp. R. & Regs. r. 510-5-.07, Representation of Services. (2004).

Georgia Telemedicine Act, O.C.G.A. § 33-24-56.4 (2015).

Hageseth v. Superior Court of San Mateo County, 150 Cal. App. 4th 1399 (2007).

Health Information Technology for Economic and Clinical Health Act, Pub. L. 111-5 (2009).

Health Insurance Portability and Accountability Act, Pub. L. No. 104-191, 110 Stat. 1936 (1996).

International Shoe Co. v. Washington, 326 U.S. 310, 319, 66 S.Ct. 154, 90 L.Ed. 95 (1945).

Joint Task Force for the Development of Telepsychology Guidelines for Psychologists. (2013). Guidelines for the practice of telepsychology. *American Psychologist, 68,* 791–800. Retrieved from https://www.apa.org/pubs/journals/features/amp-a0035001.pdf

Jones v. Williams, 660 F. Supp. 2d 1145; 2009 U.S. Dist. LEXIS 91334 (N.D.Ca. 2009).

Medicare Telehealth Parity Act of 2015, H.R. 2948, 114th Cong. (2015).

Miss. Code Ann. § 73-31-3(d)(iii) (2015).
National Council of State Boards of Nursing. (2000). *Nurse Licensure Compact.* Retrieved from https://www.ncsbn.org/nurse-licensure-compact.htm
Prince v. Urban, 49 Cal. App. 4th 1056; 57 Cal. Rptr. 2d 181; 1996 Cal. App. LEXIS 924 (Cal. App. 4th, 1996).
Servicemembers' Telemedicine and E-Health Portability Act of 2011, Pub. L. No. 112-81, § 713, 125 Stat. 1298 (2011).
Telehealth Advancement Act of 2011, Cal. Bus. & Prof. Code § 2290.5 (2011 & Supp. 2015).
TELEmedicine for MEDicare (TELE-MED) Act of 2015, H.R. 3081, 114th Cong. (2015a).
TELEmedicine for MEDicare (TELE-MED) Act of. 2015, S. 1778, 114th Cong. (2015b).
Veterans E-Health & Telemedicine Support Act (VETS) of 2015, H.R. 2516, 114th Cong. (2015a).
Veterans E-Health & Telemedicine Support Act (VETS) of 2015, S. 2170, 114th Cong. (2015b).
Wakefield, M. K. (2010). *Health Licensing Board: Report to Congress* (requested by Senate Report 111-66). Washington, DC: U.S. Department of Health and Human Services, Health Resources and Services Administration. Retrieved from https://telehealth.org/wp-content/uploads/2013/11/HEALTH-LICENSING-BOARD-Report_Final.pdf
Walsh v. Chez, 418 F.Supp.2d 781 (W.D. Pa. 2006).
Wright v. Yackley, 459 F.2d 287 (9th Cir. 1972).

Linda F. Campbell, Fred Millán, and Jana N. Martin

Afterword

There is no question that telepsychology will have an impact on the practice of psychology. As practitioners, it is up to us to ensure that the impact is positive. We have before us an opportunity to provide psychological services to people who previously either could not or would not approach the office of a psychologist. We have the opportunity to provide continuity of services to clients who travel for business or pleasure or who relocate and have difficulty finding a psychologist who specializes in their areas of need or who is available in a timely way. Telepsychology has much potential to expand the value of psychology to many. Like other modes and techniques of practice, however, telepsychology requires that the psychologist using it is competent; keeps up-to-date on ever-evolving technological changes and the standard of care regarding use of telepsychology in therapy and assessment; uses proper informed consent; protects the confidentiality of the therapeutic relationship, data, and interaction at all times; is responsible for safe storage and disposal of client information; and practices legally and ethically.

We have endeavored in this book to provide the reader with not only the set of guidelines that were developed and approved by the American Psychological Association, Association of State and Provincial Psychology Boards, and The Trust, but also descriptions of scenarios in which practitioners

http://dx.doi.org/10.1037/0000046-010
A Telepsychology Casebook: Using Technology Ethically and Effectively in Your Professional Practice,
L. F. Campbell, F. Millán, and J. N. Martin (Editors)

of telepsychology may find themselves. The practice of telepsychology presents some very different challenges due to the nature of technology, and it requires adaptation on the part of the client and the psychologist. Each described scenario, regardless of the setting or issue presented, helps psychologists interpret the relevant guidelines and ethical principles. Each situation applies a framework for providing services therapeutically, ethically, and legally. This educational approach helps readers generalize the framework so that they can apply it to future real-life situations, no matter how varied. We hope the casebook will be used in classroom settings, in consultation groups, and by individuals as a resource when considering a potential client for telepsychology and when reviewing treatment plan progress.

Although many elements of the case studies will remain representative of the practice of telepsychology, other elements will become less representative. This is due to rapid advances in technology and its intersection with psychological issues, changes in evidence-based treatment modalities, and evolving legal and regulatory requirements. Certainly, the authors of the guidelines were keenly aware of this, as reflected in their call for vigilance and competence in each guideline. This call is also reflected in the introduction to the guidelines:

> It will be important for psychologists to be cognizant and compliant with laws and regulations that govern independent practice within jurisdictions and across jurisdictional and international borders. This is particularly true when providing telepsychology services. . . . it continues to be the responsibility of the psychologist to apply all current legal and ethical standards of practice when providing telepsychology services. (Joint Task Force for the Development of Telepsychology Guidelines for Psychologists, 2013, p. 791)

We join the call for vigilance in making the practice of telepsychology a positive one for the public and for the profession. Here's to opportunities to expand the possibilities for our profession to provide ethical, effective, accessible psychological treatment for all.

References

Joint Task Force for the Development of Telepsychology Guidelines for Psychologists. (2013). Guidelines for the practice of telepsychology. *American Psychologist, 68,* 791–800. Retrieved from https://www.apa.org/pubs/journals/features/amp-a0035001.pdf

Appendix

Guidelines for the Practice of Telepsychology

Introduction

These guidelines are designed to address the developing area of psychological service provision commonly known as telepsychology. Telepsychology is defined, for the purpose of these guidelines, as the provision of psychological services using telecommunication technologies as expounded in the Definition of Telepsychology. The expanding role of technology in the provision of psychological services and the continuous development of new technologies that may be useful in the practice of psychology present unique opportunities, considerations and challenges to practice. With the advancement of technology and the increased number of psychologists using technology in their practices, these guidelines have been prepared to educate and guide them.

These guidelines are informed by relevant American Psychological Association (APA) standards and guidelines, including the following: *Ethical Principles of Psychologists and Code of Conduct* (hereafter referred to as APA Ethics Code; APA, 2017), and the "Record Keeping Guidelines" (APA, 2007). In addition, the assumptions and principles that guide the APA's "Guidelines on Multicultural Training, Research, Practice, and Organizational Change for Psychologists" (APA, 2003) are infused throughout the rationale and application describing each of the guidelines. Therefore, these guidelines are informed by professional theories, evidence-based practices and definitions in an effort to offer the best guidance in the practice of telepsychology.

The use of the term *guidelines* within this document refers to statements that suggest or recommend specific professional behaviors, endeavors or conduct for psychologists. Guidelines differ from standards in that standards are mandatory and may be accompanied by an enforcement mechanism. Thus, guidelines are aspirational in intent. They are intended to facilitate the continued systematic development of the profession and to help ensure a high level of professional practice by psychologists. "Guidelines are created to educate and to inform the practice of psychologists. They are also intended to stimulate debate and research. Guidelines are not to be promulgated as a means of establishing the identity of a particular group or specialty area of psychology; likewise, they are not to be created with the purpose of excluding any psychologist from practicing in a particular area" (APA, 2002, p. 1048). "Guidelines are not intended to be mandatory or exhaustive and may not be applicable to every professional or clinical situation. They are not definitive and they are not intended to take precedence over the judgment of psychologists" (APA, 2002, p. 1050). These guidelines are meant to assist psychologists as they apply current standards of professional practice when utilizing telecommunication technologies as a means of delivering their professional services. They are not intended to change any scope of practice or define the practice of any group of psychologists.

The practice of telepsychology involves consideration of legal requirements, ethical standards, telecommunication technologies, intra- and interagency policies, and other external constraints, as well as the demands of the particular professional context. In some situations, one set of considerations may suggest a different course of action than another, and it is the responsibility of the psychologist to balance them appropriately. These guidelines aim to assist psychologists in making such decisions. In addition, it will be important for psychologists to be cognizant and compliant with laws and regulations that govern independent practice within jurisdictions and across jurisdictional and international borders. This is particularly true when providing telepsychology services. Where a psychologist is providing services from one jurisdiction to a client/patient located in another jurisdiction, the law and regulations may differ between the two jurisdictions. Also, it is the responsibility of the psychologists who practice telepsychology to maintain and enhance their level of understanding of the concepts related to the delivery of services via telecommunication technologies. Nothing in these guidelines is intended to contravene any limitations set on psychologists' activities based on ethical standards, federal or jurisdictional statutes or regulations, or for those psychologists who work in agencies and public settings. As in all other circumstances, psychologists must be aware of the standards of practice for the jurisdiction or setting in which they function and are expected to comply with those standards. Recommendations related to the guidelines are consistent with broad ethical principles (APA, 2017) and it continues to be the responsibility of the psychologist to apply all current legal and ethical standards of practice when providing telepsychology services.

It should be noted that APA policy generally requires substantial review of the relevant empirical literature as a basis for establishing the need for guidelines and for providing justification for the guidelines' statements themselves

(APA, 2002). The literature supporting the work of the Task Force on Telepsychology and guidelines statements themselves reflect seminal, relevant, and recent publications. The supporting references in the literature review emphasize studies from approximately the past 15 years plus classic studies that provide empirical support and relevant examples for the guidelines. The literature review, however, is not intended to be exhaustive or serve as a comprehensive systematic review of the literature that is customary when developing professional practice guidelines for psychologists.

Definition of Telepsychology

Telepsychology is defined, for the purpose of these guidelines, as the provision of psychological services using telecommunication technologies. Telecommunications is the preparation, transmission, communication, or related processing of information by electrical, electromagnetic, electromechanical, electro-optical, or electronic means (Committee on National Security Systems, 2010). Telecommunication technologies include but are not limited to telephone, mobile devices, interactive videoconferencing, e-mail, chat, text, and Internet (e.g., self-help websites, blogs, and social media). The information that is transmitted may be in writing, or include images, sounds, or other data. These communications may be synchronous with multiple parties communicating in real time (e.g., interactive videoconferencing, telephone) or asynchronous (e.g., e-mail, online bulletin boards, storing and forwarding information). Technologies may augment traditional in-person services (e.g., psychoeducational materials online after an in-person therapy session) or be used as stand-alone services (e.g., therapy or leadership development provided over videoconferencing). Different technologies may be used in various combinations and for different purposes during the provision of telepsychology services. For example, videoconferencing and telephone may also be utilized for direct service while e-mail and text is used for nondirect services (e.g., scheduling). Regardless of the purpose, psychologists strive to be aware of the potential benefits and limitations in their choices of technologies for particular clients in particular situations.

Operational Definitions

The Task Force on Telepsychology has agreed upon the following operational definitions for terms used in this document. In addition, these and other terms used throughout the document have a basis in definitions developed by the following U.S. agencies: the Committee on National Security Systems (2010), the U.S. Department of Health and Human Services, Health Resources and Services Administration (Wakefield, 2010), U.S. Department of Commerce, National Institute of Standards and Technology (2011). Last, the terminology and definitions that describe technologies and their uses are constantly evolving, and therefore psychologists are encouraged to consult glossaries and publications prepared by agencies, such as the Committee on National Security Systems and the National Institute of Standards and Technology, which represent definitive sources responsible for developing terminology and definitions related to technology and its uses.

The term *client/patient* refers to the recipient of psychological services, whether psychological services are delivered in the context of health care, corporate, supervision, and/or consulting services. The term *in-person*, which is used in combination with the provision of services, refers to interactions in which the psychologist and the client/patient are in the same physical space and does not include interactions that may occur through the use of technologies. The term *remote*, which is also used in combination with the provision of services utilizing telecommunication technologies, refers to the provision of a service that is received at a different site from where the psychologist is physically located. The term *remote* includes no consideration related to distance and may refer to a site in a location that is in the office next door to the psychologist or thousands of miles from the psychologist. The terms *jurisdictions* or *jurisdictional* are used when referring to the governing bodies at states, territories, and provincial governments.

Finally, there are terms within the document related to confidentiality and security. *Confidentiality* means the principle that data or information is not made available or disclosed to unauthorized persons or processes. The terms *security* or *security measures* are terms that encompass all of the administrative, physical, and technical safeguards in an information system. The term *information system* is an interconnected set of information resources within a system and includes hardware, software, information, data, applications, communications, and people.

Need for the Guidelines

The expanding role of telecommunication technologies in the provision of services and the continuous development of new technologies that may be useful in the practice of psychology support the need for the development of guidelines for practice in this area. Technology offers the opportunity to increase client/patient access to psychological services. Service recipients limited by geographic location, medical condition, psychiatric diagnosis, financial constraint or other barriers may gain access to high-quality psychological services through the use of technology. Technology also facilitates the delivery of psychological services by new methods (e.g., online psychoeducation, therapy delivered over interactive videoconferencing) and augments traditional in-person psychological services. The increased use of technology for the delivery of some types of services by psychologists who are health service providers is suggested by recent survey data collected by the APA Center for Workforce Studies (2008) and by the increasing discussion of telepsychology in the professional literature (Baker & Bufka, 2011). Together with the increasing use and payment for the provision of telehealth services by Medicare and private industry, the development of national guidelines for the practice of telepsychology is timely and needed. Furthermore, state and international psychological associations have developed or are beginning to develop guidelines for the provision of psychological services (Canadian Psychological Association, 2006; New Zealand Psychological Association, 2011; Ohio Psychological Association, 2010).

Development of the Guidelines

The guidelines were developed by the Joint Task Force for the Development of Telepsychology Guidelines for Psychologists (Telepsychology Task Force) established by the following three entities: the American Psychological Association (APA), the Association of State and Provincial Psychology Boards (ASPPB), and The Trust. These entities provided input, expertise, and guidance to the Task Force on many aspects of the profession, including those related to its ethical, regulatory, and legal principles and practices. The Telepsychology Task Force members represented a diverse range of interests and expertise that are characteristic of the profession of psychology, including knowledge of the issues relevant to the use of technology, ethical considerations, licensure and mobility, and scope of practice, to name only a few.[1]

The Telepsychology Task Force recognized that telecommunications technologies provide both opportunities and challenges for psychologists. Telepsychology not only enhances a psychologist's ability to provide services to clients/patients but also greatly expands access to psychological services that, without telecommunication technologies, would not be available. Throughout the development of these guidelines, the Telepsychology Task Force devoted numerous hours reflecting on and discussing the need for guidance to psychologists in this area of practice, the myriad, complex issues related to the practice of telepsychology and the experiences that they and other practitioners address each day in the use of technology. There was a concerted focus to identify the unique aspects that telecommunication technologies bring to the provision

[1]The Telepsychology Task Force comprised psychologists with four members each representing the APA and the ASPPB and two members representing The Trust. The cochairs of the Telepsychology Task Force were Linda Campbell, PhD, and Fred Millán, PhD. Additional members of the Task Force included the following psychologists: Margo Adams Larsen, PhD; Sara Smucker Barnwell, PhD; Colonel Bruce E. Crow, PsyD; Terry S. Gock, PhD; Eric A. Harris, EdD, JD; Jana N. Martin, PhD; Thomas W. Miller, PhD; Joseph S. Rallo, PhD. APA staff (Ronald S. Palomares, PhD; Joan Freund; and Jessica Davis) and ASPPB staff (Stephen DeMers, EdD; Alex M. Siegel, PhD, JD; and Janet Pippin Orwig) provided direct support to the Telepsychology Task Force. Funding was provided by each of the respective entities to support in-person meetings and conference calls of Task Force members in 2011 and 2012. This draft is scheduled to expire as APA policy no later than 10 years after the initial date of recognition by the APA. After the date of expiration, users are encouraged to contact the APA Practice Directorate to confirm that this document remains in effect.

of psychological services, distinct from those present during in-person provision of services. Two important components were identified:

1. the psychologist's knowledge of and competence in the use of the telecommunication technologies being utilized; and
2. the need to ensure the client/patient has a full understanding of the increased risks to loss of security and confidentiality when using telecommunication technologies.

Therefore, two of the most salient issues that the Telepsychology Task Force members focused on throughout the document are the psychologist's own knowledge of and competence in the provision of telepsychology and the need to ensure that the client/patient has a full understanding of the potentially increased risks to loss of security and confidentiality when using technologies.

An additional key issue discussed by the task force members was interjurisdictional practice. The guidelines encourage psychologists to be familiar with and comply with all relevant laws and regulations when providing psychological services across jurisdictional and international borders. The guidelines do not promote a specific mechanism to guide the development and regulation of interjurisdictional practice. However, the Telepsychology Task Force notes that while the profession of psychology does not currently have a mechanism to regulate the delivery of psychological services across jurisdictional and international borders, it is anticipated that the profession will develop a mechanism to allow interjurisdictional practice given the rapidity by which technology is evolving and the increasing use of telepsychology by psychologists working in U.S. federal environments such as the U.S. Department of Defense and Department of Veterans Affairs.

Competence of the Psychologist

Guideline 1. Psychologists who provide telepsychology services strive to take reasonable steps to ensure their competence with both the technologies used and the potential impact of the technologies on clients/patients, supervisees, or other professionals.

RATIONALE

Psychologists have a primary ethical obligation to provide professional services only within the boundaries of their competence based on their education, training, supervised experience, consultation, study or professional experience. As with all new and emerging areas in which generally recognized standards for preparatory training do not yet exist, psychologists utilizing telepsychology aspire to apply the same standards in developing their competence in this area. Psychologists who use telepsychology in their practices assume the responsibility for assessing and continuously evaluating their competencies, training, consultation, experience, and risk management practices required for competent practice.

APPLICATION

Psychologists assume responsibility to continually assess both their professional and technical competence when providing telepsychology services. Psychologists who utilize or intend to utilize telecommunication technologies when delivering services to clients/patients strive to obtain relevant professional training to develop their requisite knowledge and skills. Acquiring competence may require pursuing additional educational experiences and training, including but not limited to a review of the relevant literature, attendance at existing training programs (e.g., professional and technical) and continuing education specific to the delivery of services utilizing telecommunication technologies. Psychologists are encouraged to seek appropriate skilled consultation from colleagues and other resources.

Psychologists are encouraged to examine the available evidence to determine whether specific telecommunication technologies are suitable for a client/patient, based on the current literature available, current outcomes research, best practice guidance, and client/patient preference. Research may not be available in the use of some specific technologies, and clients/patients should be made aware of those telecommunication technologies that have no evidence of effectiveness. However, this, in and of itself, may not be grounds to deny providing the service to the client/patient. Lack of current available evidence in a new area of practice does not necessarily indicate that a service is ineffective. Additionally, psychologists are encouraged to document their consideration and choices regarding the use of telecommunication technologies used in service delivery.

Psychologists understand the need to consider their competence in utilizing telepsychology as well as their client's/patient's ability to engage in and fully understand the risks and benefits of the proposed intervention utilizing specific technologies. Psychologists make reasonable effort to understand the manner in which cultural, linguistic, socioeconomic, and other individual characteristics (e.g., medical status, psychiatric stability, physical/cognitive disability, personal preferences), in addition to organizational cultures, may impact effective use of telecommunication technologies in service delivery.

Psychologists who are trained to handle emergency situations in providing traditional in-person clinical services are generally familiar with the resources available in their local community to assist clients/patients with crisis intervention. At the onset of the delivery of telepsychology services, psychologists make reasonable effort to identify and learn how to access relevant and appropriate emergency resources in the client's/patient's local area, such as emergency response contacts (e.g., emergency telephone numbers, hospital admissions, local referral resources, clinical champion at a partner clinic where services are delivered, a support person in the client's/patient's life when available). Psychologists prepare a plan to address any lack of appropriate resources, particularly those necessary in an emergency, and other relevant factors that may impact the efficacy and safety of said service. Psychologists make reasonable effort to discuss with and provide all clients/patients with clear written instructions as to what to do in an emergency (e.g., where there is a suicide risk). As part of emergency planning, psychologists are encouraged to acquire knowledge of the laws and rules of the jurisdiction in which the client/patient resides and the differences from those in the psychologist's jurisdiction, as well as document all their emergency planning efforts.

In addition, as applicable psychologists are mindful of the array of potential discharge plans for clients/patients when telepsychology services are no longer necessary and/or desirable. If a client/patient recurrently experiences crises/emergencies suggestive that in-person services may be appropriate, psychologists take reasonable steps to refer a client/patient to a local mental health resource or begin providing in-person services.

Psychologists using telepsychology to provide supervision or consultation remotely to individuals or organizations are encouraged to consult others who are knowledgeable about the unique issues telecommunication technologies pose for supervision or consultation. Psychologists providing telepsychology services strive to be familiar with professional literature regarding the delivery of services via telecommunication technologies, as well as competent with the use of the technological modality itself. In providing supervision and/or consultation via telepsychology, psychologists make reasonable efforts to be proficient in the professional services being offered, the telecommunication modality via which the services are being offered by the supervisee/consultee, and the technology medium being used to provide the supervision or consultation. In addition, since the development of basic professional competencies for supervisees is often conducted in person, psychologists who use telepsychology for supervision are encouraged to consider and ensure that a sufficient amount of in-person supervision time is included so that the supervisees can attain the required competencies or supervised experiences.

Standards of Care in the Delivery of Telepsychology Services

Guideline 2. Psychologists make every effort to ensure that ethical and professional standards of care and practice are met at the outset and throughout the duration of the telepsychology services they provide.

RATIONALE

Psychologists delivering telepsychology services apply the same ethical and professional standards of care and professional practice that are required when providing in-person psychological services. The use of telecommunication technologies in the delivery of psychological services is a relatively new and rapidly evolving area, and therefore psychologists are encouraged to take particular care to evaluate and assess the appropriateness of utilizing these technologies prior to engaging in, and throughout the duration of, telepsychology practice to determine if the modality of service is appropriate, efficacious and safe.

Telepsychology encompasses a breadth of different psychological services using a variety of technologies (e.g., interactive videoconferencing, telephone, text, e-mail, Web services, and mobile applications). The burgeoning research in telepsychology suggests the effectiveness of certain types of interactive telepsychological interventions to their in-person counterparts (specific therapies delivered over videoteleconferencing and telephone). Therefore, before psychologists engage in providing telepsychology services, they are urged to conduct an initial assessment to determine the appropriateness of the telepsychology service to be provided for the client/patient. Such an assessment may include the examination of the potential risks and benefits to provide telepsychology services for the client's/patient's particular needs, the multicultural and ethical issues that may arise, and a review of the most appropriate medium (e.g., video teleconference, text, e-mail, etc.) or best options available for the service delivery. It may also include considering whether comparable in-person services are available and why services delivered via telepsychology are equivalent or preferable to such services. In addition, it is incumbent on the psychologist to engage in a continual assessment of the appropriateness of providing telepsychology services throughout the duration of the service delivery.

APPLICATION

When providing telepsychology services, considering client/patient preferences for such services is important. However, it may not be solely determinative in the assessment of their appropriateness. Psychologists are encouraged to carefully examine the unique benefits of delivering telepsychology services (e.g., access to care, access to consulting services, client convenience, accommodating client special needs, etc.) relative to the unique risks (e.g., information security, emergency management, etc.) when determining whether or not to offer telepsychology services. Moreover, psychologists are aware of such other factors as geographic location, organizational culture, technological competence (both psychologist and client/patient), and, as appropriate, medical conditions, mental status and stability, psychiatric diagnosis, current or historic use of substances, treatment history, and therapeutic needs that may be relevant to assessing the appropriateness of the telepsychology services being offered. Furthermore, psychologists are encouraged to communicate any risks and benefits of the telepsychology services to be offered to the client/patient and document such communication. In addition, psychologists may consider some initial in-person contact with the client/patient to facilitate an active discussion on these issues and/or conduct the initial assessment.

As in the provision of traditional services, psychologists endeavor to follow the best practice of service delivery described in the empirical literature and professional standards (including multicultural considerations) that are relevant to the telepsychological service modality being offered. In addition, they consider the client's/patient's familiarity with and competency for using the specific technologies involved in providing the particular telepsychology service. Moreover, psychologists are encouraged to reflect on multicultural considerations and how best to manage any emergency that may arise during the provision of telepsychology services.

Psychologists are encouraged to assess carefully the remote environment in which services will be provided, to determine what impact, if any, there might be to the efficacy, privacy and/or safety of the proposed intervention offered via telepsychology. Such an assessment of the remote environment may include a discussion of the client's/patient's situation within the home or within an organizational context, the availability of emergency or technical personnel or supports, risk of distractions, potential for privacy breaches or any other impediments that may impact the effective delivery of telepsychology services. Along this line, psychologists are encouraged to discuss fully with the clients/patients their role in ensuring that sessions are not interrupted and that the setting is comfortable and conducive to making progress to maximize the impact of the service provided since the psychologist will not be able to control those factors remotely.

Psychologists are urged to monitor and assess regularly the progress of their client/patient when offering telepsychology services in order to determine if the provision of telepsychology services is still appropriate and beneficial to the client/patient. If there is a significant change in the client/patient or in the therapeutic interaction to cause concern, psychologists make reasonable effort to take appropriate steps to adjust and reassess the appropriateness of the services delivered via telepsychology. Where it is believed that continuing to provide remote services is no longer beneficial or presents a risk to a client's/patient's emotional or physical well-being, psychologists are encouraged to thoroughly discuss these concerns with the client/patient, appropriately terminate their remote services with adequate notice and refer or offer any needed alternative services to the client/patient.

Informed Consent

Guideline 3: Psychologists strive to obtain and document informed consent that specifically addresses the unique concerns related to the telepsychology services they provide. When doing so, psychologists are cognizant of the applicable laws and regulations, as well as organizational requirements that govern informed consent in this area.

RATIONALE

The process of explaining and obtaining informed consent, by whatever means obtained, sets the stage for the relationship between the psychologist and the client/patient. Psychologists make reasonable effort to offer a complete and clear description of the telepsychology services they provide, and seek to obtain and document informed consent when providing professional services (APA Ethics Code, Standard 3.10). In addition, they attempt to develop and share the policies and procedures that will explain to their clients/patients how they will interact with them using the specific telecommunication technologies involved. It may be more difficult to obtain and document informed consent in situations where psychologists provide telepsychology services to their clients/patients who are not in the same physical location or with whom they do not have in-person interactions. Moreover, there may be differences with respect to informed consent between the laws and regulations in the jurisdictions where a psychologist who is providing telepsychology services is located and the jurisdiction in which this psychologist's client/patient resides. Furthermore, psychologists may need to be aware of the manner in which cultural, linguistic, socioeconomic characteristics, and organizational considerations may impact a client's/patient's understanding of, and the special considerations required for, obtaining informed consent (such as when securing informed consent remotely from a parent/guardian when providing telepsychology services to a minor).

Telepsychology services may require different considerations for and safeguards against potential risks to, confidentiality, information security, and comparability of traditional in-person services. Psychologists are thus encouraged to consider appropriate policies and procedures to address the potential threats to the security of client/patient data and information when using specific telecommunication technologies and appropriately inform their clients/patients about them. For example, psychologists who provide telepsychology services consider addressing with their clients/patients what client/patient data and information will be stored, how the data and information will be stored, how it will be accessed, how secure is the information communicated using a given technology, and any technology-related vulnerability to confidentiality and security by creating and storing electronic client/patient data and information.

APPLICATION

Prior to providing telepsychology services, psychologists are aware of the importance of obtaining and documenting written informed consent from their clients/patients that specifically addresses the unique concerns relevant to those services that will be offered. When developing such informed consent, psychologists make reasonable effort to use language that is reasonably understandable to their clients/patients, in addition to, evaluating the need to address cultural, linguistic, organizational considerations, and other issues that may impact on a client's/patient's understanding of the informed consent agreement. When considering for inclusion in informed consent those unique concerns that may be involved in providing telepsychology services, psychologists may include the manner in which they and their clients/patients will use the particular telecommunication technologies, the boundaries they will establish and observe, and the procedures for responding to electronic communications from clients/patients. Moreover, psychologists are cognizant of pertinent laws and regulations with respect to informed consent in both the jurisdiction where they offer their services and where their clients/patients reside (see Guideline on Interjurisdictional Practice for more detail).

Besides those unique concerns described above, psychologists are encouraged to discuss with their clients/patients those issues surrounding confidentiality and the security conditions when particular modes of telecommunication technologies are utilized. Along this line, psychologists are cognizant of some of the inherent risks a given telecommunication technology may pose in both the equipment (hardware, software, other equipment components) and the processes used for providing telepsychology services, and strive to provide their clients/patients with adequate information to give informed consent for proceeding with receiving the professional services offered via telepsychology. Some of these risks may include those associated with technological problems, and those service limitations that may arise because the continuity, availability, and appropriateness of specific telepsychology services (e.g., testing, assessment, and therapy) may be hindered as a result of those services being offered remotely. In addition, psychologists may consider developing agreements with their clients/patients to assume some role in protecting the data and information they receive from them (e.g., by not forwarding e-mails from the psychologist to others).

Another unique aspect of providing telepsychology services is that of billing documentation. As part of informed consent, psychologists are mindful of the need to discuss with their clients/patients what the billing documentation will include prior to the onset of service provision. Billing documentation may reflect the type of telecommunication technology used, the type of telepsychology services provided, and the fee structure for each relevant telepsychology service (e.g., video chat, texting fees, telephone services, chat room group fees, emergency scheduling, etc.). It may also include discussion about the charges incurred for any service interruptions or failures encountered, responsibility for overage charges on data plans, fee reductions for technology failures, and any other costs associated with the telepsychology services that will be provided.

Confidentiality of Data and Information

Guideline 4. Psychologists who provide telepsychology services make reasonable effort to protect and maintain the confidentiality of the data and information relating to their clients/patients and inform them of the potentially increased risks to loss of confidentiality inherent in the use of the telecommunication technologies, if any.

RATIONALE

The use of telecommunications technologies and the rapid advances in technology present unique challenges for psychologists in protecting the confidentiality of clients/patients. Psychologists who provide telepsychology learn about the potential risks to confidentiality before utilizing such technologies. When necessary, psychologists obtain the appropriate consultation with technology experts to augment their knowledge of telecommunication technologies in order to apply security measures in their practices that will protect and maintain the confidentiality of data and information related to their clients/patients.

Some of the potential risks to confidentiality include considerations related to uses of search engines and participation in social networking sites. Other challenges in this area may include protecting confidential data and information from inappropriate and/or inadvertent breaches to established security methods the psychologist has in place, as well as boundary issues that may arise as a result of a psychologist's use of search engines and participation on social networking sites. In addition, any Internet participation by psychologists has the potential of being discovered by their clients/patients and others and thereby potentially compromising a professional relationship.

APPLICATION

Psychologists both understand and inform their clients/patients of the limits to confidentiality and risks to the possible access or disclosure of confidential data and information that may occur during service delivery, including the risks of access to electronic communications (e.g., telephone, e-mail) between the psychologist and client/patient. Also, psychologists are cognizant of the ethical and practical implications of proactively researching online personal information about their clients/patients. They carefully consider the advisability of discussing such research activities with their clients/patients and how information gained from such searches would be utilized and recorded as documenting this information may introduce risks to the boundaries of appropriate conduct for a psychologist. In addition, psychologists are encouraged to weigh the risks and benefits of dual relationships that may develop with their clients/patients, due to the use of telecommunication technologies, before engaging in such relationships (APA Practice Organization [APAPO], 2012).

Psychologists who use social networking sites for both professional and personal purposes are encouraged to review and educate themselves about the potential risks to privacy and confidentiality and consider utilizing all available privacy settings to reduce these risks. They are also mindful of the possibility that any electronic communication can have a high risk of public discovery. They therefore mitigate such risks by following the appropriate laws, regulations and the APA Ethics Code (APA, 2017) to avoid disclosing confidential data or information related to clients/patients.

Security and Transmission of Data and Information

Guideline 5. Psychologists who provide telepsychology services take reasonable steps to ensure that security measures are in place to protect data and information related to their clients/patients from unintended access or disclosure.

RATIONALE

The use of telecommunication technologies in the provision of psychological services presents unique potential threats to the security and transmission of client/patient data and information. These potential threats to the integrity of data and information may include computer viruses, hackers, theft of technology devices, damage to hard drives or portable drives, failure of security systems, flawed software, and ease of accessibility to unsecured electronic files, and malfunctioning or outdated technology. Other threats may include policies and practices of technology companies and vendors such as tailored marketing derived from e-mail communications. Psychologists are encouraged to be mindful of these potential threats, and take reasonable steps to ensure that security measures are in place for protecting and controlling access to client/patient data within an information system. In addition, they are cognizant of relevant jurisdictional and federal laws and regulations that govern electronic storage and transmission of client/patient data and information, and develop appropriate policies and procedures to comply with such directives. When developing policies and procedures to ensure the security of client/patient data and information, psychologists may include considering the unique concerns and impacts posed by both intended and unintended use of public and private technology devices, active and inactive therapeutic relationships, and the different safeguards required for different physical environments, different staff (e.g., professional versus administrative staff), and different telecommunication technologies.

APPLICATION

Psychologists are encouraged to conduct an analysis of the risks to their practice setting, telecommunication technologies, and administrative staff in order to ensure that client/patient data and information is accessible only to appropriate and authorized individuals. Psychologists strive to obtain appropriate training or consultation from relevant experts when additional knowledge is needed to conduct an analysis of the risks.

Psychologists strive to ensure that policies and procedures are in place to secure and control access to client/patient information and data within information systems. Along this line, they may encrypt confidential client/patient data for storage or transmission and utilize such other secure methods as safe hardware and software and robust passwords to protect electronically stored or transmitted data and information. If there is a breach of unencrypted electronically communicated or maintained data, psychologists are urged to notify their clients/patients and other appropriate individuals/organizations as soon as possible. In addition, they are encouraged to make their best efforts to ensure that electronic data and information remain accessible despite problems with hardware, software, and/or storage devices by keeping a secure back-up version of such data.

When documenting the security measures to protect client/patient data and information from unintended access or disclosure, psychologists are encouraged to clearly address what types of telecommunication technologies are used (e.g., e-mail, telephone, video teleconferencing, text), how they are used, and whether telepsychology services used are the primary method of contact or augments in-person contact. When keeping records of e-mail, online messaging and other work using telecommunication technologies, psychologists are cognizant that preserving the actual communication may be preferable to summarization in some cases depending on the type of technology used.

Disposal of Data and Information and Technologies

Guideline 6. Psychologists who provide telepsychology services make reasonable efforts to dispose of data and information and the technologies used in a manner that facilitates protection from unauthorized access and accounts for safe and appropriate disposal.

RATIONALE

Consistent with APA "Record Keeping Guidelines" (2007), psychologists are encouraged to create policies and procedures for the secure destruction of data and information and the technologies used to create, store, and transmit the data and information. The use of telecommunication technologies in the provision of psychological services poses new challenges for psychologists when they consider the disposal methods to utilize in order to maximally preserve client confidentiality and privacy. Psychologists are therefore urged to consider conducting an analysis of the risks to the information systems within their practices in an effort to ensure full and complete disposal of electronic data and information, plus the technologies that created, stored, and transmitted the data and information.

APPLICATION

Psychologists are encouraged to develop policies and procedures for the destruction of data and information related to clients/patients. They also strive to securely dispose of software and hardware used in the provision of telepsychology services in a manner that insures that the confidentiality and security of any patient/client information is not compromised. When doing so, psychologists carefully clean all the data and images in the storage media before reuse or disposal consistent with federal, state, provincial, territorial, and other organizational regulations and guidelines. Psychologists are aware of and understand the unique storage implications related to telecommunication technologies inherent in available systems.

Psychologists are encouraged to document the methods and procedures used when disposing of the data and information and the technologies used to create, store, or transmit the data and information, as well as any other technology utilized in the disposal of data and hardware. They also strive to be aware of malware, cookies, and so forth and to dispose routinely of them on an ongoing basis when telecommunication technologies are used.

Testing and Assessment

Guideline 7. Psychologists are encouraged to consider the unique issues that may arise with test instruments and assessment approaches designed for in-person implementation when providing telepsychology services.

RATIONALE

Psychological testing and other assessment procedures are an area of professional practice in which psychologists have been trained and are uniquely qualified to conduct. While some symptom screening instruments are already being administered online frequently, most psychological test instruments and other assessment procedures currently in use have been designed and developed originally for in-person administration. Psychologists are thus encouraged to be knowledgeable about, and account for, the unique impacts, suitability for diverse populations, and limitations on test administration and on test and other data interpretations when these psychological tests and other assessment procedures are considered for and conducted via telepsychology. Psychologists also strive to maintain the integrity of the application of the testing and assessment process and procedures when using telecommunication technologies. In addition, they are cognizant of the accommodations for diverse populations that may be required for test administration via telepsychology. These guidelines are consistent with the standards articulated in the most recent edition of *Standards for Educational and Psychological Testing* (American Educational Research Association, American Psychological Association, & National Council on Measurement in Education, 1999).

APPLICATION

When a psychological test or other assessment procedure is conducted via telepsychology, psychologists are encouraged to ensure that the integrity of the psychometric properties of the test or assessment procedure (e.g., reliability and validity) and the conditions of administration indicated in the test manual are preserved when adapted for use with such technologies. They are encouraged to consider whether modifications to the testing environment or conditions are necessary to accomplish this preservation. For example, a test taker's access to a cell phone, the Internet, or other persons during an assessment could interfere with the reliability or validity of the instrument or administration. Further, if the individual being assessed receives coaching or such information as potential responses or the scoring and interpretation of specific assessment instruments because they are available on the Internet, the test results may be compromised. Psychologists are also encouraged to consider other possible forms of distraction which could affect performance during an assessment and which may not be obvious or visible (e.g., sight, sound, and smell) when utilizing telecommunication technologies.

Psychologists are encouraged to be cognizant of the specific issues that may arise with diverse populations when providing telepsychology and make appropriate arrangements to address those concerns (e.g., language or cultural issues; cognitive, physical, or sensory skills or impairments; or age may impact assessment). In addition, psychologists may consider the use of a trained assistant (e.g., proctor) to be on premise at the remote location in an effort to help verify the identity of the client/patient, provide needed on-site support to administer certain tests or subtests, and protect the security of the psychological testing and/or assessment process.

When administering psychological tests and other assessment procedures when providing telepsychology services, psychologists are encouraged to consider the quality of those technologies that are being used and the hardware requirements that are needed in order to conduct the specific psychological test or assessment approach. They also strive to account for and be prepared to explain the potential difference between the results obtained when a particular psychological test is conducted via telepsychology and when it is administered in person. In addition, when documenting findings from evaluation and assessment procedures, psychologists are encouraged to specify that a particular test or assessment procedure has been administered via telepsychology and to describe any accommodations or modifications that have been made.

Psychologists strive to use test norms derived from telecommunication technologies administration if such are available. Psychologists are encouraged to recognize the potential limitations of all assessment processes conducted via telepsychology and to be ready to address the limitations and potential impact of those procedures.

Interjurisdictional Practice

Guideline 8. Psychologists are encouraged to be familiar with and comply with all relevant laws and regulations when providing telepsychology services to clients/patients across jurisdictional and international borders.

RATIONALE

With the rapid advances in telecommunication technologies, the intentional or unintentional provision of psychological services across jurisdictional and international borders is becoming more of a reality for psychologists. Such service provision may range from the psychologists or clients/patients being temporarily out of state (including split residence across states) to psychologists offering their services across jurisdictional borders as a practice modality to take advantage of new telecommunication technologies. Psychological service delivery systems within such institutions as the U.S. Department of Defense and the Department of Veterans Affairs have already established internal policies and procedures for providing services within their systems that cross jurisdictional and international borders. However, the laws and regulations that govern service delivery by psychologists outside of those systems vary by state, province, territory, and country (APAPO, 2010). Psychologists should make reasonable effort to be familiar with and, as appropriate, to address the laws and regulations that govern telepsychology service delivery within the jurisdictions in which they are situated and the jurisdictions where their clients/patients are located.

APPLICATION

It is important for psychologists to be aware of the relevant laws and regulations that specifically address the delivery of professional services by psychologists via telecommunication technologies within and between jurisdictions. Psychologists are encouraged to understand what the laws and regulations consider as telehealth or telepsychology. In addition, psychologists are encouraged to review the professional licensure requirements, the services and telecommunication modalities covered, and the information required to be included in providing informed consent. It is important to note that each jurisdiction may or may not have specific laws that impose special requirements when providing services via telecommunication technologies. The APAPO (2010) has found that there are variations in whether psychologists are specified as a single type of provider or covered as part of a more diverse group of providers. In addition, there is wide diversity in the types of services and the telecommunication technologies that are covered by these laws.

At the present time, there are a number of jurisdictions without specific laws that govern the provision of psychological services utilizing telecommunication technologies. When providing telepsychology services in these jurisdictions, psychologists are encouraged to be aware of any opinion or declaratory statement issued by the relevant regulatory bodies and/or other practitioner licensing boards that may help inform them of the legal and regulatory requirements involved when delivering telepsychology services within those jurisdictions.

Moreover, because of the rapid growth in the utilization of telecommunication technologies, psychologists strive to keep abreast of developments and changes in the licensure and other interjurisdictional practice requirements that may be pertinent to their delivery of telepsychology services across jurisdictional boundaries. Given the direction of various health professions, and current federal priorities to resolve problems created by requirements of multi-jurisdictional licensure, (see, e.g., FCC National Broadband Plan, 2010, Canadian Agreement on Internal Trade 1995), the development of a telepsychology credential required by psychology boards for interjurisdictional practice is a probable outcome. For example, nursing has developed a credential that is accepted by many US jurisdictions that allows nurses licensed in any participating jurisdiction to practice in person or remotely in all participating jurisdictions. In addition, an ASPPB Task Force has drafted a set of recommendations for such a credential.

Conclusion

It is important to note that it is not the intent of these guidelines to prescribe specific actions, but rather, to offer the best guidance available at present when incorporating telecommunication technologies in the provision of psychological services. Because technology and its applicability to the profession of psychology is a dynamic area with many changes likely ahead, these guidelines also are not inclusive of all other considerations and are not intended to take precedence over the judgment of psychologists or applicable laws and regulations that guide the profession and practice of psychology. It is hoped that the framework presented will guide psychologists as the field evolves.

References

American Educational Research Association, American Psychological Association, & National Council on Measurement in Education. (1999). *Standards for educational and psychological testing.* Washington, DC: American Psychological Association.

American Psychological Association. (2002). Criteria for practice guideline development and evaluation. *American Psychologist, 57,* 1048–1051.

American Psychological Association. (2003). Guidelines on multicultural education, training, research, practice, and organizational change for psychologists. *American Psychologist, 58,* 377–402.

American Psychological Association. (2007). Record keeping guidelines. *American Psychologist, 62,* 993–1004.

American Psychological Association. (2017). *Ethical principles of psychologists and code of conduct* (2002, Amended June 1, 2010 and January 1, 2017). Retrieved from http://www.apa.org/ethics/code/index.aspx

American Psychological Association Center for Workforce Studies. (2008). *2008 APA survey of psychology health service providers: Module D. Information on telepsychology, medication, and collaboration.* Retrieved from http://www.apa.org/workforce/publications/08-hsp/telepsychology/index.aspx

American Psychological Association Practice Organization. (2010). Telehealth: Legal basics for psychologists. *Good Practice, 41,* 2–7.

American Psychological Association Practice Organization. (2012, Spring/Summer). Social media: What's your policy? *Good Practice,* pp. 10–18.

Baker, D. C., & Bufka, L. F. (2011). Preparing for the telehealth world: Navigating legal, regulatory, reimbursement, and ethical issues in an electronic age. *Professional Psychology: Research and Practice, 42,* 405–411.

Canadian Psychological Association. (2006). *Ethical guidelines for psychologists providing services via electronic media.* Retrieved from http://www.cpa.ca/aboutcpa/committees/ethics/psychserviceselectronically

Committee on National Security Systems. (2010). *National information assurance (AI) glossary.* Washington, DC: Author.

New Zealand Psychological Association. (2011). *Draft guidelines: Psychology services delivered via the Internet and other electronic media.* Retrieved from http://psychologistsboard.org.nz/cms_show_download.php?id=141

Ohio Psychological Association. (2010). *Telepsychology guidelines.* Retrieved from http://www.ohpsych.org/psychologists/files/2011/06/OPATelepsychology Guidelines41710.pdf

U.S. Department of Commerce, National Institute of Standards and Technology. (2011). *A glossary of key information security terms.* Washington, DC: Author.

Wakefield, M. K. (2010). *Health Licensing Board: Report to Congress* (requested by Senate Report 111-66). Washington, DC: U.S. Department of Health and Human Services, Health Resources and Services Administration. Retrieved from https://telehealth.org/wp-content/uploads/2013/11/HEALTH-LICENSING-BOARD-Report_Final.pdf

Index

About the Editors

Linda F. Campbell, PhD, is a professor in the counseling psychology program at the University of Georgia and director of the departmental training clinic. She teaches psychotherapy, assessment, and other courses, but her primary area of study is ethics. She is coauthor of *APA Ethics Code Commentary and Case Illustrations* and has published primarily in the area of ethics. Dr. Campbell is past chair of the APA Ethics Committee and is a member of the State Board of Examiners of Psychologists in Georgia. She was a cochair of the Task Force on the Development of Telepsychology Guidelines. She grew up in West Virginia and graduated from West Virginia University before moving to Georgia.

Fred Millán, PhD, ABPP, NCC, is a Latino counseling psychologist, licensed in New York State and board certified in psychoanalysis by the American Board of Professional Psychology. He is the director of the Graduate Mental Health Counseling Program and professor of psychology at SUNY Old Westbury. He maintains a part-time private practice in Spanish and English and provides clinical supervision to doctoral students, postdoctoral fellows, and psychiatric residents. Dr. Millán serves as the vice chair of the APA Ethics Committee and president-elect of the National Latino/a Psychological Association. He is a former president of the Association of State and Provincial Psychology Boards (ASPPB), former chair of the New York State Board for Psychology, and former cochair of the APA, ASPPB, and The Trust Task Force on Telepsychology.

Jana N. Martin, PhD, received her master's and doctor of philosophy degrees from the University of Mississippi and completed a child specialty internship at Duke University Medical Center. After many years practicing as a psychologist, Dr. Martin became CEO of The Trust in 2010. As CEO, Dr. Martin focuses on providing broad professional liability coverage, financial security products, and support services for psychologists in areas such as telepsychology. She coauthored the second edition of *Assessing and Managing Risk in Psychological Practice* and has cowritten numerous book chapters and articles and presents workshops on risk management topics. Dr. Martin was cochair of the APA/ASPPB/Trust Task Force on the Development of Telepsychology Guidelines for Psychologists.